The
Biblical Basis
for the
Catholic Faith

The
Biblical Basis
for the
Catholic Faith

John Salza

Our Sunday Visitor Publishing Division

Our Sunday Visitor, Inc.

Huntington, Indiana 46750

Nihil Obstat:
Rev. Michael Heintz
Censor Librorum

Imprimatur:
✠ John M. D'Arcy
Bishop of Fort Wayne-South Bend
January 27, 2005

The *nihil obstat* and *imprimatur* are declarations that a work is free from doctrinal or moral error. It is not implied that those who have granted the *nihil obstat* and *imprimatur* agree with the contents, opinions, or statements expressed.

The Scripture citations used in this work, unless otherwise noted, are taken from the *Catholic Edition of the Revised Standard Version of the Bible* (RSV), copyright © 1965 and 1966 by the Division of Christian Education of the National Council of the Churches of Christ in the United States of America. Citations marked "DR" are from the Douay-Rheims version of the Bible, and passages marked "NIV" are from the New International Version of the Bible. Used by permission. All rights reserved.

Every reasonable effort has been made to determine copyright holders of excerpted materials and to secure permissions as needed. If any copyrighted materials have been inadvertently used in this work without proper credit being given in one form or another, please notify Our Sunday Visitor in writing so that future printings of this work may be corrected accordingly.

Our Sunday Visitor Publishing Division
Our Sunday Visitor, Inc.
200 Noll Plaza
Huntington, IN 46750

ISBN: 1-59276-146-1 (Inventory No. T197)
LCCN: 2005920075

Cover design by Troy Lefevra
Interior design by Sherri L. Hoffman

PRINTED IN THE UNITED STATES OF AMERICA

To the girls I dearly love:
Alba, Anna, Mia, and Mara

Contents

Introduction

Catholics are often confronted by God-loving "Bible Christians" who sincerely believe that the Catholic faith is not based on the Scriptures. Quoting verse after Bible verse, these well-meaning believers attempt to refute the teachings of the Catholic Church. Sadly, many Catholics do not know the Scriptures well enough to effectively answer the inquiries and allegations of their Protestant brothers and sisters.

I have written this book for ordinary Catholics who do not have a solid scriptural understanding of their Catholic faith, as well as non-Catholic Christians who want to better understand the teachings of the Catholic Church. This book will provide answers to common questions about the Catholic faith and help readers to rediscover — or perhaps discover for the first time — the basis of these truths in Sacred Scripture. In this way I hope to demonstrate that not only is the Catholic faith biblical, but Catholicism is Bible Christianity *par excellence.*

The word "Catholic" comes from the Greek word *katolikos,* which means "according to the whole" or, more colloquially, "universal." Around A.D. 110, Ignatius of Antioch used this word to describe the Church. Just before he was martyred for the faith, the bishop writes to the Smyrnaeans, "Wherever Christ Jesus is, there is the Catholic Church."

Early Church Fathers such as Ignatius are authors and heroes of our faith, for their wisdom and example guided the Church for the first seven centuries of her existence. Some of the Fathers were taught directly by the apostles.[1] Because their writings are genuinely and explicitly Catholic, and because some non-Catholic theologians and Scripture scholars recognize them as an authentic source of early Christian belief, I was tempted to quote from them in every section of this book. However, when discussing the Catholic faith with non-Catholics, I have learned that not all of them are interested in the writings of the Fathers. Some want to use the Bible alone, because their faith is based on the Bible alone.

It can be frustrating to talk with Christians who place more confidence in their own or in a pastor's ability to interpret the Scriptures than in the reliability of what the first Christians had to say about a particular teaching. Nevertheless, I found using the Bible alone to write this book was a very rewarding and faith-filled exercise, particularly because it demonstrates that every Catholic teaching on faith and morals is explicitly, or at least implicitly, taught in Sacred Scripture.

However, I must emphasize from the beginning that using the Bible alone to study and explain Christian truths is *not* a Catholic approach. When God entrusted His Word to the Church over twenty centuries ago, He did it through both the Scriptures and Tradition, as one sacred "Deposit of Faith." We therefore have two thousand years of Church teaching from which to draw when studying the truths of Christianity. These teachings include the many doctrines in which both Catholics and Protestants believe, even though they are not explicitly stated in Scripture (the Trinity, the two natures of Christ, the two wills of Christ, and so on). Therefore, we look to the Church for God's Word as revealed not only in Scripture, but also in the apostolic Tradition and teaching authority that she has received from Jesus Christ. Nevertheless, the Bible is indispensable for explaining Catholic teaching, and the essential point of commonality between Catholics and Protestants. I pray that this common-ground approach may not only facilitate fruitful dialogue between us and our non-Catholic brothers and sisters, but also help those who do not yet recognize the Catholic Church as the Church of the Bible, to see in her the fullness of the Christian faith.

From a Catholic perspective, trying to prove the Catholic faith is biblical is a bit like trying to prove the American government is Constitutional. Just as the United States Constitution came from the American Government, the Bible came from the Catholic Church. Those Christians who criticize the Catholic Church's teachings on faith and morals are therefore criticizing the very Church that gave them the Bible. On matters of Christian faith, while it is important to demonstrate that a teaching is biblical, the real question is whether or not it is consistent with the teachings of the Catholic Church, "the pillar and bulwark of the truth" (1 Tim 3:15).[2]

The purpose of growing in our knowledge of Scripture is not to win arguments, of course. It is to grow in a deeper and holier relationship with our Lord and Savior Jesus Christ. Jerome, one of the early Church Fathers (A.D. 347 – 420), said, "Ignorance of Scripture is ignorance of Christ." We must know the Scriptures to know and love Jesus Christ, for knowing and loving Jesus means knowing and loving what Jesus taught us, which comes from His written Word.

Catholics believe that Jesus established the Catholic Church in order to continue His mission of salvation in the world. At the same time, Catholics should also acknowledge that there are those who do not consider themselves Catholic but who nevertheless love Jesus, and who are often more familiar with Scripture than Catholics are. We can learn much from their witness and example. However, we who hold the Catholic faith believe that we have been given the fullness of the saving truth of Jesus Christ in His One, Holy, Catholic and Apostolic Church. By having the totality of this truth, we have the fullness of the means of salvation that God desires for each of us.

That is not to say that Catholics are inherently superior to those from other faith traditions, or that we should demean the faith of other Christians. Rather, we should be humbled by our intimate union with Christ and His Church, and moved by a spirit of charity to spread our faith to our non-Catholic brothers and sisters. We must continue to pray that all Christians will embrace the fullness of truth in Christ, which can be found only inside the Catholic Church. Only then will we be "perfectly one," as our Lord desired (Jn 17:23). With that, let us search the Scriptures (see Jn 5:39).

John Salza
May 13, 2004
Feast of Our Lady of Fatima

CHAPTER ONE

The Bible and the Problem of *Sola Scriptura*

There are certain truths that all Christians — both Catholic and Protestant — have in common. We all believe that:

- God is one in three divine persons — Father, Son, and Holy Spirit.
- Out of His infinite love, God created the human family to share in His divine life for all eternity.
- As a result of Adam's original sin, the human race fell from God's life of grace and subjected itself to death and condemnation.
- Out of His infinite mercy, God revealed a plan to redeem humanity from sin and death. Beginning with Adam and continuing with Noah, Abraham, Moses, and David, God communicated His plan of redemptive love through various covenants.
- God brought His love for humanity into perfect fulfillment in the complete and everlasting Covenant established by the Incarnate Son of God, Jesus Christ, through His death and Resurrection.
- God made His plan of salvation in Christ known through the Scriptures.

There are also differences, of course. While most non-Catholic Christians believe that God made His revelation known through the Bible alone, Catholics believe that God's revelation has also been transmitted through the oral apostolic Tradition and teaching authority of the Catholic Church.

The belief in the Bible as the exclusive source for God's infallible Word is often referred to as *sola Scriptura*, which is Latin for "Scripture alone."[3] This is a recent development in Christian teaching, coming about in the sixteenth century when Martin Luther ignited the Reformation. Today most denominations are built upon this idea. Those who believe in *sola Scriptura* conclude that any teaching about the Christian faith that is not explicitly found in the Bible is "unbiblical." If a teaching is unbiblical, the non-Catholic Christian argues that it is not part of God's revelation and, therefore, cannot be true. Because these Christians believe that many of the Catholic Church's teachings cannot be found in the Bible, they believe that the Catholic faith is unbiblical and hence not true.

Therefore, we begin our examination of the Catholic faith by addressing the issue of whether or not God has limited His divine revelation to the writings of the Bible. The importance of this issue of authority cannot be overemphasized — this is the crux of the debate between Protestants and Catholics.

If God transmitted His revelation solely through the Bible, then two things must also be true: First, God has revealed nothing that is necessary for our salvation outside of the Bible. Second, if God wanted to save us through His written revelation alone, He would have instructed us *in the Bible* to follow the Scriptures alone.

Are these things true? Let's look at these issues one at a time.

1. Is it true that God has revealed nothing outside of Scripture that is necessary for our salvation?

No, this is not true. For example, all Christians would agree that knowing which books belong in the canon of Scripture[4] (the Bible) is necessary for our salvation. Without this knowledge, non-inspired writings might be confused with divine revelation, which would be detrimental to our salvation. Truth would be mixed with error.

One problem with *sola Scriptura* is that nowhere does the Bible say which books are to be included in the Bible, or which are divinely inspired. In fact, none of the authors of the books in the New Testament, other than John in the book of Revelation,[5] even claim to be writing under divine inspiration. This fact forces us to look *outside* the Bible to understand how its canon was determined. This is a glaring contradiction to the theory of *sola Scriptura:* The canon of Scripture, so necessary for our salvation, *was defined by the Catholic Church.*

The historical record demonstrates that the Church established the canon of Scripture at regional councils in Rome in A.D. 382, Hippo in 393, and Carthage in 397.[6] Before the Church's declaration, there was no agreed-upon canon. So Christians who accept the canon of Scripture accept an infallible decision made by the Catholic Church.

On what basis did the Catholic Church have the authority to determine what was divinely inspired, and what was not? How did the Christians in the second and third centuries come to understand the gospel, without having the Bible in written form? And finally, if all Christians accept the Church's teaching on what Scriptures are inspired, why don't all Christians accept her other teachings on salvation, the Eucharist, Mary, the saints, and purgatory?

These are all excellent questions, which we will address later in the book. For now, let us simply acknowledge that not everything we need to know for our salvation comes to us through the Bible. This fact proves that *sola Scriptura*, which is believed by so many Protestant Christians, is a false doctrine.

What about the books in the Catholic canon that are not found in other Christian Bibles?

To downplay the Church's determination of the Bible canon, some non-Catholics point out that not all Christians agree upon the entire canon of Scripture. Some do not accept the Catholic Church's Old Testament canon of Scripture, and do not include (or place in a separate section) the Deuterocanonical books,[7] which have been part of the Catholic canon for two thousand years. The Deuterocanonical books (which means "second canon"), which non-Catholics sometimes call the "Apocrypha," are Old Testament Scriptures that were primarily written in Greek. This fact distinguishes them from the Protocanonical books (or "first canon"), which were originally written in Hebrew and Aramaic. Of course, this rebuttal does not explain why all Christians accept the Catholic Church's New Testament canon

(Protestant and Catholic Bibles have the same twenty-seven books), nor does it explain why God directed the Church to determine the New Testament canon if the Bible is the sole rule and guide of faith.

This argument also does not address why the Deuterocanonical books were considered divinely revealed until the sixteenth century, when Martin Luther removed these books from the Old Testament canon. In fact, the Jews held the Deuterocanonical books to be divinely revealed even before the time of Christ, which is why Jesus and the apostles used these books when preaching the gospel. These references are found throughout the New Testament:

- Jesus quotes from Tobit 7:18 when He calls His Father, "Lord of Heaven and earth" (Mt 11:25).
- Mary follows Sirach 10:14 when she says God "has put down the mighty from their thrones" (Lk 1:52).
- Elizabeth alludes to Judith 13:18 when she declares that Mary is most "blessed ... among women" (Lk 1:42).
- Mark and Luke record the Sadducees' story about the seven brothers in Tobit 3:8 and Tobit 7:11.[8]
- James follows Sirach 29:10-11 in his teaching about laying up one's true treasure instead of silver and gold that will rust (see James 5:3).
- The seven spirits before God in John's Revelation are the same seven angels who present the prayers of the saints before the Holy One in Tobit 12:15 (see Rev 1:4).
- Peter alludes to Wisdom 3:5-6 when he teaches that God will test us just as gold is tested by fire (see 1 Pet 1:6-7).
- The author of Hebrews follows Sirach 25:22 when he tells us to strengthen our "drooping hands" and "weak knees" (Heb 12:12).[10]
- Paul follows Wisdom 5:17-20 when he charges us to take up the "armor of God," the "breastplate of righteousness," the "helmet of salvation" and the "shield of faith."[*] He borrows from Baruch 4:7 when he teaches that the pagans "sacrifice to demons and not to God."[*] And he quotes from 2 Maccabees 12:15, when he calls God the "one and only Sovereign."[*][9]

- He also refers to 2 Maccabees 7:1-42, which is one of the most incredible stories of faith in Scripture, regarding the torture and murder of a mother and her children (see Heb 11:35).

These and other examples are in Appendix A.

Jesus and the apostles also used the Septuagint in their teachings. The Septuagint was the Greek translation of the Hebrew and Aramaic Old Testament Scriptures, which included the Deuterocanonical books. Of the approximately 350 Old Testament quotes in the New Testament, about three hundred come from the Septuagint. Some non-Catholic scholars, to give their rejection of the Deuterocanon a more historical basis, argue that the Jews removed these books from their canon at the Council of Jamnia, about a century after Christ's Ascension. However, these Jewish councils also rejected the Church's New Testament canon, as well as the claim that Jesus Christ was the Messiah! Therefore, Christians cannot appeal to Jewish councils, which rejected the New Testament and Christianity as a whole, as a basis for making pronouncements about the Bible.

Isn't using Scripture to prove the Church's infallibility a circular argument?

This charge is leveled at some Catholics who use the full canon of Scripture (with the Deuterocanonical books) to highlight the significant problems with *sola Scriptura.* "Circular reasoning" means the premise of the argument is restated in the conclusion. That is, the Catholic argues that the Church is infallible and therefore she gave us the Bible, but the Catholic gets this information from the Bible, and so it is the Bible, and not the Church, that is infallible.

Even knowledgeable Catholics can get stumped with this argument. However, the Catholic argument is spiral, not circular:

- Point 1. The Scriptures are historically reliable (a point of agreement for all Christians).
- Point 2. Therefore we must demonstrate the Scriptures reveal that Christ established an infallible Church. (We do this in the next chapter.)

- Point 3. Once the existence of this infallible Church is established, we may then conclude that the Scriptures are inspired *because the infallible Church says they are inspired.*

Without the existence of the Church, we would never know whether or not the Bible is inspired. As many Catholics point out, it is the Bible *and* the Church — both or neither!

Those who deny that the Catholic Church made an infallible decision concerning the canon of Scripture must conclude that the canon of Scripture is a fallible collection of infallible books. However, few Christians would say this, for if the canon is only a fallible collection, how can we be sure that the books themselves are infallible? And how can we be sure that there are not other infallible texts that should have been included? This argument necessarily undermines the reliability of the Bible on grounds of infallibility and exclusivity, which is the foundation of the Protestant faith.

Having to acknowledge the Catholic Church's infallible decision, many non-Catholics argue that the Church, after determining the canon, became apostate. This also raises many questions. For example, when did the Church drift off into apostasy? What year? Also, on what specific doctrinal issues did the Church abandon the true faith? Further, who made this judgment that the Church went into apostasy, and by what authority? Such an argument poses insurmountable problems and unanswerable questions for those who accuse the Church of apostasy. Such an argument also makes a liar of Jesus, who said that the gates of hell would never prevail against His Church (see Mt 16:18).

2.   Does the Bible instruct us to follow the Bible alone?

Again, the answer is no. This is the other insurmountable problem with *sola Scriptura*. Nowhere in Scripture does Christ or any apostle command the faithful to observe only what is found in the Scriptures. In Matthew 28:20, Jesus says, "Observe *all* that I have commanded you."[11] And yet, we also know that *not all* that Jesus taught was recorded in Scripture (see Jn 20:30). If it were, John writes, "...the world itself could not contain the books that would be written" (Jn 21:25). Therefore, if we are to be faithful to Jesus' command, we must observe all the teachings that He passed on to His apostles, and these include teachings that come to us from outside Scripture.

Here is another point to consider: If Jesus wanted us to observe only those teachings that were recorded in written form, why is it that at no time during His earthly ministry does He command any apostle to commit His teachings to writing? This is quite surprising, if He intended all of Christian teaching to be committed to a book. To the contrary, right before His Ascension into heaven, Jesus commanded His apostles to "*preach* the good news to all creation."[12]

Because Jesus was ascending to the Father and would no longer be with His apostles, it would have made sense for Jesus to instruct His apostles to memorialize His gospel message, the source of all saving truth and moral discipline, in written form. But Jesus never commanded His apostles to write anything, and only three of the original twelve apostles (Peter, Matthew and John) wrote anything down.[13] Were the other apostles less faithful to Jesus?

Of course they weren't. Each of the apostles handed on the gospel of the Lord as He intended from the beginning, through His Church. Some of the apostles committed the gospel message to writing under the inspiration of the Holy Spirit. All of them handed on the gospel through their preaching and by example, both what they received from Christ and what was given to them through the prompting of the Holy Spirit.

This living transmission of the gospel, whether oral or written, is called Sacred Tradition. This Tradition was entrusted to the Church, preserved through apostolic succession, and protected by the Holy Spirit. Before we examine the biblical basis for the Church and apostolic succession, let us address what the Scriptures say about Tradition.

Why Is Sacred Tradition Important?

In his letter to the Thessalonians, Paul says that we receive the fullness of the gospel by obeying the Tradition handed down from the apostles by word of mouth or letter:

> To this he called you through our gospel, so that you may
> obtain the glory of our Lord Jesus Christ. So then, brethren,

stand firm and hold to the traditions that you were taught by us, either by word of mouth or by letter (2 Thess 2:14-15).

Paul's instruction demonstrates that the oral and written forms of communicating the gospel, handed down to us by the apostles, are of equal value. Paul does not instruct us to obey the Scriptures alone. Therefore, to defend *sola Scriptura*, one must find a verse in the Bible that subsequently voids Paul's instructions in 2 Thessalonians 2:15 to follow oral Tradition. Otherwise that person is not being faithful to the Bible by following the Bible alone.

In fact, the Bible provides many examples of the sacred writers instructing the faithful to follow Tradition:

- "Now we command you, brethren, in the name of our Lord Jesus Christ, that you keep away from any brother who is living in idleness and not in accord with the tradition that you received from us" (2 Thess 3:6).
- "I commend you because you remember me in everything and maintain the traditions even as I have delivered them to you" (1 Cor 11:2).
- "What you have learned and received and heard and seen in me, do; and the God of peace will be with you" (Phil 4:9).

Hence, Paul instructs the various churches to follow the apostolic Tradition that came to them through preaching, and never teaches them to follow the Scriptures alone.

Paul also instructs the leaders of the Church to hold firm to the apostolic Tradition handed on to them. To Timothy, whom Paul ordained Bishop of Ephesus around A.D. 65, Paul writes, "O Timothy, guard what has been entrusted to you" (1 Tim 6:20). The Greek word for "entrusted," *paratheke*, may also be translated "deposit." Oral apostolic Tradition has always been considered part of what the Church calls the Deposit of Faith (in Latin, *Depositum Fidei*). Paul further instructs Timothy by referring to the Tradition when he says, "But as for you, continue in what you have learned and have firmly believed, knowing from whom you learned it" (2 Tim 3:14). Paul instructs Timothy to be obedient to what Paul has handed on to him, not to follow the Scriptures alone.

In the beginning of Luke's Gospel, the author acknowledges that the faithful have already received the teachings of Christ even though they didn't have the New Testament Scriptures. He was only writing that they "may know the truth concerning the things of which you have been informed" (Lk 1:4). Thus, Luke writes to verify the oral Tradition that the people had already received, which serves as an equally valuable witness to God's revealed truth. As Paul teaches, "Any charge must be sustained by the evidence of two of three witnesses" (2 Cor 13:1).

In the book of Acts, Luke also tells us that the early Christians followed the apostolic Tradition handed on to them. "And they devoted themselves to the apostles' teaching and fellowship, to the breaking of bread and the prayers" (Acts 2:42). In Peter's second epistle, he writes that he "will see to it that after my departure you may be able at any time to recall these things" (2 Pet 1:15). However, since this was Peter's last canonical epistle, this "means to recall" must refer to the apostolic Tradition and teaching authority of his office (discussed later) that he left behind.

Paul says that the Romans are "filled with all knowledge, and able to instruct one another" as he writes the epistle to them (see Rom 15:14). Thus, Paul is only writing the Romans to remind them about "some points" of the teaching that the Romans previously received through oral Tradition (v.15).

In Acts 20:27, Paul tells the elders at Ephesus that he declared to the Ephesians "the whole counsel of God." However, in Ephesians 3:3, Paul says that he has written to the Ephesians only "briefly" about the revelation made known to him. In writing to the Corinthians about celebrating the Eucharist, Paul says, "About the other things I will give directions when I come."[14] Surely, Paul did not intend the Corinthians to erase from their memories his oral instructions as soon as Scripture was completed.

Paul also warns the Thessalonians about the "son of perdition," (2 Thess 2:3) and says, "Do you not remember that when I was still with you I told you this?" (v.5). Yet there is nothing in Paul's first letter to the Thessalonians about the "son of perdition," which means that Paul had instructed them to heed his oral teaching as well.

Paul further warns the Galatians about avoiding immoral behavior, saying, "I warn you, as I warned you *before*, that those who do such things shall not inherit the kingdom of God" (Gal 5:21). But there is no written record of Paul's previous warning to the Galatians, so he must have been reminding them about his oral instructions on immorality.

Didn't Jesus condemn the "traditions of men"?

If Jesus and the apostles intended to transmit the gospel in both oral and written form, then why does Jesus condemn the use of tradition in several places in the Gospels?[15] A closer reading of these texts reveals that Jesus was actually condemning the human traditions of hypocritical Pharisees who donated their goods to the Temple (under the "Corban rule") to avoid using the goods to care for their parents. In other words, they were using mere human traditions to circumvent God's laws (to honor father and mother).

These verses have nothing to do with the oral and written Tradition of the Christian faith handed down to us from the apostles. When human traditions are at odds with Christ's teachings, we must reject them; this is different from apostolic Tradition, which we must accept. Jesus also does not condemn all human traditions.

Some also use Jesus' warning in Revelation 22:18-19 as an argument against Tradition because it adds to the written Word of God. But when Jesus warned us not to add or take away from the prophecies "in this book," He was referring only to the book of Revelation, and not all the Scriptures of the Bible (which were established nearly three hundred years later). Moreover, God commands the very same thing in Deuteronomy,[16] but this did not preclude Christians from accepting the Old Testament books that were written after Deuteronomy or the New Testament books.

Didn't oral Tradition end after all the original apostles had died?

Some Christians who acknowledge that the Bible instructs us to follow oral Tradition, defend *sola Scripura* by arguing that Christian oral Tradition had to come from the mouth of the original apostles.

Since the apostles are no longer with us, they conclude, there is no longer any oral Tradition to follow.

This position is inconsistent with what the Scriptures teach about the meaning of the word Tradition, "to hand on" (in Greek, *paradosis*), which would not stop at the second generation. For example, Paul encourages Timothy to hand on the apostolic Tradition to future generations by writing "and what you have heard from me before many witnesses entrust to faithful men who will be able to teach others also" (2 Tim 2:2).

This verse demonstrates that oral Tradition need not come from the mouth of an apostle; it is entrusted to successors who are able to teach with the same apostolic authority. In this case, the apostolic Tradition is handed on from Paul (first generation), to Timothy (second generation), to other faithful men (third generation) who will be able to teach others as well (fourth generation). There is nothing in the Scriptures about oral Tradition ending with the apostolic age.

The manner in which the Catholic Church determined the canon of Scripture at the end of the fourth century also proves that oral Tradition did not have to come from the mouth of an apostle. During the first century after Christ's Ascension, there were many writings about Jesus circulating about Judea. Early documents such as the Didache, the Shepherd of Hermas, and the Epistle of Clement were long debated, as it was not evident to fallible minds that these writings weren't divinely inspired. Similarly, there is little in Paul's letter to Philemon that immediately stands out as divine revelation from God. The inspiration of such works as John's third epistle and the book of Revelation were also subjected to centuries of debate until the Church determined the canon. How was the Church to determine which writings were inspired and which writings were not inspired? The answer is *apostolic Tradition.*

When the bishops of the Church reviewed the various writings that claimed to be authentic teachings of Christ, they did not have any written guidance to help them make the determination. There was no apostolic manual on how to discern divine inspiration. The last apostle, John, died around A.D. 100, and there was no Bible during the first centuries of the early Church. Instead, the bishops drew from the Tradition they were given by their predecessors, who drew from the bishops before them, and so on. This process was guided by the Holy Spirit, whom Christ promised would be with the Church forever.[17] Oral Tradition effectively communicated God's Word and kept Christianity alive for nearly four hundred years. Therefore, oral Tradition does not have to come from the mouth of an apostle — only from an apostle's successor.

How did the Jews know which books were inspired, without the Catholic Church?

This inquiry, often made to challenge oral Tradition and the authority of the Church, actually highlights the truth of the Catholic position. For example, the Jews didn't know the book of Isaiah was Scripture because the book of Isaiah told them so. The book of Isaiah, like every other book in the Old Testament, does not claim to be "God-breathed" (in Greek, *theopneustos*) Scripture.

Instead, the Jews knew Isaiah was Scripture because the traditions handed down to them told them Isaiah was Scripture. The Jews also knew Isaiah was Scripture because the divinely appointed authorities over them, which Jesus acknowledged in Matthew 23:3, told them it was Scripture. Therefore, the Jews knew Isaiah was Scripture because of tradition and authority (the Catholic position), and not because of Scripture (the non-Catholic position).

In reality, nothing in Scripture suggests that the Jews knew the book of Isaiah was God-breathed. Such infallible knowledge could come only from an infallible source. This is a principle of logic: *an effect can never be greater than its cause.* No one would argue that the Jewish authorities who rejected Jesus Christ were infallible. Clearly they were not. Thus, in the absence of a direct revelation from God, no fallible mind could ever have known for certain what Scriptures were inspired until an infallible source told them. God provided this infallible source to discern the infallible Scriptures when He gave us the Catholic Church, which Scripture, Tradition, and history affirm.

Was "sola Scriptura" given to us by the Holy Spirit after the canon was complete?

To skirt the inherent biblical and historical problems of *sola Scriptura*, some non-Catholic Christians argue that the doctrine was not a concept of faith during the period of revelation, but that this rule of faith developed over time. This argument actually proves that *sola Scriptura* is not taught in the Scriptures. This is because the Scriptures were written during this very period of revelation. If the Scriptures didn't teach the concept of *sola Scriptura* during the period of revelation, then they don't teach the concept of *sola Scriptura* at all. We cannot divide the meaning of Scripture between revelation and post-revelation periods; God's revelation can never contradict itself.

Nowhere in the Bible does God reveal that the apostolic Word in its entirety would eventually be committed to writing, either with the compilation of the Bible or any other event. Jesus never said, "Preach the good news to all creation until the Bible canon is determined; then, stop preaching, because the written Word will become the exclusive means to convey the good news." Similarly, Paul never said, "Stand firm and hold fast to the tradition which you received from us, whether oral or written, until the Bible canon is determined. Then only obey the written Tradition." Nothing in Scripture rescinds the command to obey oral Tradition, nor reveals that the oral Word handed down from the apostles' preaching would eventually cease to be authoritative.

On the contrary, the Scriptures tell us that the Word of God handed down to us orally through preaching lasts forever: "The word of the Lord abides for ever. That word is the good news which was preached to you" (1 Pet 1:25). If we were to follow oral Tradition during the apostolic age, we should follow the same Tradition today. The Bible expresses the living Word of God, and this living Word is the same yesterday, today and forever (see Heb 13:8). Scripture teaches us that this living Word is both written and oral.[18] Although heaven and earth will pass away, the words Jesus gave to His apostles will "not pass away" (Mk 13:31).

Are there other examples of God's Word in oral apostolic Tradition?

Certainly. The apostles and the other sacred writers understood that they were to hand down the gospel message orally. In fact, some indicated that they even preferred teaching the gospel orally as opposed to writing letters.

- Paul prayed earnestly night and day that he and the other leaders of the Church could see the Thessalonians face-to-face, and supply what was lacking in their faith (see 1 Thess 3:10). His letters were not enough.
- Paul tells Timothy that he is coming to see his spiritual son "soon" in order to give him apostolic instruction in person, and that he is only writing Timothy in the event that Paul is delayed (see 1 Tim 3:14-15).
- Similarly, John tells the faithful, "Though I have much to write to you, I would rather not use paper and ink, but I hope to come to see you and talk with you face to face, so that our joy may be complete" (2 Jn 12). In his third epistle, John also says, "I had much to write to you, but I would rather not write with pen and ink" (3 Jn 13).

Throughout the Bible, the sacred writers emphasize that the gospel comes to us through the oral apostolic Word. When the faithful hear the apostolic Word, they hear Christ Himself, for the Lord says, "He who hears you, hears me" (Lk 10:16).

- Luke writes that the Holy Spirit appeared to the apostles in the form of "tongues of fire" so that they could "speak" the gospel message (see Acts 2:3-4). Luke also emphasizes how the apostles sent Judas and Silas out to preach the gospel "by word of mouth" (Acts 15:27).
- Paul teaches in Romans (10:8) that the word of God comes orally from the apostles when he writes, "The word is near you, on your lips and in your heart (that is, the word of faith which we preach)." Paul further writes, "So faith comes from what is heard, and what is heard comes by the preaching of Christ" (v.17).

- Paul teaches the Corinthians that it is because of his preaching that they believe in Christ* and are saved.*[19] Paul tells the Galatians that the gospel he preaches is not a man's gospel, but a revelation of Jesus Christ (see Gal 1:11-12).

- Paul tells the Ephesians that the gospel of their salvation comes from what they heard from the apostles (see Eph 1:13). Paul tells the Colossians that what they heard before in the Word of truth is the saving gospel (see Col 1:5). Paul teaches the Thessalonians that what they have heard from the apostles is not from men, but actually the Word of God (see 1 Thess 2:13).

- Paul encourages Timothy to follow the sound words that he heard from Paul, and to guard these truths by the power of the Holy Spirit.[20] Paul tells Titus that God's Word is manifested through preaching (see Titus 1:3). Finally, at the end of his life, Paul charges Timothy to preach the Word.[21] Although Paul was completing his ministry and preparing for death, he gave no commandment to Timothy to write anything down.

We also see in the Old Testament that oral tradition was the principal way in which God chose to communicate His Word to His people. For example, in Deuteronomy we see that Moses had the law read only every seven years (see Deut 31:9-12). Of course, the Word was not absent during the seven-year interval. It was communicated orally, by God's chosen ones, and sought by the faithful. "For the lips of a priest should guard knowledge, and men should seek instruction from his mouth, for he is the messenger of the LORD of hosts" (Mal 2:7).

In fact, many of the events in the Pentateuch that Moses authored occurred centuries before Moses' birth. Moses, as well as many of the other Old Testament writers, had to rely upon oral tradition to communicate the Word of God in writing.

The prophets taught that the Word of God should be passed on orally. Joel writes: "Tell your children of it, and let your children tell their children, and their children another generation" (Joel 1:3). Isaiah also teaches that the oral Word endures forever when he says, "The grass withers, the flower fades; but the word of our God will stand for ever" (Is 40:8). Isaiah further reveals that God has promised a living voice to hand on the Word of God to generations by word of mouth (not a book):

> And as for me, this is my covenant with them, says the LORD: my spirit which is upon you, and my words which I have put in your mouth, shall not depart out of your mouth, or out of the mouth of your children, or out of the mouth of your children's children, says the LORD, from this time forth and for evermore (Is 59:21).

This prophecy was fulfilled by the oral apostolic Tradition of the Catholic Church.

Oral Tradition was not just a way for the apostles to hand on Christ's teaching to future generations. Jesus and the apostles used oral tradition themselves to teach the gospel during their lives.

- When Matthew wrote the prophecy, "He shall be called a Nazarene" (Mt 2:23), he was relying on Jewish oral tradition. This prophecy is not found in the Old Testament.[22]
- Paul relies on oral apostolic Tradition when he quotes Christ's statement, "It is more blessed to give than to receive" (Acts 20:35). This popular statement of Jesus is not found in the Gospels.
- Paul also draws from apostolic Tradition when he explains Jesus' teaching that a wife should not separate from her husband (1 Cor 7:10), and when he quotes an early Christian hymn — "Awake, O sleeper, rise from the dead and Christ shall give you light" (Eph 5:14).
- Paul draws from Old Testament tradition when he writes that "Jannes and Jambres opposed Moses" (2 Tim 3:8-9), for neither of them is mentioned in the Old Testament. He draws on Old Testament oral tradition again when he writes about the rock who was Christ following Moses during the Exodus (see 1 Cor 10:4). This is also not recorded in the Old Testament.[23]
- The author of Hebrews relies on Old Testament oral tradition when he writes about the Maccabean martyrs being

sawed in two, which is not recorded in Maccabees or else-where in the canon (see Heb 11:37).

- Jude relies on Old Testament oral tradition when he writes about the Archangel Michael's dispute with Satan over Moses' body* and Enoch's prophecy.*24
- Finally, our Lord Jesus relies upon oral tradition when He acknowledges Moses' seat of authority being occupied by the Sanhedrin (Mt 23:2). Nothing about "Moses' seat" is recorded in the Old Testament.

These verses demonstrate that Jesus and the sacred writers used oral tradition to teach the gospel, and not the Scriptures alone. In addition, we also find the sacred writers appealing to writings outside of the New Testament canon to teach the Word of God.

- In 1 Corinthians 5:9-11, Paul refers to a prior letter he wrote to the Corinthian church, which he clearly considered as authoritative as his writings that became part of the New Testament canon. Paul also tells the Colossians to read his letter from Laodicea,25 which is not part of the New Testament canon.
- Peter says that all of Paul's letters are inspired by the wisdom given to him by God,26 but as we have seen, not all these letters are in the Bible.
- James also appeals to a document outside the Old Testament canon as he cites: "He yearns jealously over the spirit which he has made to dwell in us?" (James 4:5).
- Paul quotes even the writings of the pagan poets when he preached the gospel at the Aeropagus (Acts 17:28). For the sacred writers to appeal to writings outside of the Bible is further devastating to the *sola Scriptura* position.

One of the most compelling examples of the early Church's use of apostolic Tradition to teach the faith came at the Council of Jerusalem, as recorded in Acts 15. At this regional council, the Church had to resolve its first doctrinal question regarding whether or not Christians had to be circumcised. If the Church took a *sola Scriptura* approach to this question, she would have undoubtedly imposed a circumcision requirement on new Christians. After all, the Scriptures demonstrated that circumcision was the sign of God's everlasting covenant with Abraham (see Gen 17:11; Rom 4:11). This sign of the covenant was also renewed and reinforced in the Law of Moses (Lev 12:3). Hence, all the Patriarchs and prophets were circumcised, the apostles were circumcised, and even the Lord Jesus Himself was circumcised (Lk 2:21). Based on the Scriptures alone, the case for requiring Christians to be circumcised seemed clear.

As we know, the Church did not impose a circumcision requirement upon newly converted Christians. Based on a teaching of Christ that He entrusted to the apostles, *and not the Scriptures*, Peter declares that both Jews and Gentiles are not saved by the yoke of circumcision, but through the grace of the Lord Jesus (see Acts 15:10-11). Peter's decision, guided by the Holy Spirit, was based upon the apostolic Tradition, and *not* on *sola Scriptura*. In fact, Peter never even mentions the Scriptures in rendering his decision, which was a monumental one for the early Church as more and more Gentiles converted to Christianity.

Based on the foregoing Scripture passages, it is clear *sola Scriptura* was never taught by Jesus or the apostles, and is therefore unbiblical. Scripture alone disproves "Scripture alone" theology. The fullness of the gospel has been handed down to us through the Sacred Tradition of the Church, whether oral or written.

Texts Used to Prove *Sola Scriptura*

Despite the mountain of scriptural evidence refuting *sola Scriptura*, some Christians appeal to a few favorite verses to defend their position. Perhaps their favorite passage to make the argument is 2 Timothy 3:16-17:

> All scripture is inspired by God and profitable for teaching, for reproof, for correction, and for training in righteousness, that the man of God may be complete, equipped for every good work.

Upon examining the context of Paul's statement, however, we see the text cannot be used in this way. There are several reasons for this. First, right before this passage, Paul appeals to apostolic Tradition to instruct Timothy in the ways of the faith. He writes:

But as for you, continue in what you have learned and have firmly believed, knowing from whom you learned it (2 Tim 3:14).

Later in the epistle (3:15), Paul then appeals to the Old Testament Scriptures, with which Timothy had been raised, when he writes,

...and how from childhood you have been acquainted with the sacred writings, which are able to instruct you for salvation through faith in Christ Jesus.

In other words, Paul first instructs Timothy to obey Tradition, and then teaches Timothy that one can come to faith in Jesus Christ without reading the New Testament (since Paul is referring to the Old Testament Scriptures only). Both these teachings are at odds with *sola Scriptura.*

Paul then writes, "All Scripture is inspired by God and profitable for teaching" (2 Tim 3:16). The word for "profitable" in Greek, *ophelimos,* means "useful" — *not "exclusive."* In fact, the use of the word profitable actually underscores the fact that Scripture is not mandatory or exclusive. For example, Paul uses the same word *ophelimos* in his letter to Titus when he writes that good deeds are "profitable to men" (Titus 3:8). If "profitable" does not mean "exclusive" in Titus 3:8, it cannot mean "exclusive" in 2 Timothy 3:16.

Another significant problem in using this verse to prove *sola Scriptura* is that the phrase "all Scripture" comes from the Greek phrase *pasa graphe. Pasa graphe* actually means "every Scripture," not "all Scripture." This means that every *passage* of Scripture is useful. To translate *ophelimos* as "exclusive" would mean that *every single Scripture passage,* independent of the rest of God's revelation, is our exclusive source for teaching and instruction. But if this were true, Christians could not only use *sola Scriptura,* but could use *sola* Matthew or *sola* Mark, or even a single Scripture verse, and be assured of having the fullness of the gospel. Clearly, this is untrue.

Finally, Paul's use of "every Scripture" is in reference to the Old Testament Scriptures of Timothy's childhood, not the Bible in its present form (as there was no New Testament canon at the time of Paul's writing). For all these reasons, 2 Timothy 3:16-17 does not support the idea of *sola Scriptura*. In addition, there are several other important points to consider regarding this passage.

First, we must remember for whom the letter was written. In 2 Timothy 3:17, Paul writes that "the man of God may be complete, equipped for every good work." Who is this "man of God"? Paul was giving instructions to Timothy, a bishop of the Church, so the "man of God" is a clergyman. Thus, the passage is not addressed to the lay faithful. In addition, the word "complete" (in Greek, *artios*) simply means "suitable or fit." *Artios* also describes the "man of God," *not* the Scriptures as some would argue. Therefore, this passage cannot be used to prove that the Scriptures are "complete."

Another issue to consider is what Paul meant when he says in 2 Timothy 3:17 that Scripture may equip the man of God for "every good work." Paul uses this same phrase in 2 Timothy 2:21: "If any one purifies himself from what is ignoble, then he will be a vessel for noble use, consecrated and useful to the master of the house, ready for *any good work.*" These verses show that Paul is teaching Timothy to draw on *different* sources to achieve the *same* goal: being ready for every good work. Therefore, if purification, *independent* of the Scriptures, can make the man of God ready for "every good work," then 2 Timothy 3:16-17 cannot be teaching *sola Scriptura*.

Finally, many non-Catholic Christians contend that the apostles taught *sola Scriptura* to the first-century Church. If this is true, why in 1 Thessalonians 2:13 does Paul teach that he is giving revelation from God orally? This is a critical point. If the apostles were teaching that the "Bible *alone*" contains God's authoritative revelation, then why is Paul *also* giving the faithful *oral* revelation? Either Paul is contradicting his own teaching on *sola Scriptura* with his statement in 1 Thessalonians 2:13, or Paul was not teaching *sola Scriptura* in 2 Timothy 3:16-17. The much-quoted 2 Timothy 3:16-17, instead of proving *sola Scriptura*, actually disproves it.

Other passages commonly used to "prove" sola Scriptura

While 2 Timothy 3:16-17 is the principal passage used to defend *sola Scriptura*, non-Catholic Christians refer to other Scripture passages as well. However, these passages are also misinterpreted or taken entirely out of context.

- *Matthew 4:1-11.* Here Jesus is being tempted by the devil in the wilderness, and He appeals to the authority of Scripture by first quoting Deuteronomy 8:3: "Man shall not live by bread alone, but by every word that proceeds from the mouth of God."

Once again, we must consider context. In this verse, Jesus is resisting temptation, not giving a dogmatic definition about the formal sufficiency of Scripture. Jesus quotes from Deuteronomy 8:3 to contrast His forty faithful days in the desert with Israel's forty years of sin and rebellion.

As we have already learned, "every word that proceeds from the mouth of God" is not limited to Scripture. *All* God's revelation must be heeded, and Scripture is one of the sources of that revelation. Finally, we should note that the devil quotes from Psalm 91:11-12 in tempting Jesus to throw Himself off the mountain, since God "will give His angels charge of you" (Mt 4:6). This is an example of how a person not under proper authority (here, the devil) can falsely interpret Scripture to his own destruction.[27]

- *John 5:39-40.* In this Gospel passage, Jesus tells the Jews, "You search the scriptures, because you think that in them you have eternal life, and it is they that bear witness to me; yet you refuse to come to me that you may have life."

Here Jesus rebukes Jews who did not believe that He was the Messiah, and instructs them to search the Scriptures for the Old Testament Messianic prophecies of which He was the fulfillment, and to verify His oral teaching. In fact, the Scriptures were *not* sufficient to teach the Jews about Jesus as Messiah, for they rejected Jesus after searching the Scriptures. Thus, the passage demonstrates precisely the opposite of what the *sola Scriptura* advocate is trying to prove. Moreover, Jesus does not say, "Search the Scriptures alone."

- *John 10:35.* In this passage, Jesus proclaims that "scripture cannot be broken."

Once again, this verse does not make a case for *sola Scriptura.* Jesus is rebuking disbelieving Jews and calling their attention to the Scriptures that prophesied of His coming, which they were obviously not interpreting correctly. Note also that the "Scripture" Jesus refers to in verse 35 is Psalm 82:6 of the Old Testament. Jesus' comments have nothing to do with the New Testament canon or the exclusivity of the Bible.

- *John 20:31.* Here John writes, "...but these are written that you may believe that Jesus is the Christ, the Son of God, and that believing you may have life in His name."

This verse is also used to "prove" that the Bible is the only source for God's Word. However, this passage says nothing of the sort. At most, John is saying that his Gospel has been written to help people believe in Jesus, but this verse does not say that Scripture is the exclusive source for gospel truth. In fact, the verse does not even say Scripture is necessary to come to faith in Christ.

- *Acts 17:11.* Here Luke writes about the people of Berea, who "received the word with all eagerness, examining the Scriptures daily to see if these things were so."

Again, this passage simply explains that the Bereans used the Old Testament Scriptures to confirm the oral teachings they received about Jesus the Messiah. The passage also does not say that the Bereans "examined the Scriptures alone." In fact, this text shows that the Bereans accepted the oral teaching from Paul as the Word of God even before searching the Scriptures. Hence, the verse proves too much for the Christian who is arguing for *sola Scriptura.*

Why, then, in this same passage are the Bereans described as "more noble than those in Thessalonica?" Is it because they used Scripture, which therefore elevates the written Word over that of the oral Word? Not at all. The Bereans' greater nobility was not because of their use of Scripture, which Paul directed his listeners to consult as a common practice in order to prove Christ was the Messiah (see

Acts 17:3). Instead, when the passages are read in their proper context, we see that the Bereans were nobler than the Thessalonians because they accepted Paul's oral teaching as the Word of God. While only "*some* of them were persuaded" in Thessalonica,[*] Paul says that "*many* of them therefore believed" in Berea.[*28] The Bereans were also more reasonable and less violent than the Thessalonians as described in Acts 17:5-9. For all these reasons, the Bereans were nobler than the Thessalonians.

- *1 Corinthians 4:6.* Paul writes, "I have applied all this to myself and Apollos for your benefit, brethren, that you may learn by us not to go beyond what is written, that none of you may be puffed up in favor of one against another."

This is a confusing passage in Scripture. Both Protestant and Catholic exegetes agree that the meaning is ambiguous, and much has been written about it. Many scholars say that Paul was warning the Corinthians not to fall into the sin of pride about their religion, as the Jews had done, by quoting a proverb about children learning to write by tracing letters. By saying, "Don't go above the line," Paul is instructing them not to be arrogant (or "puffed up").[29]

Nevertheless, even a literal translation of the verse does not prove that all of God's revelation has been committed to the Bible. The phrase does not even identify the document to which "what is written" refers: Old Testament Scriptures? Mosaic Law? The Talmud? Or something else? Since there was no New Testament canon at the time Paul wrote this letter, it can't possibly be used to prove *sola Scriptura.* Further, Paul says in the same verse "learn by us" (v.6) just as he similarly says, "Be imitators of me" a few verses later (v.16). Paul is actually instructing the Corinthians to follow his apostolic example, and not take some narrow view of God's Word. If Paul were really teaching *sola Scriptura* in 1 Corinthians 4:6, then Paul would be contradicting himself by urging the Corinthians to go beyond Scripture by "learning by us" and being "imitators of me."

To what, specifically, does the term "apostolic Tradition" refer?

After proving that the Bible instructs us to follow Sacred Tradition and not the Scriptures alone, the Catholic Christian may be asked for a list of these Traditions. This is a legitimate question. We have already demonstrated that the canon (or list) of Scripture is among the Traditions of the Catholic Church. Other important apostolic Traditions that came out of the early Church include:

- the Creeds of our Christian faith (such as the Apostles' Creed and the Nicene Creed),
- doctrines related to the Blessed Trinity (that God is one in three persons) and Christology, including the hypostatic union (that Jesus is a divine person with both a divine and a human nature).
- Marian Traditions, including the Immaculate Conception of Mary (that she was conceived without original sin), her perpetual virginity (that Mary remained a virgin before, during and after the birth of Jesus), and her Assumption (that Mary was taken up body and soul into heaven).

These Traditions were written down by the early Church Fathers during the first seven centuries of the Church, and were used to combat various heresies that sprung forth during the early Church concerning the nature of Jesus and His relationship to the Father. Although some Marian Traditions were formally defined much later, they also have a scriptural basis, and are alluded to in the writings of the Church Fathers.

These writings can be read by anyone who makes a trip to the local diocesan library or studies the many good websites about the Fathers on the Internet. Any Christian who wants to learn more about the Tradition handed down to us from the apostles should also obtain a copy of the *Catechism of the Catholic Church,* which can be found in any Catholic bookstore.

Sola Scriptura and Private Judgment

We close this chapter by examining a practical problem with *sola Scriptura* — having to make private judgments about what is true and what is not true concerning the Christian faith. To be an advocate of Bible-only Christianity, one must hold the view that the written Word of God is clear and understandable, notwithstanding its varied literary genres, historical backdrops, and mystical revelations. Those holding this view argue that no resource outside of the Bible is needed to help Christians interpret the Bible correctly. This presumed clarity of God's written Word is often called "perspicuity."

Of course, if God's written Word were so clear, Christians would be united in the doctrines of the faith. In reality, more than *thirty thousand* denominations exist today, all with different interpretations of Scripture on even the most basic doctrines of Christian teaching, such as baptism. This alone proves that the written Word of God is not always clear. This is also one of the most compelling arguments against Protestant Christianity, and one of the main reasons Protestants leave their Bible churches and come home to the Catholic Church.

The Scriptures themselves teach us that the Word of God is not clear. For example, in the Old Testament, the Lord speaks directly to Samuel three times, but Samuel does not recognize the voice.[30] The Word of God is not always clear, even when He speaks directly to us. In 1 Kings 13:1-32, we see that the man of God cannot discern between God's Word (His commandment to refrain from eating and drinking) and the erroneous word of a prophet (who said that God had rescinded His command to refrain from eating and drinking). The Word of God is not perspicuous.

In Acts 8:29-39, Philip encounters the Ethiopian eunuch reading Isaiah the prophet, and asks, "Do you understand what you are reading?" (v.30). The eunuch responds, "How can I, unless someone guides me?" (v.31). We need an authority outside of Scripture to help us understand God's Word. Even those in authority need to be guided and corrected from time to time. For example, the author of Hebrews writes, "For though by this time you ought to be teachers, you need someone to teach you again the first principles of God's word" (Heb 5:12).

I have always wondered how non-Catholic Christians argue that Scripture is so clear, and yet so often depart from the literal and obvious meaning of Scripture. The Catholic Church has always taught that we are to interpret the Scriptures in the literal and obvious sense, unless reason makes the interpretation untenable or necessity requires. God has chosen His words very carefully, and He means what He says. God is not trying to deceive us, for He cannot lie.[31]

This is why the Church interprets literally, for example,

- Matthew 16:18 (Peter is the rock);
- Matthew 19:9 (remarriage after divorce is adultery);
- Matthew 26:26-28 ("this is my body," "this is my blood");
- John 3:5 (born of water and Spirit means baptism);
- John 6:51-58 ("eat my flesh," "drink my blood");
- John 20:23 ("If you forgive the sins ... they are forgiven");
- 1 Peter 3:21 ("Baptism ... saves you");
- James 2:24 ("man is justified by works and not by faith alone"); and,
- James 5:14-15 (anoint the sick with oil to save them and forgive their sins).

The Church interprets these verses literally because there is no compelling reason to interpret them otherwise. God means what He says; to say otherwise is to accuse Him of poor communication.

Bible Christians talk a lot about "truth," and often accuse Catholics of "defecting from the truth." This poses an interesting question: What, exactly, constitutes "the truth" of the Christian faith? Which doctrines, and what version of those teachings? For example, what is the truth regarding baptism? The priesthood? Salvation? Sexual morality?

Furthermore, how can we know the truth about anything not explicitly taught in the Scriptures? For example, how can we take a stand on bioethical issues such as in-vitro fertilization or stem cell research, if the Bible is silent about them? And how can anyone claim that Catholics and other Christians have "defected from the truth," if they cannot define absolute truth themselves?

The truth is that, apart from the teaching authority and Tradition of the Church, no one can ever know the absolute truth about any Christian doctrine. Instead, truth is reduced to private judgment, which has led to religious relativism and indifferentism that has infected our churches and our society as a whole.

Peter's admonitions regarding private judgment Christianity are clear:

First of all you must understand this, that no prophecy of Scripture is a matter of one's own interpretation, because no prophecy ever came by the impulse of man, but men moved by the Holy Spirit spoke from God (2 Pet 1:20).

If Scripture is not a matter of one's own private interpretation, this means that Scripture is a matter of *public* interpretation, a gift that has been entrusted by Christ to the Holy Catholic Church. Those who interpret the Scriptures privately outside of the living Tradition of the Church become their own arbiters of truth. This is like taking a fish out of water. Scripture needs to breathe in its natural environment, which is the Church. Private interpretation can lead people to fall into serious error, and jeopardize their salvation.

In reference to Paul's inspired letters, Peter warns:

There are some things in them hard to understand, which the ignorant and unstable twist to their own destruction, as they do the other scriptures (1 Pet 3:16).

Thus, the divine Word needs a divine interpreter, the Church, who is guided by the Holy Spirit into all truth. God loves us too much to simply give us a book to let us figure it out on our own. Moreover, our loving God is bound by His justice to provide us with a reliable mechanism for discerning truth and error. This way, we can be obedient to His will and attain the salvation He wishes for us. Absent such a mechanism, we would be confused, to which the thousands of Christian denominations testify. God is not the author of such confusion.[32]

Before closing, we must emphasize that demonstrating that *sola Scriptura* is unbiblical by no means diminishes the role of Scripture in the Catholic faith. On the contrary, all Catholics (should) know that the Church exalts Scripture to its rightful place as the living Word of God. The Church venerates the Scriptures as she venerates the Lord's own body. This is why Scripture takes a pre-eminent place in Catholic spirituality, as we see in praying the Liturgy of the Hours, the Psalms, the Rosary, and especially the Holy Mass, where the Bible is read in full every three years.

We now look at the biblical basis for the Catholic Church.

CHAPTER TWO

The Church

Most non-Catholic Christians do not believe that Jesus Christ established a visible Church that is governed by a hierarchy of leaders who can teach with authority. Instead, they believe that the Church is an invisible association of believers in Christ, loosely connected by a common belief in the Bible alone as the rule and guide of faith. They believe this despite the fact that this understanding of "church" was not espoused by any Christian figure until 1517, when Martin Luther broke away from the Catholic Church and developed the novel doctrine of *sola Scriptura*. In this chapter, we will consider what the Bible has to say about the Church that Christ established while He was on earth, and demonstrate that this Church is the One, Holy, Catholic, and Apostolic Church.

An Introduction to the Biblical Church

The Scriptures teach us that Jesus Christ left behind a visible and hierarchical Church with bishops, priests and deacons on whom He conferred His own divine teaching authority and instructed to perpetuate His mission by passing on their authority to successors. We will examine the scriptural basis for this later in the chapter.

The Scriptures also teach us that Jesus specifically built His Church upon the Apostle Peter,* to whom He gave the keys to the kingdom of heaven,* and the special mandate to rule over His flock.[33]

Jesus also invested Peter with His own divine teaching authority, declaring to Peter that whatever he bound and loosed on earth would be bound and loosed in heaven (Mt 16:19). While Jesus also established His Church on the foundation of the other apostles, and gave them binding and loosing authority,[34] Jesus designated Peter alone as the rock on which He would build the Church, and gave Peter alone the keys to the kingdom of heaven.

Because of Peter's status as the rock of the Church and the keeper of the keys, Christ invested Peter with special authority to govern the visible Church on earth. Further, by virtue of the keys, Christ established a mechanism of apostolic succession, whereby Peter's office of supreme pastor would be passed on to successors, thereby providing a perpetual and visible source of unity for the Church from one generation to the next.

Only the Catholic Church claims to be the one Church that Christ built upon Peter. The Catholic Church can in fact demonstrate an unbroken lineage of 263 successors to Peter since the birth of the Church over twenty centuries ago. Moreover, the bishops of the Church can all trace their lineage back to the original apostles. No other church can make these claims.

Because the apostolic roots of the Church are so historically compelling, non-Catholic Christians are forced to challenge the claims of the Church, saying that Jesus did not intend to build a visible Church on Peter or to create an office of supreme pastor that would endure beyond the apostles. To remain faithful to their tradition of *sola Scriptura*, however, they must do this using the Scriptures alone. While there is substantial extra-biblical evidence of Peter's supremacy in the Church (the historical reality of the Church's lineage, the writings of the Church Fathers, the etchings in the Roman catacombs, etc.), Catholics must be prepared to answer these inquiries using the Scriptures as well. We provide biblical answers in the next sections.

The Papacy

We begin by examining passages of Matthew 16:13-19 that provide the biblical basis for the papacy. When Jesus came into the district of Caesarea Philippi with His apostles, He asked them, "Who do men say that the son of man is?"[35]

They said, "Some say John the Baptist, others say Elijah, and others Jeremiah or one of the prophets."

Then Jesus said to them, "But who do you say that I am?"

Simon Peter replied, "You are the Christ, the Son of the living God."

And Jesus answered him:

> Blessed are you, Simon Bar-Jona! For flesh and blood has not revealed this to you, but my Father who is in heaven. And I tell you, you are Peter, and on this rock I will build my church, and the powers of death shall not prevail against it. I will give you the keys of the kingdom of heaven, and whatever you bind on earth shall be bound in heaven, and whatever you loose on earth shall be loosed in heaven.[36]

We see that after Simon receives a revelation from the Father and confesses that Jesus is the Christ, Jesus blesses him and changes his name to Peter, which means "rock" ("Peter" comes from the Greek word *Petros*). "Rock" was not a name in Jesus' time, so this was an extraordinary thing for Jesus to do. Jesus did this in response to Simon's confession of Jesus' true identity, which was also extraordinary.

What is the significance of this exchange? Jesus gave Simon this new name to identify his new status as the rock foundation of the Church and chief shepherd among the apostles. Simon's pronouncement about Jesus was evidence of his supernatural insight, given by the Spirit, which he needed to fulfill his new role. This exchange of titles perhaps comes out even more forcefully in the Greek language — Jesus, you are the *Christos*! — Simon, you are the *Petros*!

We see the significance of a divine name change elsewhere in Scripture. God changes Abram's name to Abraham and Sarai to Sarah,* Jacob's name to Israel,* and Eliakim's name to Jehoiakim.*[37] In each instance, when God changes a person's name, He changes the status of that person as well; he or she becomes a special agent of God. Similarly, when Jesus changes Simon's name to Peter, he became God's special agent.

Is Peter really the rock?

Because the Catholic Church can demonstrate through apostolic succession that her foundation was built upon the rock of Peter, anti-Catholics have taken great pains to disprove that Christ built His

Church on Peter at all. Otherwise the Catholic Church's claim of having a Christ-appointed central authority figure is convincing.

Some attempt to discredit the Catholic position by correctly pointing out that there are many places in Scripture where God is called "rock."[38] From this fact, they conclude that God, and not Peter, is the rock that Jesus is referring to in Matthew 16:18.

This argument, however, assumes that attributions used in Scripture can be applied to only one individual. This, of course, is not true. For example...

- in Ephesians 2:20, the apostles are called the foundation of the Church;
- in 1 Corinthians 3:11, Jesus is called the foundation of the Church.
- In Acts 20:28, the apostles are called the shepherds of the flock;
- in 1 Peter 2:25, Jesus is called the Shepherd of the flock.

Moreover, we don't need to rely on Matthew 16:18 to conclude that Simon is the "rock" because Jesus also calls Simon the "rock" in Mark 3:16 and John 1:42.[39]

Of course, Catholics believe Jesus is the "real" rock foundation of the Church, for without Him, there would be no Church. By conferring this attribute to Peter, Jesus designates Peter as the foundation of the earthly Church, over which Peter would rule as chief shepherd after Jesus ascended into heaven (Jesus speaks in the future tense in Matthew 16:18-19).[40] Therefore, Peter is the rock on which Christ would build His Church after He ascended to the Father.

We have further proof of this when we analyze Matthew 16:18 in the Greek. The Scriptures use the adjective *tautee* to describe "rock." The Greek word *tautee* is a demonstrative adjective, underscoring that Peter himself — as opposed to any other person or thing — is the rock on which Jesus builds the Church.

We can see this by eliminating the noun (*Petros*) that the demonstrative adjective (*tautee*) describes: "You are Peter, and upon *this* I will build my Church." This shows that the referent of the adjective is the person of Peter. Without the demonstrative adjective, the meaning would be ambiguous; for example: "You are Peter, and upon *the* I will build my Church"; or, "You are Peter, and upon *a* I will build my Church." This is further demonstrated by the fact that Jesus turns the dialogue upon the *person* of Peter after the apostle professes the Father's revelation:

> Blessed are *you* Simon, for flesh and blood has not revealed this to *you*, and I tell *you*, *you* are Peter, and on this rock I will build my Church. I will give *you* the keys to the kingdom, and whatever *you* bind and loose on earth will be bound and loosed in heaven (see Mt 16:17).

Another way Protestants attack Peter's status as the rock foundation of the Church is by attempting to redefine the Greek word *Petros*. They argue that, because the Greek translation of rock in Matthew 16:18 is *Petros*, and the word *petra* in Greek could mean a pebble, *Petros* must mean a small pebble (rather than a large foundation stone). Because Jesus called Peter a "small pebble," the apostle cannot be the foundation of the Church.[41]

There are considerable problems with this perspective:

- It cannot be reconciled with Jesus' three-fold blessing of Peter in Matthew 16:18-19.

We have already seen that, upon Simon's confession, Jesus blesses Simon for having received divine revelation, changes Simon's name to Peter, and finally gives Simon Peter the keys to the kingdom of heaven and the power to bind and loose. To argue that Jesus was renaming Simon "small pebble" is to conclude that Jesus was attempting to diminish Peter right after blessing him, only to build Peter back up again by giving him the keys to the kingdom and the binding and loosing authority. In other words, Jesus would be saying, "Blessed are you Simon, Bar-Jona, but you are an insignificant little pebble and I am the real rock on which I will build my Church; nevertheless, I will give you the keys to the kingdom of heaven, and whatever you bind and loose on earth will be bound and loosed in heaven." This argument does not stand to reason.

- The original languages do not support the "pebble" theory.

Petros is the Greek translation of the Aramaic word *kepha*. Since Jesus spoke Aramaic (as did all Palestinian Jews at the time), Jesus did not call Simon *Petros*. Jesus called Simon *Kepha*, and said, "On this *kepha* I will build my Church."[42] See also Mark 3:16 and John 1:42, where Simon is called *Cephas*, a transliteration of the word *kepha*. In Aramaic, *kepha* means a massive stone, and *evna* means little pebble. Using the Greek word *petros* to translate *kepha* was done simply to reflect the masculine noun of Peter. If the translator wanted to identify Peter as the small pebble, he would have used *lithos* (which means pebble in Greek), not *petros*. But this was not the case, because Jesus used *kepha*, not *evna*. Therefore, Jesus, like the wise man, "built His house upon the rock, and the rain fell, and the floods came, and the winds blew and beat upon that house, but it did not fall, because it had been founded on the rock" (Mt 7:24-25).

Peter's Keys to the Kingdom

What is the significance of the keys that Jesus gave to Peter? Most Protestants believe that Jesus' gift somehow relates to Peter's duties in the heavenly kingdom as the official gatekeeper for those entering eternal paradise. But this is not what Jesus meant, and this is a most critical point to understanding the meaning of Jesus Christ's kingship.

By giving Peter the keys to the kingdom, Jesus was announcing to the Jews that that He had come to fulfill His Father's promise by restoring the kingdom previously established by David, which had been lost through war, rebellion and sin. Therefore, by giving Peter the keys, Jesus was giving Peter authority over the *earthly* kingdom. This kingdom is the Holy Catholic Church, whose glory will only be made manifest at the end of time.[43] To understand this more fully, we look at the Scriptures.

In the Old Testament, God enters into a covenant with David, whom God describes as "a man after his own heart" (1 Sam 13:14). God tells David that He will make the nations his heritage (see Ps 2:8) and promises David that from his lineage would come a king who would bring all the nations under the kingship of God. This king would be not only the son of David, but also the Son of God, whose kingdom on earth would be established forever:

I will raise up your offspring after you. . . I will be his father, and he shall be my Son. . . And your house and your kingdom shall be made sure forever before me; your throne shall be established forever.[44]

Even after the Davidic line appeared to be lost, Israel's prophets continued to echo God's promise that the righteous one from David's lineage would restore the kingdom of God.[45]

With the coming of Christ, the evangelists made it clear that Jesus was the one who had come to fulfill God's promise by re-establishing and perfecting the Davidic kingdom as the worldwide household of God.

Matthew and Luke make a point of tracing Jesus' royal pedigree back to King David.[46] The archangel Gabriel announces to Mary that her Son would be given the throne of His father David (see Lk 1:32). Luke points out that Jesus was also born in the city of David (see Lk 2:11). The Gospels also show that some recognized Jesus' kingship. For example, Nathaniel declares to Jesus, "Rabbi, you are the Son of God! You are the King of Israel!" (Jn 1:49). Many people also cried out to Jesus, calling Him the "Son of David."[47] The Jewish people were waiting for the Messiah to come from the line of David and to restore the kingdom that had been lost.

In the old Davidic kingdom, the king had royal ministers who performed the priestly duties of conducting liturgical worship and offering sacrifice. The king also had a prime minister, or chief steward, who would rule and govern the household in the king's absence. The chief steward would act as the king's representative and would have the authority to establish rules of conduct for the members of the kingdom he served. The chief steward's authority was represented by his "keys," as we read in the prophet Isaiah:

Thus says the Lord GOD of hosts, "Come, go to this steward, to Shebna, who is over the household, and say to him: I will thrust you from your office, and you will be cast down from your station. In that day I will call my servant Eliakim the son of Hilkiah, and I will clothe him with your robe, and will bind your girdle on him, and will commit your authority to his hand; and he shall be a father to the inhabitants of

Jerusalem and to the house of Judah. And I will place on his shoulder the key of the house of David; he shall open, and none shall shut; and he shall shut, and none shall open."[48]

In describing the Old Covenant kingdom, Isaiah tells us that Shebna, King David's chief representative, has an office and a station (see Is 22:5,19). In the next verse, Eliakim succeeds Shebna as the chief steward of the household (see v.20). King David, by this time, had been dead for three centuries, but his kingdom was preserved through a succession of representatives. We also see that Shebna's authority is fully transferred to Eliakim, who is called a "father" to God's people (v.21). Finally, we see that the keys to the kingdom pass from Shebna to Eliakim, and whenever Eliakim opens, "none shall shut; and he shall shut, and none shall open" (v.22). Thus, *the keys to the kingdom are a symbol of authority, and are used to facilitate dynastic succession.* Jesus was referring to this passage in Isaiah when giving Peter the keys to the kingdom of heaven, and most Jews immediately recognized the connection.

This passage in Isaiah is the only other place in Scripture where keys are mentioned in the context of a kingdom. Jesus came not to abolish the Old Covenant, but to fulfill it (see Mt 5:17). Thus, Jesus, after establishing Peter as the rock foundation of the Church, appoints Peter as His chief steward and invests Peter with His own authority to rule and govern while Jesus is in heaven. In fact, Jesus begins to talk about His death and departure only after He appoints Peter as the chief steward of the kingdom (see Mt 16:21). Peter's office as chief steward provided a visible and perpetual source of unity for the Church from one generation to the next, a fact that was not seriously questioned for 1,500 years — until the Protestant Reformation.

As the chief steward, Peter also becomes the father of the inhabitants of the Church. This is why Catholics call the successor of Peter "the pope" and his office "the papacy" (the word "pope" simply means father or papa in Italian). Further, whatever Papa binds or looses (opens or shuts) on earth is bound or loosed (open or shut) in heaven. Binding and loosing are rabbinical terms that describe the authority to make rules of conduct (in Hebrew, *halakah*) for the faithful. Thus,

Peter can enact laws and make disciplinary decisions for the Church. Jesus also gives the authority to bind and loose to the other apostles,[49] but He gives Peter alone the keys.

Binding and loosing authority also connotes the supernatural ability to make doctrinal pronouncements and forgive sins. We see elsewhere in Scripture that keys represent supernatural authority.[50] For example, Jesus says in the book of Revelation that He has "the keys of Death and Hades" (Rev 1:18).[51] The keys represent Jesus' power over death and His authority to forgive and punish sins. Jesus gives these keys to Peter as the chief shepherd of the Church.

Thus, not only do Peter's keys symbolize his governing authority over Christ's earthly kingdom, but they also represent his pastoral authority over souls. Peter's keys fit into the gates of Hades, which can bind sin and punishment, and loose sin through the sacrament of forgiveness. Hence, the gates of Hades will never prevail against the Church (see Mt 16:18). Further, because Peter's declarations on earth are ratified in heaven, Christ is giving Peter the authority to teach infallibly (which means without error).

Whose authority?

In an effort to disprove Peter's authority, some point out that Jesus is also described in the book of Revelation as the one "who has the key of David, who opens and no one shall shut, who shuts and no one opens" (Rev 3:7). But this verse does not say anything about Jesus stripping Peter of his earthly duties, and such a divestiture would not make any sense in light of other Gospel texts.[52] Instead, the verse reminds us that the resurrected Christ is the source of all power and authority, and that His conferral of the keys to Peter is a divine appointment. While Jesus is the rock and the holder of the keys, He has conferred these distinctions upon Peter as the chief steward of the earthly kingdom.

The Jews quickly understood the "binding and loosing" terminology Jesus used to describe Peter's authority. For example, Jesus uses similar words to describe the authority of the Pharisees when He says, "They bind heavy burdens, hard to bear... but they themselves will not move [loose] them with their finger" (Mt 23:4). In this situation, Jesus acknowledges that the Pharisees sit on Moses' seat and have the legitimate authority to teach, but warns the Jews not to follow their hypocritical example (see Mt 23:2-3). This verse also shows that Jesus recognized that Moses' authority was preserved through succession to his chair.[53] But while the Pharisees had the old binding and loosing authority under the Old Covenant kingdom, Peter and the apostles (and their successors) exercise the new binding and loosing authority of the New Covenant kingdom of God, which is the Catholic Church.

We see elsewhere in Scripture where Jesus makes it clear to Peter and the other apostles that Peter is the chief steward of the kingdom and chief shepherd of the flock. For example, Peter asks Jesus if the parable of the master and the kingdom was meant just for the apostles or for all people. Jesus, perhaps with a bit of humor, rhetorically confirms to Peter that he is the chief steward over the Master's household of God.[54] In the Garden of Gethsemane, Jesus asks Peter, and no one else, why he was asleep (Mk 14:37). Jesus holds Peter accountable for his actions on behalf of the other apostles because he has been appointed their leader. Jesus also prays that Peter's faith may not fail and charges Peter to be the one to strengthen the other apostles.

While this is not evident in the English translation, the Greek makes clear that Jesus emphasizes Peter's leadership among the apostles by using the singular "you" in referring to Simon Peter, and the plural "you" when referring to the other apostles.

> Simon, Simon, behold, Satan demanded to have you [plural] that he might sift you [plural] like wheat, but I have prayed for you [singular] that your [singular] faith may not fail; and when you [singular] have turned again, strengthen your [singular] brethren.[55]

After the Resurrection, Jesus asks Simon Peter in front of the other apostles if he loves Jesus "more than these," referring to the other apostles (Jn 21:15). After Peter's three-fold affirmation, reversing his three-fold denial of Jesus during the Passion, Jesus then charges Peter to be the chief shepherd among the apostles by telling him, "Feed my lambs," "Tend my sheep," and "Feed my sheep" (Jn 21:15-17). The word for "tend" (in Greek, *poimaine*) also means to rule or govern. This is the same word that is used to describe how Jesus will "rule the nations with a rod of iron."[56] Jesus gives Peter the supreme authority to rule over the other apostles.

What "kingdom?"

Those who deny that Christ left a visible, hierarchical and authoritative Church are forced to argue that the kingdom of heaven Jesus was talking about in Matthew 16:19 refers to the heavenly kingdom of eternal glory (as if Peter's keys relate to a gate-keeping duty of letting people into heaven). Otherwise, the Catholic understanding of a visible, earthly, kingdom-Church built upon Peter and invested with Christ's divine authority is compelling.

Of course, this interpretation does not explain how Christ fulfilled the Father's promise to restore the earthly kingdom of David, although Protestants don't argue that God's promise remains unfulfilled. Nevertheless, the New Testament Scriptures are clear that when Jesus spoke of the kingdom of heaven, He was referring to the earthly Church.

- Jesus compares the kingdom of God to a field of good and bad seeds in reference to good and bad people.[57] This kingdom must refer to the earthly Church and not eternal state of glory, for there are no bad people in heaven.
- Jesus also says the kingdom of heaven is like a mustard seed that grows into a tree.[58] This refers to the growth of the universal Church on earth — not heaven, which is eternal.
- Jesus says the kingdom of heaven is like bread that is mixed with three measures of flour to become leavened.[59] This refers to the earthly kingdom of God, which grows in holiness. The metaphors "mustard seed" and "bread" also demonstrate that the Church would change in appearance over time, but would be in essence the very same Church of Jesus Christ and His apostles.
- Jesus also says the kingdom of heaven is like a net which catches fish of every kind.[60] This describes the universal ("Catholic") Church, which unites people of every kind into the body of Christ.

- Jesus compares the kingdom of heaven to ten maidens, five of whom were foolish.[61] Again, this kingdom refers to the Church on earth, because there are no fools in the glorious kingdom of heaven!

When Jesus declares that the kingdom of God "has come upon you"* or "is at hand,"*[62] He is referring to the earthly kingdom of God, and not the eternal state of glory. Similarly, when Jesus gives Peter the keys to the kingdom of heaven, He is referring to God's kingdom on earth.

The Scriptures in the Old Testament also demonstrate that the "kingdom of God" refers to the earthly kingdom. For example, we see that Solomon sits "upon the throne of the kingdom of the Lord" (1 Chron 28:5). Later we see that "Solomon sat on the throne of the LORD as king instead of David his father" (1 Chron 29:23). Hence, the kingdom of the Lord means God's earthly kingdom, and Jesus was referring to the earthly kingdom of the Catholic Church when He gave Peter the keys "to the kingdom of heaven" (Mt 16:19).

When Jesus gave Peter the keys, the Jews also understood that He was instituting in His kingdom a plan for a succession of chief stewards from one generation to the next. Through the prophet Ezekiel, God declares, "David shall be king over them; and they shall all have one shepherd" (Ez 37:24-25). In the kingdom established in the New Covenant, Jesus is our King, and Peter is our earthly shepherd. Just as the key of David passed from Shebna to Eliakim in the Old Covenant kingdom, the keys of the kingdom in the New Covenant have passed from Peter to Linus to Cletus to Clement, all the way to our current pope.

The papacy is an office with a two thousand year history, facilitated by the passing of the keys from one chief steward to the next.[63] Hence, when Paul says that Jesus Christ's Church will exist in every generation (see Eph 3:21), he can only be referring to the Catholic Church. No other church has existed in every generation.

Other examples of Peter's primacy among the apostles
The Scriptures make evident Peter's primacy among the apostles and in the early Church. Peter is mentioned about 155 times in the

New Testament. The rest of the apostles combined are mentioned less frequently. Peter is almost always mentioned first among the apostles.[64] Peter is mentioned even before the Apostle John, whom Jesus loved.[65] In addition, we see Peter's formation as the leader of the apostles occurring during Jesus' earthly ministry, particularly when Peter speaks on behalf of the apostles:

- Peter is the first among the apostles to confess the divinity of Christ.[66]
- In the presence of the disciples, Peter asks Jesus about the rule of forgiveness,* and recalls Jesus' curse on the fig tree.*[67]
- Peter also speaks on behalf of the apostles, telling Jesus that they have left everything to follow Him.[68]
- Jesus speaks directly to Peter regarding the parable of the two debtors, and Peter answers on behalf of the disciples.[69]
- When Jesus asks who touched His garment, Peter answers on behalf of the disciples.[70]
- Peter is the only one among the apostles to speak at the Transfiguration of Jesus.[71]
- Peter asks Jesus to clarify a parable on behalf of the disciples.[72]
- Peter speaks out to the Lord in front of the apostles concerning the washing of feet.[73]
- When a tax collector approaches Peter for Jesus' tax, Jesus pays the half-shekel tax with one shekel, for both Himself and Peter.[74] Peter is treated as the spokesman for Christ and His representative on earth.

In Luke's Gospel, Jesus instructs Peter to let down his nets, and the miraculous catch of fish follows (see Lk 5:4,10). This event is a metaphor for Peter's role as the fisher of men. In John's Gospel, after the Resurrection Jesus instructs Peter to cast his net over the right side of the boat, and another miraculous catch follows (see Jn 21:6). The catch is a metaphor for gathering the people of God into the Church, whose net will never break (v.11). Peter's boat, from which Jesus taught (see Lk 5:3), is also a metaphor for the Church, which is often referred to as the "barque of Peter." Peter is also the only apostle to get out of the boat, run to the shore, and lead the other apostles to Jesus (see Jn 21:6-7). Peter is the earthly shepherd leading his flock to the Lord.

After Jesus' Ascension, we see Peter exercising his authority as the chief shepherd of the early Church:

- Peter initiates the selection of a successor to Judas, and no one questions him.[75]
- Peter is the first to preach the gospel after the descent of the Holy Spirit on Pentecost Sunday, which has always been celebrated as the birth of the Church.[76]
- Peter is the first to preach about repentance and baptism in the name of Jesus Christ.[77]
- Peter is also the first to teach that Jesus Christ is the Messiah and that there is no salvation other than through Him.[78]
- Peter is the first apostle to teach about salvation in Christ for both Jews and Gentiles.[79]
- Peter is the first to exercise his binding authority by condemning Anaias and Sapphira, resulting in their death.[80]
- Peter is mentioned first in conferring the sacrament of confirmation.[81]
- Peter also binds Simon under pain of sin for requesting to receive the Holy Spirit by the laying on of hands.[82]

As we have seen, Peter also resolves the first doctrinal debate of the Church regarding circumcision at the Church's first Council at Jerusalem, and no one questions his authority (see Acts 15:7-12). Teaching that Jews no longer had to observe the Mosaic Law was a colossal decision for the infant Church. But after Papa Peter decided the matter, all kept silent. Notice that only *after* Peter makes his declaration do Paul and Barnabas, both bishops, speak in support of Peter's teaching. Thereafter, James, another bishop, speaks to further acknowledge Peter's definitive teaching by stating "Simeon (Peter) has related..." (Acts 15:13-14).[83]

Peter further acts as the chief bishop by "exhorting" all the other bishops and elders of the Church,[*] and by making a judgment on the proper interpretation of Paul's letters.[*84] The other apostles acknowledge Peter's primacy in Scripture. For example, in describing the events of the Resurrection, the Gospel writers note that John arrived at the tomb first but stopped and waited for Peter. Peter then arrived and entered the tomb before John.[85] The two disciples of Emmaus also specify that Peter saw the risen Jesus, though they had seen Jesus themselves the previous hour (see Lk 24:33-34). Paul also distinguishes Jesus' post-Resurrection appearances to Peter from those of the other apostles (see 1 Cor 15:4-8). Paul spends fifteen days with Peter privately before beginning his ministry, even though He was chosen directly by Christ in the revelation on the road to Damascus.[86] Luke writes that the "whole Church" offered earnest prayers for Peter during his imprisonment (see Acts 12:5).

In many cases, Peter is uniquely the object of divine intervention. For example, only Peter has faith to walk on water.[87] Peter alone is told that he has received a revelation from God the Father (see Mt 16:17). An angel, who is a messenger of God, identifies Peter as the leader of the apostles as he confirms the Resurrection of Christ (Mark 16:7). Peter works the first healing of the apostles,[*] and even his shadow had healing power[*].[88] Peter both heals Aeneas and raises Tabitha from the dead.[89] An angel tells Cornelius to call upon Peter,[*] and frees Peter from jail[*][90]

What about verses that seem to minimize Peter's authority?

In spite of the overwhelming scriptural evidence of Peter's supremacy in the early Church, some non-Catholics point to several verses that seem to minimize Peter's authority. For example:

Mark 8:33. In this verse, Jesus rebukes Peter along with the other apostles for their failure to understand who Jesus is, as well as the importance of His Messianic role as the Savior of humanity. Since none of the other apostles understood, either, Jesus' rebuke of Peter actually emphasizes Peter's importance among the apostles. Moreover, at this point, Peter was not yet the pope — that is, he had not yet been given the keys to the kingdom of heaven. Hence, the rebuke has nothing to do with Peter's teaching authority.

Galatians 2:11-14. These verses are also sometimes used to diminish Peter's authority over the Church. Again, Paul does not rebuke Peter for his teaching, but his failure to live by that teaching. Peter had been the one who taught infallibly about the gospel being preached to the Gentiles (Acts 10, 11), and yet Peter distanced himself from the Gentiles. Paul thus rebukes Peter for his conduct, as if to say, "Peter, you are our leader, you taught infallibly about the Gentiles, and yet your conduct is inconsistent with your teaching. You of all people!" Paul's rebuke of Peter and his conduct once again underscores, not diminishes, the importance of Peter's leadership in the Church.

Some Christians also deny that Peter was ever in Rome to diminish the authority of the bishop of Rome, who is considered Peter's successor. Whether Peter ever went to Rome is irrelevant to whether Jesus instituted the papacy. Nevertheless, the Scriptures indicate that Peter was in fact in Rome. In 1 Peter 5:13, Peter says he is writing from "Babylon" which was a code name for Rome (the early Christians used code names for their faith to avoid Roman persecution). Several verses in the book of Revelation also demonstrate that Babylon meant Rome.[91] Rome was the only "great city" of the New Testament period after the destruction of the Temple in Jerusalem. Paul also writes to the Romans that he doesn't want to "build on another man's foundation," referring to Peter who built the Church in Rome (Rom 15:20). Because Rome was considered the center of the ancient world, Jesus wanted His Church to be established in Rome.

In addition, the historical record demonstrates that Peter was martyred in Rome around A.D. 67, crucified upside down. This was the death Jesus predicted[*] and Peter wrote about[*92] as he embraced the eventual martyrdom he would suffer. Peter's bones are kept beneath the altar of the church in Saint Peter's Basilica in Rome. Thus, Peter, as the first of the apostles, humbled himself as the servant of all servants.[93]

Apostolic Authority and Succession

In addition to establishing the office of prime minister, Jesus instructed the apostles to appoint and train additional bishops, priests and deacons to spread the gospel message throughout the world. In this way, the work of the Church would continue from generation to generation.

References to these offices within the Church are found throughout the Scriptures. For example, Paul writes that Christ's Church has bishops (in Greek, *episkopoi*) who serve the Church in a particular location,* priests (in Greek, *presbyteroi*) who serve the bishops,* and deacons (in Greek, *diakonoi*) who serve the priests.[94]

These formal positions of authority within the Church demonstrate that Christ intended to leave behind a visible and hierarchical Church.[95] This is why Jesus uses the word *ecclesia* to describe His Church. *Ecclesia* is the Greek word for a formal, hierarchical assembly with visible leadership. Jesus only uses this word twice in the New Testament, each time in reference to His Church.[96] The hierarchical and visible nature of the early Church contravenes the common Protestant view of church as an invisible community of believers linked together by faith in the Bible alone.

The apostles clearly understood that, to accomplish the mandate Christ had given them, they would need to pass on to others both the task and the authority He had granted them. They were to "appoint elders . . . in every church, with prayer and fasting" (Acts 14:23).

In the Acts of the Apostles (1:15-26), we see that the first thing Peter did after Christ's Ascension into heaven was to appoint a successor to Judas Iscariot. Notwithstanding Judas' egregious sin of betraying Christ, the authority of his office[97] (or *bishopric*) was respected and preserved (v.20). Thus, Matthias succeeded to Judas' office with full apostolic authority (v.15-26).

In connection with choosing the successor to Judas, Peter declares to the early Church that "one must be ordained to be a witness with us of his resurrection" (Acts 1:22). Hence, the implementation of succession was effected through a formal, ceremonial act called ordination or the "laying on of the hands." This is also known as the sacrament of holy orders, discussed later. This process of ordination ensured a legitimate, apostolic transfer of teaching authority to other jurisdictions and from one generation to the next. Catholics refer to this process as apostolic succession, and every validly ordained Catholic bishop has an unbroken lineage of predecessor bishops all the way back to the original twelve apostles, and, hence, to Christ Himself.

The Scriptures provide many examples of sacramental ordination. For example, in Acts 6, the twelve apostles expanded the apostolic college by an additional seven men: "They chose Stephen, a man full of faith and of the Holy Spirit, and Philip, and Prochorus, and Nicanor, and Timon, and Parmenas, and Nicolaus, a proselyte of Antioch. These they set before the apostles, and they prayed and laid their hands upon them" (Acts 6:5-6).

A few chapters later, the Church ordained Barnabas and Saul at the direction of the Holy Spirit.

> While they were worshiping the Lord and fasting, the Holy Spirit said "Set apart for me Barnabas and Saul for the work to which I have called them." Then after fasting and praying they laid their hands on them and sent them off (Acts 13:2-3).

Paul reminds Timothy, his newly ordained bishop, about the awesome gift he received through holy orders: "Do not neglect the gift you have, which was given you by prophetic utterance when the council of elders laid their hands upon you"* and, "Hence I remind you to rekindle the gift of God that is within you through the laying on of my hands."*[98]

Paul also urges Timothy to be careful about ordaining others. "Do not be hasty in the laying on of hands, nor participate in another man's sins; keep yourself pure" (1 Tim 5:22). Paul is emphasizing that the gift of supernatural authority is a reality that cannot be used indiscriminately.

How the Old Testament priesthood foreshadows the New

The Old Covenant practices of appointing priests over the people of God foreshadowed the sacramental ordination of priests of the Catholic Church. For example, Moses appoints various heads over God's people, establishing a hierarchy and transfer of authority.[99] God commanded Moses to lay his hands upon Joshua before the assembly to formally commission him and invest him with authority, so that all the people might obey him.[100] Moses laid his hands upon Joshua, and because of this, Joshua is recognized as Moses' successor, full of the spirit of wisdom (see Deut 34:9).

God further commands Moses to "anoint them as you anointed their father, that they may serve me as priests: and their anointing shall admit them to a perpetual priesthood throughout their generations" (Ex 40:15). Moses also ordained Aaron and "anointed him with holy oil; to minister to the Lord and serve as priest and bless his people in his name" (Sir 45:15).

This "sacramental" ordination conferred special graces and power from God, and all future priests had to be ordained by a legitimate successor of Moses, or they did not have a valid priesthood. For example, only a priest ordained by Aaron and his descendants had authority to burn incense before the Lord (Num 16:40). Those anointed by Aaron and his successors were called "anointed priests, whom he ordained to minister in the priest's office" (Num 3:3). Throughout the Old Testament, we continually see the words "priest," "authority," "laying on of hands," "anointed," and "office," all in reference to the perpetual priesthood of God.

In the New Testament, the sacramental priesthood of God is described in the same way.

Thus, we see three offices of priesthood in both the Old and New Testament: the high priest, the ministerial priests, and the universal priests. In the Old Testament, Aaron was the high priest,* Aaron's sons were ministerial priests,* and Israel acted as the universal priests.* [101] In the New Testament, Jesus is our High Priest,* the ordained bishops and priests serve as the ministerial priesthood,* and all those who are baptized serve as royal or universal priests.*[102]

The Scriptures teach us that the ministerial priests of the New Covenant share in the ministry and authority of our High Priest, Jesus Christ. Jesus declared to His apostles:

- "He who receives you receives me, and he who receives me receives him who sent me" (Mt 10:40).
- "Truly, truly, I say to you, he who receives any one whom I send receives me; and he who receives me receives him who sent me" (Jn 13:20).
- "He who hears you hears me, and he who rejects you rejects me, and he who rejects me rejects him who sent me" (Lk 10:16).

Jesus thus teaches us that when we accept those whom He sends (through the sacrament of holy orders), we accept Christ Himself. If we reject those He sends (the apostles and their successors), we reject Jesus.

The apostles recognized their divinely appointed authority. Paul writes that the priests of the Church have been called by God and are commissioned by Him.[103] They are ambassadors for Christ and exercise Christ's own authority.[104] Paul thus instructs the faithful to respect those who have authority over their souls.[105] Paul also charges bishop Timothy to exhort and reprove with all authority, which he received by the laying on of hands (see Titus 2:15). John also writes about his divinely appointed authority (see 3 Jn 9).

Peter and Jude similarly charge the members of the Church to be subject to the elders,* and Peter warns the faithful about despising priestly authority.*[106] While Peter calls Jesus the Shepherd and Guardian,* Paul also declares that the apostles are shepherds and guardians appointed by the Holy Spirit.*[107]

The priesthood and our call to obedience
In the Old Testament, God called His people to obey those He had put in charge of them. For example, the Lord commanded Israel to obey His appointed priests, and warns that those who do not obey His priests shall die.[108] This was the fate of Korah and his followers after their rebellion against Moses and his priests (see Num 16:1-35). "With all your soul fear the Lord, and honor his priests. With all your might love your Maker, and do not forsake his ministers" (Sir 7:29-30).

God calls us to the same obedience in the New Testament. The author of Hebrews says,

> "Obey your leaders and submit to them; for they are keeping watch over your souls, as men who will have to give account. Let them do this joyfully, and not sadly, for that would be of no advantage to you" (Heb 13:17).

The Scriptures repeatedly instruct the faithful to be obedient to those God put in authority, for to obey them is to obey Christ. This call to obedience has serious implications for Christians today. If

Christianity is just about "Jesus, the Bible, and me," God's command to obey His appointed leaders, who have authority over our souls, would be meaningless.

The authority Jesus gives His priests to preach the Word and celebrate the sacraments is part of the mystery of the Incarnation. God became flesh in Jesus Christ so that we could become one with God. This mystery of Emmanuel (God with us) is perpetuated through the priesthood. What the priests have received from Christ, Christ received from God the Father. Jesus taught that all the Father has is given to the Son, and the Son gives it to the apostles (see Jn 16:14-15). The Father assigned the kingdom to the Son, and the Son has assigned it to the apostles (see Lk 22:29).

Jesus also continually taught that He did nothing on His own authority, but acted with the authority of the Father,[*] and what He taught was not His own teaching, but the teaching of the Father who sent Him.[*][109] In prayer to His Father, Jesus declared, "As thou didst send me into the world, so I have sent them into the world"; He commissioned His apostles by saying, "As the Father has sent me, even so I send you."[*][110] The apostles and their successors have divinely appointed authority, and this authority is not lessened or mitigated, for it comes directly from Jesus Christ.

The Church's gift of infallibility

As we have already touched upon, because the apostles' authority comes from Jesus Himself, the authority they enjoy is not simply one of Church governance, but of teaching those things that are necessary for our salvation. Referring to the successors to the apostles, John writes, "Whoever knows God listens to us. . . . By this we know the spirit of truth and the spirit of error" (1 Jn 4:6). Notice that John does not say that whoever knows God reads the Scriptures, and that knowing the Scriptures is the way we discern truth and error. John says listening to those chosen to lead is the way we know truth and error.

But if listening to mere human beings is the way God wants us to know truth and error, God must endow His chosen leaders with a special ability to discern truth and error. Moreover, if Jesus really gave Peter and the apostles the authority to bind and loose in heaven what they bound and loosed on earth, God must have given them the special charism of teaching His revealed truth, for God cannot lie (see Titus 1:2).

This gift is called infallibility. Infallibility means that the Holy Spirit prevents the Church from teaching error on matters relevant to our salvation. Thus, whenever the successor of Peter, either in his capacity as the chief shepherd of the Church (*ex cathedra* teaching) or together with the bishops throughout the world united to him in a gathering called a council (conciliar teaching), definitively teaches a matter on faith and morals to be believed by the universal Church, the teaching is free from error. God protects His Church from going "off the rails." This, however, is only a negative protection. The Holy Spirit does not inspire the pope to teach infallibly; He only protects the pope from teaching error on faith and morals when the pope manifestly invokes His protection. Popes have used this protection sparingly throughout the centuries, and usually only when it was necessary to end speculation about a doctrine, or to combat heresy.

The Church's two-thousand-year history of consistent, dogmatic teaching bears witness to the reality of the Church's infallibility. The fact that many denominations have broken away from the Church, and have even splintered away from the Protestant tradition from which they came, over matters of the faith (especially on issues of sexual morality), also bears witness to this reality. *Jesus teaches that the Church, not the Scriptures, is the final arbiter on matters of the Christian faith* (see Mt 18:17-18). This is why it is gravely sinful to disobey the teachings of the Church on matters of faith and morals.

We should note that the special gift of infallibility has nothing to do with the moral perfection of the Church's members (which refers to "impeccability"). Even so, Protestant Christians should have no problem with the concept that sinners can teach infallibly. The Bible is a perfect example. All its writers were sinners, but their writings are infallible. Just look at Peter. He denied Christ, was rebuked by one of his bishops (Paul), and yet wrote two infallible encyclicals. Moses was a murderer and David was an adulterer and murderer, but they too wrote infallibly. God even allowed Caiaphas to prophesy infallibly, even though he was evil and helped to plot Jesus' death. God allows sinners to teach infallibly, just as He allows sinners to become saints.

This gift of infallibility was prophesied by Isaiah when he referred to the Church as the "Holy Way" where sons will be taught by God and not err.[111] The early Church was called "the Way," which was the subject of Isaiah's prophecy.[112] But the only human beings who will not err are those who are specially guided by God. Hence, Jesus promises His apostles that it will not be they who speak, but the Spirit of their heavenly Father speaking through them.[113] Jesus promises His apostles that the Holy Spirit would be with the Church forever, and would teach her all things regarding the faith.[114] Jesus also said the Holy Spirit would guide the Church into all truth (see Jn 16:13). While He had much to say to the apostles, they could not bear to learn everything while Jesus was on earth (v.12). The apostles knew that the Holy Spirit would guide their teaching (see Acts 15:28). Through the Holy Spirit, the Church would grow in her understanding of the truth over time. The Church calls this process the *"development of doctrine."*

"Development of doctrine" does not mean that the Church invents new doctrine, or that the Church's doctrine changes over time. That would be impossible because the Church's doctrine is the immutable teaching of Christ, which He gave to the apostles. The development of doctrine simply means that the Church's *understanding* of Christ's revelation, as reflected in the depth and clarity of her teaching, evolves as she is guided "into all truth."[115] This process is necessary as the subjective and human side of the Church strives to expound the objective and divine truth of God. Jesus sent the Holy Spirit to the Church after His Ascension for this very purpose.

Paul's letter to the Ephesians gives us powerful insights into Paul's understanding of the Church. Paul writes that the ineffable wisdom of God is made known, even to the intellectually superior angels, through the Church (see Eph 3:9-10). This verse tells us that God's infinite wisdom comes to us through the Church, which cannot teach error. Paul even alludes that this is a mystery hidden for all ages — that God manifests His wisdom through one infallible Church for all (v.9). Paul also says that God's glory is manifested in the Church by the power of the Spirit who works within the Church's leaders (see Eph 3:20).

Later in the letter, Paul again calls the Church a "mystery" (Eph 5:32). The Church is not just a building full of believers; that is not a mystery. The Church is a mystery because her significance as the kingdom of heaven in our midst cannot be understood by reason alone. Understanding the Church also requires faith. She is a supernatural truth. That is why belief in the "One, Holy, Catholic and Apostolic Church" is an article of faith in the 1,700 year-old Nicene Creed.

The Church's gift of unity

Jesus told us why He left us a hierarchical Church with a chief representative: *to prove to the world that He was sent by the Father* (see Jn 17:21). Jesus was linking the credibility of His message to the worldwide unity of the Church. This is how incredibly important Jesus viewed the unity of the Church. A united Church in the midst of our chaotic world would cause people to believe in its divine institution. If the Church were divided, she would be like every other human organization. Jesus said that a kingdom divided against itself is laid waste and will not stand.[116] Unity, therefore, subsists in the truth, and this is why Paul called the Church "the pillar and bulwark of the truth" (1 Tim 3:15).

Because the unity of the Church was such an important sign, Jesus prayed that His followers might be perfectly one, as He is one with the Father.[117] Jesus' oneness with the Father could never be less than perfect. Thus, the oneness Jesus prays for is attained through a unified Church, which cannot include over thirty thousand different divisions of Christianity. Jesus said that there must be one flock and one shepherd (see Jn 10:16). That Jesus' prayer is answered by the Father is evidenced by the miraculous two thousand years of unity in the Catholic Church. This unity is brought about by the charity of the Holy Spirit, who gives the members of the Church various gifts in order to attain to the unity of faith (see Eph 4:11-14).

We must not lose faith in the Church's teaching authority and divine institution when her members commit sin. This may be especially difficult today, where Church scandal is rampant. But God has taught us through the Scriptures that His mysterious plan requires:

- the wheat and the weeds to be side by side in the Church until the end of time[118];
- the Church be like a net that catches fish of every kind, good and bad[119] ;
- that a great house have not only gold and silver, but also wood and earthenware, some for noble use, and some for ignoble use[120]; and
- both good figs that will be rewarded, and bad figs that will be discarded.[121]

Paul also warns that Church elders might be unfaithful (1 Tim 5:19). Jesus' deliberate choice of Judas Iscariot as among His first twelve apostles should constantly remind us of this reality. Unfaithful members do not nullify the faithfulness of God and the work of the Holy Spirit in the Church.[122] Even if we are faithless, God remains faithful, for He cannot deny Himself.[123] No matter how sinful her members, Jesus promised that the gates of hell would not prevail against the Church.[124] This two-thousand-year miracle of unity in faith and morals, especially in such a confused and divided world, demonstrates that Jesus kept His promise in the Holy Catholic Church.

CHAPTER THREE

The Sacraments

Jesus Christ instituted seven sacraments to be celebrated by His Holy Catholic Church, to communicate His grace to the members of His body. The sacraments are: baptism, penance (also called reconciliation or confession), Eucharist (also called Holy Communion), confirmation, holy matrimony, holy orders and anointing of the sick. Jesus gave us these sacraments to nourish the whole of our spiritual lives. Consequently, the sacraments correspond to periods in our natural lives. For example, at the beginning of life we receive baptism; in childhood and beyond we receive reconciliation and Holy Communion; as teenagers or young adults we receive confirmation[125]; in early adulthood we may get married or, if male, receive holy orders; and in our senior years we may receive the sacrament of anointing.

The word "sacrament" comes from the Latin word *sacramentum,* which means "oath." Swearing an oath provides the foundation for a covenant relationship. A covenant is an intimate, personal relationship between two individuals or groups. While a contract is an exchange of property or services, a covenant is an exchange of persons. When a person swears an oath to someone else, he binds himself to that person beyond mere legality. In making a covenant, God says, "I am yours and you are mine." At the Last Supper, Jesus spoke of our "New Covenant" with God as He offered His body and blood to us under the appearance of bread and wine.

In this eternal New Covenant of love, Jesus gives Himself to us in all the sacraments, but most especially in the Eucharist. In all seven sacraments, we encounter the risen Christ in an interpersonal communion, and we receive His grace by the power of the Holy

Spirit. Thus, the seven sacraments are "salvific" (which means they bring about our salvation). By the merits of the Passion, death, and Resurrection of Christ, we receive God's divine life, which we had lost through the sin of Adam.

While the Catholic Church has been celebrating these seven sacraments for two thousand years, most Protestant churches recognize only one or two (baptism, and a version of Holy Communion). Moreover, because the Eucharist — the source and summit of the Christian faith — must be confected by a validly ordained priest (i.e., with apostolic succession), Protestant churches cannot celebrate this sacrament, even if they believe in it.[126] This is perhaps the saddest consequence of being outside the Catholic Church. Those who love Jesus but are not in full communion with His Church do not enjoy, to the fullest extent, the divine graces God offers in the sacraments. On the other hand, many Catholics who are in communion with the Church (always by God's grace and through no special merit of their own) do not seek these divine graces to the extent they need them.

We now look at the biblical basis for the seven sacraments.

Baptism

Right before Jesus ascended into heaven, He commanded the apostles to "make disciples of all nations, baptizing them in the name of the Father, and of the Son, and of the Holy Spirit" (Mt 28:19). Jesus also said, "He who believes and is baptized will be saved; but he who does not believe will be condemned" (Mk 16:16).

The Catholic Church has always taught that Christian baptism, administered in accordance with Jesus' instructions, washes away the original sin we inherited from Adam and Eve, and brings about our adoption as sons and daughters of God through Jesus Christ. That is why, in the Nicene Creed, we say, "We believe in one baptism for the forgiveness of sins." Thus, baptism in Christ is supernatural and salvific — even though many Protestant Christians today believe that baptism is only a symbolic act, and that it confers nothing supernatural to the baptized. As we see below, the Scriptures clearly support the Catholic teaching on baptism.

Born again in water baptism

In John's Gospel (3:3-5), Jesus tells Nicodemus, "Truly, truly, I say to you, unless one is born anew, he cannot see the kingdom of God." When Nicodemus asks Jesus how one could possibly re-enter his mother's womb to be born again, Jesus further clarifies His teaching: "Truly, truly, I say to you, unless one is born of water and the spirit, he cannot enter the kingdom of God" (v.5).

While Nicodemus was referring to a natural rebirth, Jesus was talking about a supernatural rebirth. The Greek word for the phrase "born again," *anothen*, literally means "begotten from above." Jesus even refers to Himself as *anothen*, or begotten from above, in John 3:31. Hence, by "water and the Spirit," a clear reference to baptism, we become "begotten from above."

Christians who believe that baptism is only symbolic argue that Jesus was not speaking about baptism in John 3:3-5, and that being "begotten from above" means accepting Jesus as personal Lord and Savior. Once someone repents of sin and accepts Jesus as Lord and Savior, they believe, that person is saved, or "born again." If being "begotten from above" by water and the Spirit means baptism, as we will demonstrate, then baptism cannot be merely symbolic and the Catholic understanding of John 3 is correct.

As we look at the verse in context, we will see that in John 3:3-5, Jesus is in fact talking about baptism. For example, in John 3:22, after Jesus' teaching about being born of water and Spirit, the Scripture says that "Jesus and his disciples went into the land of Judea; there he remained with them *and baptized*." Further, the Scriptures say, "Now when the Lord knew that the Pharisees had heard that Jesus was making and *baptizing* more disciples than John (although Jesus himself did not *baptize*, but only his disciples), he left Judea and departed again to Galilee" (Jn 4:1-3). These verses about baptism naturally flow from Jesus' teaching about baptism in John 3:3-5.

Notice that the verses say *nothing* about accepting Jesus or professing a faith in Christ as personal Lord and Savior. In this passage, Jesus connects being "born again" to water, and not a profession of faith.[127]

The Scriptures always link "water" and the "Spirit" to baptism. For example, in the book of Acts, the eunuch recognizes the necessity of water for his baptism when he says, "See, here is water! What is to prevent my being baptized?" (Acts 8:36). Peter also says, "Can anyone forbid water for baptizing these people who have received the Holy Spirit just as we have?" (Acts 10:47). The Lord says through Isaiah, "I will pour water on the thirsty land, and streams on dry ground; I will pour my Spirit upon your descendants, and my blessing on your off-spring" (Is 44:3).

In his letter to Titus, Paul writes:

> He saved us, ... by the washing of regeneration and renewal in the Holy Spirit, which he poured out on us richly through Jesus Christ, so that we might be justified by his grace and become heirs of eternal life (Titus 3:5-7).

The word for "washing" (in Greek, *loutron*) generally refers to a ritual washing with water. This, coupled with being renewed in the Holy Spirit, links the passage to baptism. This washing, which involves the use of water, is what saves us. The words "He saved us," of course, refer to our salvation in Jesus Christ. The word "regeneration" is also never used symbolically in the Bible; it refers to the supernatural regeneration or rebirth of our souls in Christ. In other words, what is contracted by generation (original sin) is washed away by regeneration (baptism).

Hence, in baptism, we become "justified by his grace" (which is an interior change), and "heirs of eternal life" (filial adoption). We are "begotten from above." Because this passage refers to baptism, it is about the beginning of life in Christ. This is why Paul says that no righteous deeds done before baptism could save us. Righteous deeds after baptism, when done by the grace of Christ, do save us (more on this in the chapter on justification).

We can also see a definite parallel on the teaching of baptism between John 3:5 and Titus 3:5:

- in John 3:5, we enter the kingdom of God / in Titus 3:5, we are saved;
- in John 3:5, we are born of water / in Titus 3:5, we are washed;

- in John 3:5, we are born of the Spirit / in Titus 3:5, we are renewed in the Spirit.

Peter also expressly teaches that baptism saves us. In his first epistle, he writes, "Baptism, corresponding to this [Noah's ark], *now saves you*; not as a removal of dirt from the body but as an appeal to God for a clear conscience" (1 Pet 3:21).[128] When Peter says baptism "now saves you," he is referring to salvation in Christ. This verse shows that baptism, which is the sign of the New Covenant, is not about the exterior, but the interior life of the person. This is how baptism can give us a "clear conscience." The conscience deals with a person's interior life, which is animated by the soul and washed clean of original sin in baptism. But unlike circumcision, which was the sign of the Old Covenant, the waters of baptism now spiritually save us, just as Noah and his family were physically saved through the waters of the flood.

The author of Hebrews writes that "since we have a great priest over the house of God, let us draw near with a true heart in full assurance of faith, with our hearts sprinkled clean from an evil conscience, and our bodies washed with pure water" (Heb 10:21-23). This is another verse about baptism: our hearts are "sprinkled clean" (with water) and purified from "an evil conscience" (interiorly), as "our bodies are washed with pure water" (in baptism).

Notice also the parallels between 1 Peter 3:21 and Hebrews 10:22:

- in 1 Peter 3:21, we are saved / in Hebrews 10:22, we draw near to the sanctuary of heaven;
- in 1 Peter 3:21, we are saved through water / in Hebrews 10:22, we are sprinkled clean and washed with pure water;
- in 1 Peter 3:21, we are given a clear conscience; in Hebrews 10:22, we are purified from an evil conscience.

Paul writes to the Corinthians, "But you were washed, you were sanctified, you were justified in the name of the Lord Jesus Christ and in the Spirit of our God" (1 Cor 6:11). Once again, we see the link between "water" and the "Spirit," in reference to baptism.[129] This verse further shows that baptism brings about sanctification and justification (the interior cleansing of the person's soul). Baptism is not just symbolic.

As we alluded to above, right before Jesus ascended into heaven, He commanded the apostles to baptize (see Mt 28:19). He would not have been giving His apostles instructions to perform an insignificant ritual at this climactic event. Jesus also said, "He who believes *and* is baptized will be saved" (Mk 16:16). Jesus is teaching that, for adults, believing is not enough to be saved. They must also be baptized. Peter, the chief shepherd of the Church, sure got the message, for after Jesus ascended to the Father, Peter declared to the people, "Repent and be baptized every one of you in the name of Jesus Christ *for the forgiveness of your sins*; and you shall receive the gift of the Holy Spirit" (Acts 2:38). Peter clearly teaches that the purpose of baptism is to forgive sins, and not merely perform a pious, symbolic ritual.

Some of the most compelling proofs of the salvific nature of baptism are found in the book of Acts. For example, even though Paul was converted to Christianity directly by Jesus Christ Himself, Ananias commands Paul to "rise and be baptized, and wash away your sins."[130] This verse proves that Paul's acceptance of Jesus as personal Lord and Savior was not enough to save Paul and forgive his sins. In spite of his heavenly revelation, Paul *had to be baptized* to be cleansed of his sins.

The word for "wash away" (in Greek, *apolouo*) that is used in Acts 22:16, and is also used in 1 Corinthians 6:11, refers to an actual cleansing away of sin. There are many other examples in Acts where people, after coming to faith in Jesus, are immediately baptized.[131] One must ask the question: If believing in Jesus is all one needs to be saved, then why does everyone in the early Church, after accepting Jesus as Savior, immediately seek baptism for the forgiveness of their sins? One can only conclude that this is because baptism is salvific, not just symbolic.

The salvific nature of baptism was foreshadowed in the Old Testament. For example, in 2 Kings 5, Naaman dipped himself seven times in the waters of the Jordan, and his flesh was restored "like the flesh of a little child" (v.14). This restoration foreshadows the regenerative function of baptism. God also tells us through the prophet Ezekiel:

I will sprinkle clean water upon you, and you shall be clean from all your uncleanness, and from all your idols I will cleanse you. A new heart I will give you, and a new spirit I will put within you; and I will take out of your flesh the heart of stone and give you a heart of flesh. And I will put my spirit within you, and cause you to walk in my statutes and be careful to observe my ordinances.[132]

This prophecy that God will sprinkle clean water upon us to spiritually cleanse us and change our hearts is fulfilled with Christian baptism as taught in Hebrews 10:22 (sprinkle); John 3:5; Acts 8:36, 10:47; 1 Peter 3:21 (water); Acts 22:16; 1 Corinthians 6:11; Titus 3:5-7; Hebrews 10:22; (cleanse); John 3:5; Titus 3:5-7; (Spirit); and, Hebrews 10:22 (hearts).

Infant baptism

The Catholic Church has been baptizing babies ever since Christ commanded His apostles to baptize all people in the name of the Father, Son, and Holy Spirit. This has been the practice of the Orthodox and many Protestant churches as well. Parents bring their babies to the waters of baptism by professing a belief in Christ on behalf of the child, and promising to raise him or her in the faith. For adults who are to be baptized,[133] the Church also requires them to profess their faith in Christ. Because baptism is salvific, the earlier one comes to baptism, the better.

On what basis does the Church believe the faith of one person may "cover" someone else? The Scriptures are full of examples where Jesus extends healing grace to people based on the faith of others. For example, Jesus forgives the sins of the paralytic based on the faith of those who brought him.[134] Jesus heals the centurion's servant based on the faith of the centurion.[135] Jesus exorcises the child's unclean spirit based on the father's faith.[136] In the Old Testament, God spared the first-born child's life during the Passover based on the parent's faith.[137] We must ask ourselves: If God is willing to effect spiritual and physical cures for children based upon the faith of their parents, *how much more* will He give the grace of baptism to children based upon the faith of their parents?

Why do children need baptismal grace for salvation? They inherit original sin from the moment of conception. Psalm 51:5 says, "Behold, I was brought forth in iniquity, and in sin did my mother conceive me." Job writes, "Man that is born of woman is of few days, and full of trouble. . . . Who can bring a clean thing out of an unclean? There is not one" (Job 14:1,4). Paul writes that "sin came into the world through one man and death through sin" (Rom 5:12). Paul does not say that this sin is manifested only when the person reaches the age of reason. Hence, Paul writes that "we were by nature children of wrath, like the rest of mankind" (Eph 2:3).

Because babies are born with original sin, they need baptism to cleanse them, that they may become adopted sons and daughters of God and receive the grace of the Holy Spirit. Jesus said that the kingdom of God also belongs to children.[138] Jesus never put an age limit upon those eligible to receive His grace.[139] When Paul addresses the "saints" of the Church,[140] these include the children, whom he addresses in Ephesians 6:1 and Colossians 3:20. Children become saints of the Church and members of the body of Christ only through baptism.

The Scriptures also demonstrate that the early Church baptized babies. In the book of Acts, Peter preached to the crowd, "Repent, and be baptized every one of you in the name of Jesus Christ for the forgiveness of your sins; and you shall receive the gift of the Holy Spirit. For the promise is to you *and to your children* and to all that are far off, every one whom the Lord our God calls to him" (Acts 2:38-39).[141] When Peter said the promise of baptism is for children, the word "children" (from the Greek, *teknon*) also includes infants. This same word *teknon* is used later in Acts 21:21 to describe the circumcision of eight-day old infants. This proves that the promise of baptism is for infants.

The book of Acts also shows whole households being baptized, which necessarily included infants and children. In Acts 16:15, Paul baptizes Lydia "with her household." The Greek word for "household," *oikos,* includes infants and children.[142] In 1 Corinthians 1:16, Paul baptizes "also the household [*oikos*] of Stephanus." In the book of Acts, Peter baptizes the entire household of Cornelius,* and Paul baptizes the jailer "with all his family."[*][143] There is never any indication that infants and children are excluded from baptism.

It is also important to remember the correlation between the Old Covenant and the New Covenant when discussing infant baptism. Babies were circumcised when they were eight days old;[144] this was the sign by which they entered into the Mosaic Covenant. Paul calls baptism the "new circumcision" when he writes:

> In him you were circumcised with a circumcision made without hands, by putting off the body of flesh in the circumcision of Christ, and you were buried with him in baptism, in which you were also raised with him through faith in the working of God, who raised him from the dead (Col 2:11-12).

Since baptism is the new circumcision of the New Covenant, baptism is for babies as well as adults (just as circumcision in the Old Covenant was for babies as well as adults). God did not make his New Covenant narrower than the Old Covenant. From a Jewish perspective, it would have been unthinkable to exclude infants and children from God's New Covenant; infants and children were always part of God's covenant family.

A covenant that excluded children would be inferior to the original covenant. In reality, the grace of Jesus Christ and the New Covenant *surpasses* that of the Old Covenant (see Rom 5:15), to include not only infants, but Gentiles as well.

Does Scripture teach that one must be a believer before being baptized?

Christians who believe that one must first be a believer in Christ before being baptized have a few favorite passages to support their position. Let's take a look at them.

Acts 2:38. Peter said, "Repent and be baptized." Thus, the non-Catholic argues, "See, repentance must come before baptism." However, this is not what it means in the original Greek. Acts 2:38 literally says, "If you repent, then each one who is a part of you and yours must each be baptized" (*Metanoesate kai bapistheto hekastos hymon*). This actually proves that babies are baptized based on their parents' faith, and not their own faith. This is confirmed in the next verse, when Peter says "the promise is to you and to your children" (Acts 2:39).

Acts 16:30-31. In this passage, Paul and Silas tell the jailer that he must believe in the Lord Jesus in order for him and his household to be saved. Then the jailer "was baptized at once, with all his family" (Acts 16:33). But notice that only the adult candidates for baptism had to profess a belief in Jesus. This, as we have previously mentioned, is the way the Church has always celebrated baptism. There is no scriptural mandate that all candidates for baptism must first profess a belief in Christ. To the contrary, as we have seen in Acts 16:15 (the baptism of Lydia and her household) and Acts 16:33 (the baptism of the jailer and his household), the Church gives the gift of baptism to entire families, based on one parent's faith (not the children's faith). Thus, Paul says that children are sanctified through the belief of one of their parents.[145]

Mark 16:16. Non-Catholics also raise Jesus' statement: "He who believes and is baptized will be saved." However, this verse actually supports the Catholic position. First, Jesus' statement refers to those who are able to profess a belief in Christ, either on behalf of themselves or on behalf of their children. Second, Jesus' statement proves the connection between baptism and salvation. Third, in reference to the same people Jesus was addressing, Jesus says, "He who does not believe will be condemned" (Mk 16:16). This second statement of Jesus demonstrates that one can be baptized and still not be a believer, which disproves the contention that one must be a believer to be baptized.

What about those who profess faith in Christ but die before they can be baptized? The Church has always taught that water baptism is a normative but not absolute necessity for salvation. Throughout her history the Church has taught that, in addition to water baptism, one can be saved by either a "baptism of desire" or a "baptism of blood." The baptism of desire is for those who explicitly desire baptism for themselves or their children, as demonstrated by repentance for their sins and acts of charity. They will receive the salvific graces of the sacrament even if they die before they receive water baptism. We see this with the good thief in Luke 23:40-43, who rebukes the bad thief and expresses his faith in Jesus. Jesus says to him, "You will be with me in paradise" (v.43). The good thief was baptized by his desire to be with Jesus in heaven as he repented of his sins, even though he died before receiving a water baptism.

Similarly, the Church has always taught that those who suffer death for the sake of the faith without having received baptism are baptized by their death for and with Christ. This baptism of blood, like baptism of desire, brings about the fruits of water baptism without the actual sacrament. Jesus refers to this type of baptism when He says, "I have a baptism to be baptized with," in reference to His death.[146] John also teaches us that He "came by water and blood, Jesus Christ, not with the water only but with the water and the blood" (1 Jn 5:6). This is why the Church celebrates the feast of the Holy Innocents on December 28 of each year. The baby boys who were slaughtered by Herod in Bethlehem (see Mt 2:16) were martyred for Christ, and so they were baptized by blood.

Pouring and sprinkling versus immersion

The preferred method of baptism is also debated among Christian churches. Some believe that baptism must be performed by immersion (immersing the entire person under the water). These churches criticize the Catholic Church because, in addition to baptizing by immersion, she also baptizes by pouring or sprinkling water over the newly baptized. The Catholic Church, in obedience to the apostles' instructions, has practiced baptism by immersion, affusion (pouring) and aspersion (sprinkling) for two thousand years.

What do the Scriptures say about this? In 2 Kings 5:14, where the regenerative function of baptism is foreshadowed, Naaman went down and dipped himself in the Jordan. The Greek word for "dipped," *baptizo,* can mean "immersion." But, as we will see, this is not always the case.

For example, in Numbers 19:18, when the Lord instructs Moses and Aaron to take hyssop, dip it in water and sprinkle it on the tent, the verbs for "dipping" (*baptisantes*) and "sprinkle" (*bapsei*) refer to affusion (pouring) and aspersion (sprinkling), not immersion.

Ezekiel's prophecy of baptism also says that God will "sprinkle clean water upon you" (Ezek. 36:25). Here the word used is *rhaino,* which means "sprinkle," not "immerse" (*Kai rhaino eph hymas hydor katharon*).

In the New Testament, John the Baptist prophesies that Jesus will baptize (in Greek, *baptisei*) with the Holy Spirit and fire.[147] In this case, *baptisei* refers to a "pouring" out over the head. This is confirmed by Matthew 3:16, where the Holy Spirit descends upon Jesus' head like a dove, and Acts 2:3-4, where the Holy Spirit descends upon the apostles' heads in the form of tongues of fire. In each case, in fulfillment of John the Baptist's prophecy, the Lord and the apostles are baptized (*baptizo*) in the form of pouring, not immersion. The pouring of water is just like the pouring out of the Holy Spirit.[148]

Pouring is connected with baptism in Titus 3:6 as well, where Paul writes that the washing of regeneration and renewal in the Holy Spirit is "poured out on us richly through Jesus Christ." We are also reminded of the "pouring out" of water and the Spirit in Isaiah 44:3, where the prophet writes that the Lord "will pour water on the thirsty land" and "pour [his] Spirit upon [our] descendants." The author of Hebrews also describes baptism as "hearts sprinkled clean."[149] There is nothing about immersion in these verses.

Mark writes that the Pharisees do not eat unless they "wash" (in Greek, *baptizo*) their hands (see Mk 7:3). This also demonstrates that *baptizo* does not always mean immersion. Similarly, when Luke writes that Jesus had not "washed" (in Greek, *ebaptisthe*) His hands before dinner, the derivative of *baptizo* in this case also means washing up, but not immersion. Mark also writes that the Jews "washed" (in Greek, *bapto*) cups, pitchers, vessels, and, in some translations, couches, but this does not mean they actually immersed these items (see Mk 7:4). Certainly with respect to couches, they would have only sprinkled them.

Paul says the Israelites were "baptized" (in Greek, *baptizo*) in the cloud and in the sea (see 1 Cor 10:2), but they could not have been immersed: Exodus 14:22 and Exodus 15:9 say they went dry shod. When Jesus talks about His baptism of blood, He is referring to how His blood will be shed, poured out, and sprinkled during His Passion.[150] This type of baptism also cannot mean a literal immersion. The point of this analysis is to demonstrate that being baptized (*baptizo* and its derivative words) does not always refer to an immersion, and, in fact, generally means a pouring out upon or sprinkling of the person.

Looking specifically at how Christian baptisms were celebrated indicates that pouring or sprinkling was often used, and not immersion. For example, at Peter's first sermon, three thousand people were baptized (see Acts 2:41). There is archeological proof that baptism by immersion would not have been possible for this many people in this area. Paul was baptized in the house of Judas, and possibly while standing up.[151] This had to be done by sprinkling or pouring, since hot tubs and swimming pools were not part of homes at this time. Peter also baptized in the house of Cornelius,* and Paul likely baptized the jailer and his family in his house.*[152] Once again, these baptisms had to be done by sprinkling or pouring.

Some non-Catholic Christians point to Acts 8:38-39 to prove baptism must be done by immersion. In verse thirty-eight, Luke writes that Philip and the eunuch "went down into the water." The verb used to describe Philip and the eunuch going down into the water (in Greek, *katabaino*) is the same verb used in 8:26 to describe the angel's instruction to Philip to stop his chariot and "go down to Gaza." The verb refers to the direction he was going, not what he did once he got there. While the eunuch could have been immersed in the water, the Greek text does not say that he was *necessarily* immersed. In fact, when people were baptized in lakes and rivers, they generally stood knee deep in the water, while the priest would pour water over them.

Similarly, some Christians insist that baptism must be done by immersion because in Acts 8:39, the verse says, "... they came up out of the water." However, the verb used here for "coming up out" of the water (in Greek, *anebesan*) is plural. So, while the verb tells us that both Philip and the eunuch both ascended out of the water, it does not prove that they were immersed. In fact, Philip could not have baptized the eunuch if they were both underwater. Finally, even if this was a baptism by immersion, the verse obviously does not say that baptism by immersion is the only way to baptize.

Was Jesus immersed in the Jordan? It isn't clear.[153] However, even if He was immersed, Jesus' baptism was not the Christian baptism He commanded the apostles to administer. So the form of His baptism is not relevant to the manner in which Christian baptism must be administered. Moreover, Jesus' baptism was a royal anointing. Jesus, the Son of David, was anointed by the Levite John the Baptist to reveal His glory to Israel, just as Solomon, the son of David, was anointed by the Levite priest Zadok in 1 Kings 1:39.

Based on the foregoing, the Scriptures are clear that Christian baptism can be celebrated by sprinkling, pouring or immersion. It also appears that baptism by sprinkling or pouring was the method of choice for the early Church.

Penance

Jesus Christ instituted the sacrament of penance (also called reconciliation or confession) as the normative way to forgive sins. In the early Church, penitents had to confess their sins orally before the Church assembly. In Acts 19:18 Luke writes, "Many also of those who were now believers came, confessing and divulging their practices" before the apostles. This verse alludes to the practice of the early Church, where people had to confess their sins publicly. The disciples of John the Baptist also confessed their sins to John as he baptized them in the Jordan River.[154]

Over time the administration of the sacrament gradually evolved to allow the penitent to privately confess sins to the priest. We see evidence of this at the end of the first millennium. Thus, today, the sacrament is administered by having the penitent privately confess his sins to the priest (sometimes this is called "auricular" confession). The priest gives the penitent a penance (prayers or works of charity) and gives the penitent absolution, which is the priestly act of forgiving the sins "in the name of the Father, and of the Son, and of the Holy Spirit."

Non-Catholic Christians immediately look at this and, like the scribes and Pharisees,[155] say, "But only God forgives sins!" They are correct. However, when Catholics confess their sins to the priest in this sacrament, they *are* confessing their sins to God. *Only God can forgive sins, but He decides how He wants us to obtain that forgiveness.* As we have seen in the chapter on the Church, Jesus Christ gave His apostles the authority to bind and loose, and entrusted to them His power to forgive sins. This is why Jesus emphasized that He forgave sins as a man, when He says, "But that you may know that the *Son of man* has the authority on earth to forgive sins"[156] Just as God entrusted the forgiveness of sins to Jesus as a man, so Jesus entrusts the forgiveness of sins to His apostles and their successors, as men. Hence, in explaining the gift of forgiving sins, Matthew writes that God "had given such authority *to men*" (Mt 9:8).

One of the most powerful Scripture passages demonstrating that Jesus gave His apostles the authority to forgive sins is in the Gospel of John. When Jesus appeared to His apostles after His Resurrection, He authorized this:

> Jesus said to them again, "Peace be with you. As the Father has sent me, even so I send you." And when he had said this, he breathed on them, and said to them, "Receive the Holy Spirit. If you forgive the sins of any, they are forgiven; if you retain the sins of any, they are retained" (Jn 20:21-23).

Even the most ardent disbelievers in the sacrament of confession have trouble with this passage. When Jesus says, "As the Father has sent me, even so I send you," He is giving His apostles notice that they will be doing the same things Jesus did during His earthly ministry (here, forgiving sins). As Christ was sent by the Father to forgive sins, so the apostles are sent by Christ to forgive sins.

Then Jesus breathes on His apostles. The only other time in Scripture where God breathes on man is in Genesis 2:7, when He breathes divine life into him. When God breathes on the apostles, a significant transformation takes place in them. They become "other Christs," endowed with the Holy Spirit and empowered to continue Jesus' divine work on earth. Jesus gives them, being so empowered, the authority to forgive and retain sins by saying, "If you forgive the sins of any, they are forgiven. If you retain the sins of any, they are retained."

It is clear from Jesus' instruction that, in order for the apostles to exercise this authority to forgive sins, people must orally confess their sins to them. Jesus knew we would most likely come to grips with our sinfulness if we knew we would have to confess our sins to another person. He also knew that we would be best assured of our forgiveness if we actually heard that we were forgiven.

Forgiveness of sin depends on the sinner's desire to be forgiven (a desire that is expressed aloud, as the apostles could not read the minds of penitents). If oral confession were not required, the way that Jesus granted the gift to the apostles would not make any sense. Hence, John says, "If we confess our sins, he is faithful and just, and will forgive our sins and cleanse us from all unrighteousness" (1 Jn 1:9). In describing this priestly gift, Paul says that God "gave us the ministry of reconciliation" (2 Cor 5:18).

The Apostle James also writes about the sacraments of reconciliation and anointing in James 5:14-16. In verse fourteen, James writes, we must call for the priests of the Church to pray over the sick person and anoint the person with oil. In verse fifteen, James writes that the actions of the priest through the prayer of faith will save the sick man. Then, in verse sixteen, James writes, "Therefore, confess your sins to one another, and pray for one another, that you may be healed."

Because verse sixteen begins with the word "therefore," the verse must be read in the context of verses fourteen and fifteen. In the first two verses, James is writing about how the priests of the Church forgive the man's sins in the sacrament of the sick. "Therefore," just as the priests forgive sins through the sacrament of anointing (verses fourteen and fifteen), so the priests also forgive sins if we "confess our sins to one another" in the sacrament of confession (verse sixteen). James' instruction to confess our sins to one another means to confess our sins to the priests of the Church, who will forgive our sins in the sacrament of confession, just as they forgive our sins in the sacrament of anointing.

What is an indulgence?

The apostles were given the authority not only to forgive sin, but to retain sin as well. What does this mean? This means that the apostles were given the gift of rendering judgment on the sincerity of the penitent, and binding the penitent to works of penance in order to be forgiven. If, in the apostles' judgment, the penitent was not sincere, or should be required to perform acts of penance in reparation for his sins, the apostles could retain the sin (withhold forgiveness) until the conditions were satisfied. While such authority is reserved to God alone, Christ shared this authority with the apostles.

The power to retain sin is extremely important because it gives priests the authority not only to forgive sin, but to remove the temporal punishments due to sin. The Church calls the removal of temporal punishments due to sin already forgiven an "indulgence."

For every sin we commit, we can be forgiven (by God's mercy), but we also incur punishment due to the sin (by God's justice). For example, in 2 Samuel 12, when David committed adultery with Bathsheba, David was forgiven (by God's mercy), but was punished by the child's death (by God's justice). Certainly, if a priest can forgive a mortal sin in the sacrament of confession (which, if it remained unconfessed and unforgiven, would destine the person to hell), the priest can certainly remove the temporal punishments due to sin. This is part of the priests' binding authority (retaining sin and imposing penance) and loosing authority (forgiving sin and removing punishment due to sin).

What's the difference between mortal and venial sin?

The Church has always taught that, if one has committed mortal sin, such sin must be confessed and absolved, with very few exceptions, in the sacrament of reconciliation.

The Apostle John discusses the difference between mortal and non-mortal (or venial) sins in his first epistle:

> If anyone sees his brother committing what is not a mortal sin, he will ask, and God will give him life for those whose sin is not mortal. There is sin which is mortal; I do not say that one is to pray for that. All wrongdoing is sin, but there is sin which is not mortal (1 Jn 5:16-17).

Mortal sin requires three elements:

- grave matter;
- knowledge with sufficient reflection; and
- full consent of the will.

The sin must be grave (idolatry, abortion, adultery, major theft), the person must know the sin is grave and sufficiently reflect upon committing the sin, and then must deliberately engage his will and commit the act. A sin is called "mortal" when it brings about spiritual death in the soul of person who committed the sin.

Mortal sin must be absolved in the sacrament of penance. If a person dies with mortal sin on the soul, he or she chooses to be eternally separated from God (which is called "hell").

If the sin does not meet those three requirements, it is venial sin. Venial sin does not have to be confessed in the sacrament of penance. Nevertheless, a pious Catholic practice is to confess even venial sins in the sacrament of reconciliation to grow in holiness as we open our hearts up to the risen Christ and receive His grace and mercy.

Even in the Old Testament, we see the practice of orally confessing sins to one another.

- Leviticus 5:5-6 says that a man guilty of sin "shall confess the sin he has committed. . . and the priest shall make atonement for him for his sin." Here, the priest not only forgives the sin but makes atonement for the sin by removing its temporal punishment.
- In Numbers 5:7, the Lord tells Moses that if anyone in Israel commits sin, "he shall confess his sin which he has committed, and he shall make full restitution for his wrong."
- In Nehemiah 9:2-3, we see that the Israelites "stood and confessed their sins and the iniquities of their fathers" orally in the Temple where they also read the book of the Law.
- In Baruch 1:13-14, the people who "have sinned against the LORD our God" are again instructed "to make your confession in the house of the LORD."
- In the book of Sirach, it says, "Do not be ashamed to confess your sins, and do not try to stop the current of a river" (Sir 4:26).[157]

Those Christians who acknowledge that the apostles had the authority to forgive and retain sins generally disregard passages such as Matthew 9:8, John 20:22-23, and James 5:16, claiming that this authority terminated at the apostles' death. The problem with their argument is that *they cannot prove it from Scripture.* Neither can they prove this argument from any historical record (the Church has been celebrating the sacrament of reconciliation throughout her history).

Why would Jesus grant such an incredible gift of forgiveness to the apostolic age and then remove the gift from future generations? The answer, of course, is that He didn't. This gift was preserved through priestly succession by the sacrament of holy orders, as Christ intended.

The Eucharist

The Church teaches that the Eucharist is the source and summit of the Christian faith. Jesus Christ instituted this sacrament with His apostles the night before He died, conferring upon them the office of priesthood, and commanding them to offer the Eucharist in His memory. Jesus took bread, blessed and broke it, and said, "This is my body," and a cup of wine and said, "This is my blood."[158]

When a validly ordained priest celebrates this sacrament in the Holy Mass, he makes present on the altar the very same sacrifice that our Lord offered two thousand years ago on the cross, to make atonement for the sins of humanity. In so doing, the priest also makes truly, really, and substantially present the body and blood, soul and divinity of Jesus Christ under the appearance of bread and wine. The Church calls this miraculous process "transubstantiation."[159] Catholics receive into their own bodies Christ's body and blood, which is called "Holy Communion" or the "Eucharist."[160]

While the Eucharist is the central point of Catholic worship, it is a scandal to many non-Catholic Christians who do not understand it, and who believe we worship the elements themselves. If the bread and wine offered in the Holy Mass did not actually become Christ's body and blood, adoring the bread and wine would indeed be idolatrous. Such an act would be gravely sinful and deeply offensive to God. That is why Christians cannot be "on the fence" when it comes to the Eucharist.

Either Jesus Christ's eternal sacrifice becomes present on the altar of the Holy Mass and the bread and wine become Jesus' body and blood, or they don't. It is either true or it is false. It is that simple. If it is true, then the Eucharist is the greatest gift that a loving God has given His children this side of heaven (because the Eucharist is Jesus Christ Himself). If it is false, then the central point of Catholic worship, and the Catholic Church herself, falls apart.

With that in mind, we now examine the Scriptures.

The Eucharist makes present Jesus' one eternal sacrifice

Catholics believe that the celebration of the Eucharist at Holy Mass, which the Scriptures often refer to as "the breaking of bread" (Acts 2:42), miraculously makes present Jesus Christ's sacrifice on the cross. It is not a new sacrifice, or a simple commemoration of the sacrifice. It is the *same* sacrifice, RE-presented in an unbloody and sacramental way. How can Catholics possibly believe this? Because this is how Jesus instituted the sacrament at the Last Supper. This will become clearer as we proceed.

When Jesus took bread, gave thanks, broke it, and gave it to His disciples, He said, "This is my body which is given for you."[161] Jesus' phrase "is given for you," describing the offering of His body, is a present participle in Greek *(didomenon)*. This use of the present participle means that, as Jesus spoke the words, He was literally giving His body to His disciples. Such grammatical usage in New Testament Greek would never refer to a future event.

In certain translations, Paul similarly records Jesus' words, "This is my body which is broken for you."[162] The Greek word for "broken" *(klomenon)* also confines Christ's words to the strictly present, and demonstrates that Jesus was offering His broken body to His disciples in the Upper Room as an unbloody, sacramental sacrifice.

Jesus' subsequent offering of His blood, which He offers separately from His body, further demonstrates that Jesus was offering the sacrifice of His body and blood at the Last Supper. When Jesus took the cup and gave thanks, He said, "Drink of it, all of you; for this is my blood of the covenant, which is poured out for many for the forgiveness of sins."[163] Matthew and Mark use the present tense for both the finite verb "is" (in Greek, *estin*) and the participle "is poured out" (in Greek, *ekchynnomenon*) to describe Jesus' blood. As we saw with the phrase "is given for you," when such a double present tense is used in New Testament Greek, the time described is always the present tense, and not the future. This means that Jesus was pouring out His blood in the Upper Room, before He went to the cross.

Luke's recording of Jesus' words makes this even more striking: "This cup which is poured out for you, is the new covenant in my blood."[164] In Luke's account, Jesus' shedding of blood (in Greek, *ekchynnomenon*) actually takes place in the cup (in Greek, *poterion*). In other words, Jesus connects the shedding with the cup, instead of with His blood (in Greek, *to haimati*). This further underscores that Jesus was offering His body and blood separately, to make present his death sacramentally, as death occurs when blood is separated from the body. Paul records a similar translation in 1 Corinthians 11:25.

In Matthew's and Mark's Gospels, when Jesus offers His blood, He says that He is offering it as the "blood of the covenant."[165] This phrase exactly parallels the phrase Moses used when he sprinkled the people with the blood of the animal sacrifices: "Behold, the blood of the covenant. . ."[166] Jesus deliberately used this phrase to emphasize that He was currently offering His blood in sacrifice, just as Moses had offered the blood of the sacrifices when he said, "This is the blood of the covenant."

After Jesus offered His body and blood to the disciples, He said, "Do this in remembrance of me."[167] In commanding His apostles to "do this," Jesus instituted the office of ministerial priesthood. Thus, Jesus acts through His ministerial priests in sacramentally offering His body and blood to the heavenly Father in the Holy Mass.

Jesus' command is also more evidence that He instituted the Eucharist as a sacrifice. When we examine the original Greek text (*touto poieite eis ten emen anamnesin*), Jesus' literal words were: "Offer this as my memorial sacrifice." The word "remembrance" or "memorial" comes from the Greek word *anamnesis,* which is translated literally as "reminder." This "reminder" refers to a sacrifice that is currently offered. For example, in Hebrews 10:3, regarding the Old Testament sacrifices, the author writes, "But in these sacrifices there is a reminder [*anamnesis*] of sin year after year." In other words, the sacrifice, currently offered in time, is the memorial or reminder (*anamnesis*).[168]

The Scriptures also show us that there were two types of memorials that could be offered — a sacrificial memorial and a non-sacrificial memorial. A sacrificial memorial, for example, would involve slaughtering an animal.[169] A non-sacrificial memorial would involve, for example, offering incense* or prayers.*[170] As Scripture demonstrates, Jesus instituted the Eucharist as a sacrificial memorial. Jesus did this to implore God's immediate attention to His suffering and move Him to have mercy on His faithful ones. If Jesus did not intend to institute the Eucharist as sacrificial memorial, Luke and Paul would have used the word *mnemosunon*, which is the word used to describe non-sacrificial memorials. This can be seen in Acts 10:4, when the angel tells Cornelius, "Your prayers and your alms have ascended as a memorial before God." The offering of prayers and alms is a non-sacrificial memorial.[171]

As we will later see, Jesus explicitly connects the sacrifice of the Eucharist to His sacrifice on the cross. This is because, as we have mentioned and will further demonstrate, Jesus' Eucharistic sacrifice and His death on the cross *are one and the same sacrifice*. Therefore, anytime a priest offers the memorial sacrifice of the Eucharist in the Holy Mass, he offers the very sacrifice of Christ. When the Father sees the perfect and voluntary sacrifice of His divine and sinless Son, it appeases His wrath, restores His dignity, and moves Him to mercifully forgive our many sins.

This process, whereby God is moved from wrath to mercy, is called *propitiation*. Because God is perfect, He could only be propitiated by the most perfect expression of love that His Incarnate Son could give — laying His life down for us.[172] Thus, John says, "If anyone sins, we have one who speaks to the Father in our defense, Jesus Christ, the Righteous One. He is the *propitiation* for our sins"[173]

Notice that John says, ". . . *if* anyone sins," then Jesus "*is* the propitiation for our sins." John is not focusing on all sins, but only on *future sins*, and says that Jesus is currently the propitiation for those sins *if and when they occur*. But in order to avail ourselves of Jesus' propitiation, John says, we must first confess our sins. "If we confess our sins, he is faithful and just, and *will* forgive our sins and cleanse us from all unrighteousness" (1 Jn 1:9, emphasis added). This ongoing process of confession, propitiation, and forgiveness is inconsistent with the non-Catholic view that all sins — past, present, and future — have been forgiven by Christ's one-time sacrifice.

Wasn't Christ's sacrifice a one-time event?

Scripture teaches us that Christ's propitiation of the Father for the forgiveness of our sins *is an ongoing action, not a one-time event.* As we read in Hebrews, "Consequently, he is able for all time to save those who draw near to God through him, since he always lives to make intercession for them" (Heb 7:25). Similarly, Paul says to the Romans, "Is it Christ Jesus, who died, yes, who was raised from the dead, who is at the right hand of God, who indeed intercedes for us?" (Rom 8:34).

Christ's ongoing intercession before the Father, to bring about the forgiveness of our sins, poses problems for many non-Catholic theologians, who view Jesus Christ's sacrifice as completed on Calvary. To receive the benefits of His sacrifice, they argue, we simply need to accept Jesus as personal Lord and Savior. But if this were true, we would not need to confess our sins and have an ongoing Intercessor to propitiate God and plead for our forgiveness.

What happens if we sin after we have been forgiven? The author of Hebrews says, "For if we sin deliberately after receiving the knowledge of the truth, *there no longer remains a sacrifice for sins*, but a fearful prospect of judgment, and a fury of fire which will consume the adversaries" (Heb 10:26-27). Thus, to avail ourselves once again of the benefits of Christ's sacrifice, we have to confess our new sins. Then Christ's ongoing intercession before the Father will bring about our forgiveness. Note that this warning is being given to full-fledged Christians who have already been sanctified* and have confidence in Christ.*[174] Such a warning poses a fundamental problem with the view that sanctified Christians have already been forgiven for their sin by Jesus' sacrifice.

From a Catholic perspective, the warning makes perfect sense when we understand that the propitiatory sacrifice of Christ only applies to *confessed* sins, and not *future* sins, which may not be confessed and accompanied by repentance. Thus, in Hebrews 10:18, the author can say, "Where there is forgiveness of these, there is no longer any offering for sin." Peter also says, "For whoever lacks these things is blind and shortsighted and has forgotten that he was cleansed from his *old sins*" (2 Pet 1:9). This is because, under the New Covenant, our past confessed sins no longer require atonement, *but our present and future un-confessed sins do.* If we confess our sins, Christ's ongoing propitiation brings about our forgiveness, and the Father expiates our sins in His mercy (see Heb 2:17). This is how we become "perfected" in the New Covenant (see Heb 10:14). This also demonstrates how important it is to attend Mass every week, even daily, to receive God's mercy and forgiveness.

Why does God require a sacrifice to atone for sin?

Why does God require a sacrifice? Why does He need to be propitiated? Because God is an intensely personal being and our sins deeply offend and anger Him. In fact, God is so offended by sin that He condemned the whole human race to suffering and death for the sin of one man (see Rom 5:12).[175] As much as God wants to save us, He cannot simply overlook our sins without being moved to forgive them. Since sin is an offense against God' nature (namely, truth), He must first be appeased in order to forgive the offense.

As human beings made in God's own image and likeness, we can relate to the idea of propitiation in our own interactions. When someone offends us, we are more willing to accept that person back into our good graces if he or she repents of the offense and makes some kind of sacrifice for us.

God also desires to be propitiated continually, because we sin continually. Though God is eternal, when He created Adam He bound Himself to time and space. Therefore, God deals with our sinfulness moment by moment. This can be seen throughout Scripture.[176] Because we sin moment by moment, God must be propitiated moment by moment to relent of His anger and forgive our sins. If God were not propitiated this way, He would condemn the world immediately.

Because God desires a perfect and ongoing propitiation to move Him to forgive our sins, God could not accept on their own merit the many centuries of Jewish animal sacrifices to atone for sin. Those bloody sacrifices appeased God's wrath momentarily, but only because they foreshadowed the one perfect sacrifice of His Son.

The Old Testament sacrifices also did not bring about the holiness that God desired in His people. Instead, God revealed that, at some point in the future, He was only going to accept the pure offering of

Christ which He would make present in time, from the rising of the sun to its setting, in every place around the world, as an ongoing propitiation. This is exactly what the prophet Malachi prophesied.

In Malachi 1:10, God expresses His displeasure with the Jewish animal sacrifices by saying, "I have no pleasure in you, says the LORD of hosts, and I will not accept an offering from your hand." Then, in the next verse, God says:

> For from the rising of the sun to its setting my name is great among the nations, and in every place incense is offered to my name, and a pure offering; for my name is great among the nations, says the LORD of hosts (Mal 1:11).

Therefore, God, through Malachi, says that He would eventually reject animal sacrifices, and instead accept a pure offering around the clock and in every place. The pure offering can only be the memorial sacrifice of Jesus Christ, our Lamb without blemish.[177]

Malachi goes on to say that, with the coming of the Messiah, "Then the offering of Judah and Jerusalem will be pleasing to the LORD as in the days of old and as in former years" (Mal 3:4). Jeremiah similarly prophesies "David shall never lack a man to sit on the throne of the house of Israel, and the Levitical priests shall never lack a man in my presence to offer burnt offerings, to burn cereal offerings, and to make sacrifices for ever" (Jer 33:17-18). In both Malachi 3:4 and Jeremiah 33:17-18, the word for "offering" (in the Hebrew, *minchah*) is singular, just as it is in Malachi 1:11. We thus conclude that either these prophecies of a single and perpetual sacrifice to forgive sins have been fulfilled in the Holy Mass of the Catholic Church, or Malachi and Jeremiah are false prophets.

The author of Hebrews confirms our conclusions about these prophecies. In Hebrews 9, the author describes the animal sacrifices of the Old Covenant, and how the High Priest would take the blood of the sacrifices into the Temple once a year as an offering for sin (v.7). While these sacrifices would temporarily appease God (and *only* because the Father foresaw the future sacrifice of Christ), the author says that these sacrifices did not "perfect the conscience of the worshiper" (v.9).[178]

The author then compares the Old Covenant sacrifices with the New Covenant sacrifice of Christ by saying:

> Indeed, under the law almost everything is purified with blood, and without the shedding of blood there is no forgiveness of sins. Thus it was necessary for the copies of the heavenly things to be purified with these rites, *but the heavenly things themselves with better sacrifices than these.* For Christ has entered, not into a sanctuary made with hands, a copy of the true one, but into heaven itself, now to appear in the presence of God on our behalf (Heb 9:22-24).

In this passage, the author explains that the "shedding of blood" requirement exists under both the Old and New Covenants. Since the author is describing the rite of purification with blood under the Old Covenant (v.22), he is referring to this same purification rite under the New Covenant (v.23) when he says, "purified with these rites."

In connection with this shedding of blood, the author says that the Old Covenant blood sacrifices were only "copies of the heavenly things." Now, in the New Covenant sacrifice, the author says that the heavenly things are purified "with better sacrifices" than those in the Old Covenant (v.23). In other words, the author says that there are blood sacrifices in both the Old and the New Covenant, but the blood *sacrifices* of the New Covenant are better.

Why is Jesus' New Covenant blood sacrifice described as "sacrifices," in the plural?

Jesus only died once, right? Correct. But as we have seen, because Jesus instituted the Eucharist as a sacrificial memorial, He presents His eternal blood sacrifice to the Father perpetually, in heaven and on earth in the Holy Mass, from sunrise to sunset around the world, as prophesied by Malachi and Jeremiah. Thus, Jesus' sacrifice is described as "sacrifices" (plural) *in the context of its sacramental re-presentation on earth in the Holy Mass.* The author first writes about the earthly sacrifices of animals, and then the earthly offerings of Jesus Christ's one eternal sacrifice.

We should also note that the "things" that were purified in the Old Covenant sacrifices were "the people" of the Covenant (Heb 9:19). In the same way, in the New Covenant, it is the people who are purified "with better sacrifices than these" (v.23). This is because Jesus continues to present His shed blood "in the presence of God on our behalf" (v.24) for the "forgiveness of sins" (v.22).

The author of Hebrews also explains how Jesus makes His sacrifice eternally present to us: "after the order of Melchizedek."[179] Melchizedek is described in the book of Genesis as a priest and king of Salem who offered a bread and wine sacrifice and called out God's blessings upon Abram.[180] The author of Hebrews describes Jesus Christ as our new King and High Priest who instituted the Eucharist at Salem (now Jeru-salem) with a bread and wine sacrifice to bless the world, in the same manner as Melchizedek (see this prophecy in Psalm 110:4).

Thus, Jesus, through His priests at the Holy Mass, offers His eternal sacrifice from the rising of the sun to its setting in every place, under the appearance of bread and wine, in the same manner as Melchizedek. The Eucharistic sacrifice also fulfills God's promise that His earthly kingdom would consist of a sacrificial priesthood forever,* and His people would drink blood like wine and be saved.*[181]

The author of Hebrews finishes his letter by instructing us to "continually offer up a sacrifice of praise to God" (Heb 13:15). This "sacrifice of praise" refers to the thanksgiving sacrifices (as we have seen in Greek, *eucharistein*; in Hebrew, *toda*) that were offered in the Old Covenant, where animals were sacrificed and eaten.[182] Peter thus says that God made us "a holy priesthood, to offer spiritual sacrifices to God through Jesus Christ" (1 Pet 2:5). Peter is referring to the earthly offerings[183] of Jesus Christ's one eternal sacrifice. We can join in offering this sacrifice of Christ with the ministerial priests because, by virtue of our baptism, we participate in Christ's royal priesthood.[184]

Paul also emphasizes that the Eucharist is a sacrifice. In 1 Corinthians 10:16-17, Paul is teaching us that the Eucharist is a participation in the body and blood of Christ. Paul emphasizes the sacrifice in the next verse by saying, "are not those who eat the sacrifices partners in the altar?" (v.18). Paul is saying that what the priests have offered on the altar has indeed been sacrificed, and we become, in Holy Communion, partakers of the sacrifice. Paul then distinguishes the Eucharistic sacrifice from pagan sacrifices by saying, "No, I imply that what pagans sacrifice they offer to demons and not to God" (1 Cor 10:20). Paul is saying that both are sacrifices, but only one is offered to God. Therefore, in connection with celebrating the Eucharistic sacrifice, Paul admonishes the Galatians by saying "O foolish Galatians! Who has bewitched you, before whose eyes Jesus Christ *was publicly portrayed as crucified*?" (Gal 3:1).

Paul further says, "You cannot partake of the table of the Lord and the table of demons" (1 Cor 10:21). The Jews always understood "the table of the Lord" to be an altar of sacrifice.[185] Again, Paul affirms the Eucharist is a sacrifice and distinguishes it from the sacrifices of pagans. The celebration of the Eucharist is not just a mere fellowship meal.

How can the Eucharist be a sacrifice, if no blood is shed?

The doctrine of the Eucharist as Christ's sacrifice is rejected by some Christians because the Lord's blood is not literally shed in the Mass, and Hebrews 9:22 says, "without the shedding of blood there is no forgiveness of sins." It is true that the Lord's blood was shed only once. However, Scripture says that Jesus takes His shed blood into heaven to offer it to the Father (see Heb 9:12). And so, this heavenly offering is sacramentally made present to us on earth in the same manner as Melchizedek's offering when the priest offers the memorial sacrifice.

Scripture also teaches that not all sacrifices are bloody and result in death. Paul instructs us to offer ourselves "as a *living* sacrifice, holy and acceptable to God, which is your spiritual worship" (Rom 12:1). Aaron offered the Levites as a wave offering to God, which was an unbloody sacrifice.[186] Therefore, the Bible also teaches that sacrifices can be unbloody and life-giving. The Eucharistic sacrifice celebrated in the Holy Mass is the supreme and sacramental thanksgiving wave offering of Christ, unbloody and life-giving, offered at the table of the Lord, in every place, from the rising of the sun to its setting.

How does Jesus offer the Father His sacrifice on our behalf?

As we have seen, the Scriptures teach us that Jesus continually propitiates the Father in heaven with His perpetual sacrifice. But how is this possible? Why is it possible? While it is impossible to explain a miracle, the Scriptures do give us some very special insights. They teach us that Jesus Christ, in all His heavenly glory, makes His sacrifice present to the Father on our behalf.

This makes sense, for if the Father could only be propitiated by the sacrifice of Jesus while He was on earth, it follows that the Father would need to be propitiated by the same sacrifice of Jesus while He is in heaven. This must mean that Jesus is interceding for us by presenting that *same* sacrifice to the Father. If not, then the Father would now be appeased by something other than Christ's sacrifice (in fact, by something *less* than Christ's sacrifice). This cannot be true because God is immutable. He cannot change His nature and now somehow accept something less than Christ's sacrifice to be appeased. The book of Revelation and the Letter to the Hebrews further demonstrate that Jesus presents the sacrifice of Himself to His Father in heaven.

In Revelation, Jesus in all His heavenly power and glory is described as "a Lamb standing, as though it had been slain" (Rev 5:6). In fact, throughout the book of Revelation, Jesus is described as a Lamb *thirty* times. Why? John is telling us that Jesus' sacrifice as our paschal Lamb is emphasized in heaven. While lambs that are slain lie down, in Revelation Jesus is portrayed as a slain Lamb standing up, acting as both our eternal High Priest and Victim on the heavenly altar, forever offering Himself to the Father for our salvation.

Jesus is also clothed in heaven with a long robe and a golden girdle (see Rev 1:13). These were the same vestments worn by the Old Testament priests who offered animal sacrifices (see Ex 28:4). Jesus is also described as "clad in a robe dipped in blood,"* and this "blood of the Lamb" is offered to the saints to "[wash] their robes and [make] them white."*[187] These verses emphasize that the blood of Jesus' sacrifice is forever present in heaven.

Jesus also says, "To him who conquers, I will give some of the hidden manna" (Rev 2:17). This manna, hidden by our senses but revealed by faith, is offered to us in the Eucharistic sacrifice of the Holy Mass. This is the "daily bread" we pray for in the Lord's

Prayer.[188] Thus, from heaven Jesus invites us into full communion with Him when He says, "Behold, I stand at the door and knock; if any one hears my voice and opens the door, I will come in to him and eat with him, and he with me" (Rev 3:20). Since those in heaven are already in eternal communion with Christ, Jesus is talking about giving His heavenly manna to those on earth. Jesus also says, "Blessed are those who are invited to the marriage supper of the Lamb" (Rev 19:9). Jesus indeed comes into us at the marriage supper of His body and blood, where we become one with Him in a nuptial covenant communion of divinity and humanity.

As our High Priest, Jesus can offer His priestly sacrifice through-out eternity.[189] A priest's principal duty is to offer sacrifice. This is why the author of Hebrews says, "It is necessary for this priest also to have something to offer" (Heb 8:3).

What is Jesus offering to the Father in heaven? He is offering the sacrifice of His body and blood. Jesus, our sacrifice, "has passed through the heavens" (Heb 4:14), just like Solomon's sacrifices were taken up into heaven.[190] "He entered once for all into the Holy Place, taking not the blood of goats and calves, *but his own blood*, thus secur-ing an eternal redemption" (Heb 9:12).

How can Jesus take His own blood into heaven, since He was no longer bleeding? Jesus can do this because "he holds His priesthood permanently, because He continues forever" (Heb 7:24). Just as the High Priest of the Old Covenant took the blood of the sacrifice once a year into the Holy Temple to present it to God, Jesus the High Priest of the New Covenant takes the blood of His sacrifice once and for all into the Temple not made with hands, to present it to God. Just as Jesus' priesthood is forever, His sacrificial offering is also for-ever. Since Jesus' priesthood is heavenly, His offering is also heavenly.

Doesn't Jesus' "once-for-all" sacrifice mean "over and done-with"?

Non-Catholic Christians rebut the Catholic position by saying "Jesus died once and for all! His suffering is over!" This is true. But while Jesus' suffering and death is always described in the past tense,[191] Jesus' priestly presentation of His sacrifice in heaven is never so described. In fact, as the letter to the Hebrews demonstrates, "once-for-all" means "perpetual," not "over and done-with." As we have seen in Hebrews 9:12, it says Jesus "entered once for all into the Holy Place, . . . taking his own blood." This refers to Jesus' appearance as High Priest in heaven, which is confirmed by Hebrews 9:24. "For Christ has entered, not into a sanctuary made with hands, a copy of the true one, but into heaven itself, now to appear in the presence of God on our behalf." Unlike the Old Covenant priests, who had to go in and out of the Holy place every year to present their sacrifice,* Jesus enters the Holy place to present His sacrifice once and for all, there to stay and never to leave again.*[192] In this case, "once-for-all" describes Jesus' *appearance* in heaven in the presence of God on our behalf. It cannot mean "over and done-with" because Jesus is in the heavenly sanctuary to mediate on our behalf for all eternity.[193] While Jesus' suffering and death is always described in the past tense, His mediation of the New Covenant as our High Priest is always described in the present tense. Jesus established the eternal Covenant with His sacrifice on the cross, which He continues to mediate through its ongoing propitiatory offering to the Father. We have already seen that Jesus is described as our ongoing "propitiation,"* and that He "always lives to intercede for us."*[194] Further, in Hebrews 8:6 it says that "Christ has obtained a ministry which is as much more excellent than the old as the covenant *he mediates* is better." Hebrews 9:15 says, "Therefore he *is the mediator* of a new covenant."

In Hebrews 9:14, we read that the blood of Christ shall "*purify* your conscience from dead works to serve the living God." In Hebrews 13:20-21, it says the blood of the eternal Covenant may "*equip* you with everything good that you may do his will." John also says, ". . . the blood of Jesus his Son *cleanses* us from all sin" (1 Jn 1:7). This is because "Jesus Christ is the same yesterday and today and for ever,"* whose "works were finished from the foundation of the world."*[195] Thus, the mediation of the Covenant is the ongoing propitiatory offering of Jesus' body and blood, and this mediation *is always described in the present tense*. Of course, if Christ's sacrifice was completed and we were eternally secure, He would not need to mediate the Covenant before the Father on our behalf.

Because Jesus is our eternal High Priest in heaven, offering the Father His body and blood for us, the author of Hebrews says "we have confidence to enter the sanctuary by the blood of Jesus" (Heb 10:19). This is in reference to the celebration of the Eucharistic sacrifice on earth. This sanctuary into which we enter at the Holy Mass in Hebrews 10:19 is the very same sanctuary where Jesus is our minister in Hebrews 8:2, offering Himself to the Father at the altar in heaven. Thus, the author says, "We have an altar from which those who serve the tent have no right to eat" (Heb 13:10).

Because we eat at the heavenly altar when we celebrate the Eucharistic sacrifice on earth, we are actually entering into the heavenly liturgy, where Jesus Christ is our High Priest. This is why the sacred writer of Hebrews says:

> But you have come to Mount Zion and to the city of the living God, the heavenly Jerusalem, and to innumerable angels in festal gathering, and to the assembly of the first-born who are enrolled in heaven, and to a judge who is God of all, and to the spirits of just men made perfect, and to Jesus, the mediator of a new covenant, and to the sprinkled blood that speaks more graciously than the blood of Abel (Heb 12:22-24).

In the celebration of the Eucharist, we come to Jesus and His sprinkled blood and worship before God with the angels and saints in heaven. We are no longer offering "copies of the heavenly things" (Heb 9:23). We are participating in the same Eucharistic offering of heaven itself. The author of Hebrews connects this festal gathering to Mount Zion, where Jesus established the Eucharist and which was miraculously preserved after the destruction of the Temple in Jerusalem.[196] John also connects the Lamb's heavenly liturgy in the book of Revelation to Mount Zion (see Rev 14:1). We thus see that the admonition of "neglecting to meet together" in Hebrews 10:25 is in connection with the Eucharistic celebration that Paul describes in 1 Corinthians 11.[197]

The early Church understood that the heavenly liturgy and the earthly liturgy were one and the same priestly action of Christ. This is why the Church has always incorporated in the Holy Mass the liturgical elements of the heavenly liturgy as seen in John's Revelation. For example, John witnesses the following:

- heaven's liturgy on Sunday;[198]
- lamp stands or Menorahs as part of the liturgical worship;[199]
- priests* who are celibates* and who wear special vestments;*[200]
- the "tau" (or sign of the cross) is on the foreheads of the saints;[201]
- a penitential right;[202]
- the recitation of the "Gloria"* and the "Alleluia";*[203]
- a book of God's Word* and incense;*[204]
- the "Holy, Holy, Holy" chant* and other antiphonal chants* and prayers conclude with "Amen";*[205]
- a tabernacle*; and a chalice* and spiritual manna;*[206]
- an altar* and martyrs (relics) under the altar;*[207]
- the liturgy's invitation to "come up here" is like the priest's invitation to "lift up your hearts";[208]
- silent contemplation;[209]
- an emphasis on the Blessed Virgin Mary* and the intercession of Michael the Archangel and the saints;*[210]
- the catholicity or universality of the assembly is revealed;[211]
- Jesus is repeatedly declared "the Lamb of God;[212] and,
- the liturgy is consummated in the marriage supper of the Lamb.[213]

All of these are part of the Catholic Church's Eucharistic liturgy on earth.

The Eucharistic sacrifice must be consumed.

We have seen how Scripture teaches that the celebration of the Eucharist makes present on earth Jesus' once and for all sacrifice in the Holy Mass. But now what do we do? Just accept Jesus as personal Lord and Savior? No. We must eat the Lamb. We must enter into the New Covenant communion with Christ. Paul writes:

> For Christ, our paschal lamb has been sacrificed. Let us, therefore, celebrate the festival, not with the old leaven, the

leaven of malice and evil, but with the unleavened bread of sincerity of truth (1 Cor 5:7-8).

Throughout the Scriptures, God commanded His people to consume their sacrifices to make atonement for their sins and restore communion with God. "They shall eat those things with which atonement was made, to ordain and consecrate them, but an outsider shall not eat of them, because they are holy" (Ex 29:33).

However, only validly consecrated priests could offer the sacrifice (2 Chron 26:18). The consummation of the sacrifice also symbolized the covenant bond that God had with His people. For example, the Mosaic Covenant was consummated with a meal in the presence of God (Ex 24:9-11). The Aaronic sacrifices also had to be consumed to restore communion with God.[214] We also remember how God saved Abraham's first-born son on Mount Moriah with a substitute sacrifice that had to be consumed (Gen 22:9-13). God would later offer His only begotten Son on a hill on that same Mount Moriah, a sacrifice that must also be consumed.

The most important sacrifice that foreshadowed the Eucharistic sacrifice was that of the Passover lamb. To commemorate Israel's exodus from slavery in Egypt, God required each family to sacrifice an unblemished lamb* without breaking its bones* and sprinkle its blood on the doorposts with hyssop.*[215] But the sacrifice was not enough. God also commanded His people to eat the sacrificed lamb.[216] The lamb was slaughtered, roasted and eaten to atone for sin and restore communion with God.[217] If God's people sacrificed the lamb but did not eat it, He would slay their first-born sons.[218]

Notice also that no one outside the family of God could eat the lamb, which corresponds to non-Catholics who cannot partake of the Eucharist until they are in full communion with the Church;* no uncircumcised person could eat the lamb, which corresponds to non-baptized people who cannot partake of the Eucharist;* and the feast of the paschal lamb was a perpetual memorial that would last forever, which is why we celebrate its fulfillment in the Eucharistic sacrifice forever.*[219] After God freed His people from the slavery of Egypt, He sustained them on their journey to the Promised Land with bread from heaven.[220] This raining of manna from heaven and the bread of angels foreshadows the true bread from heaven who is Jesus Christ.[221] This bread is suited to every taste (see Wis 16:20). Thus, God says, "Those who eat me will hunger for more, and those who drink me will thirst for more" (see Sir 24:21).

The Passover lamb of Exodus, which was slaughtered and consumed to commemorate Israel's freedom from the slavery of Egypt, foreshadows the true Passover Lamb, Jesus Christ,[222] who was also slaughtered, and who must also be consumed. He is consumed as bread from heaven, offered in the same manner as the offering of Melchizedek, to free God's people from the slavery of sin. Jesus' teaching on eating His flesh and drinking His blood is the most powerful and, to some, the most scandalous of all His teachings. Let us now examine His teaching in detail.

"I am the bread of life…"

On the eve of Passover, when the Passover lambs were sacrificed, Jesus performs the miracle of multiplying the loaves.[223] Jesus then reminds the Jews that God gave them bread from heaven on their journey to the Promised Land, and now will give them the true bread from heaven (Jn 6:31-33). Then Jesus says, "I am the bread which came down from heaven" (v.41). After the Jews question Him, Jesus goes on to say "I am the bread of life…. I am the living bread from heaven; if any one eats of this bread, he will live forever; and the bread which I shall give for the life of the world is my flesh" (vv.48,51).

The Jews understand Jesus' words literally and immediately question His teaching by saying, "How can this man give us his flesh to eat?" (v.52). Jesus does not correct their literal understanding. Instead, Jesus swears an oath and speaks even more literally about eating His flesh and drinking His blood:

> Truly, truly, I say to you, unless you eat the flesh of the Son of man and drink His blood, you have no life in you; he who eats my flesh and drinks my blood has eternal life, and I will raise him up at the last day. For my flesh is food indeed, and my blood is drink indeed. He who eats my flesh and drinks my blood abides in me, and I in him. As the living Father sent me, and I live because of the Father, so he who eats me

will live because of me. This is the bread which came down from heaven, not such as the fathers ate and died; he who eats this bread will live forever (Jn 6:53-58).

In John 6:12-52, John uses the Greek word *phago* nine times for the verb "to eat" or "to consume" to describe what we must do to Jesus' flesh. This word literally means to eat something, and would generally not invite metaphorical interpretations. This is demonstrated by the fact that the Jews understand Jesus literally and question how He could give them His flesh to eat. But if the Jews misunderstood Jesus, and Jesus was really speaking metaphorically, now would have been the time for Jesus to correct their erroneous interpretation.

Instead, in John 6:53-58 cited above, Jesus switches to an even more literal verb, *trogo*, which means to chew, gnaw, nibble or crunch to describe what we must do to Jesus' flesh.[224] Jesus increases the literalness of His message. Not one verse in Scripture uses *trogo* symbolically, and yet this is the only way to deny the Catholic understanding of Jesus' words. Moreover, the Jews knew Jesus was speaking literally even before Jesus used the verb *trogo* to describe eating His flesh, when they asked "How can this man give us His flesh to eat?" (Jn 6:52).

For those who still question whether Jesus' body and blood could possibly be food and drink, Jesus drives His message home and says, "For my flesh is food indeed, and my blood is drink indeed" (Jn 6:55). This phrase can only be understood as being responsive to those who do not believe that Jesus' flesh is food indeed, and His blood is drink indeed. Further, the Greek word for "real" (food and drink) is *alethes*, which means "really," or "truly." Such a word would have only been used if there were doubts concerning the reality of Jesus' flesh and blood being food and drink. To further bolster a literal interpretation, Jesus uses the word *sarx* for His "flesh" (not *soma* for body). This would also be an odd use of such a literal word if Jesus were only speaking symbolically about spiritually accepting Him or His teaching. Scripture, instead, shows that *sarx* is invariably used literally.[225]

For those Christians who still insist that Jesus was speaking metaphorically (even though they provide no biblical support for their position), such a metaphorical interpretation causes them further problems. Every time the Scriptures talk about symbolically eating someone's body and blood, it is always in the context of a physical assault. It always means, "destroying an enemy," not becoming intimately close to him.[226] Thus, if Jesus were speaking symbolically in John 6:53-58, He would be saying, "He who reviles or assaults me has eternal life." This, of course, is absurd.

On the surface, we can relate to Jesus' disciples who, after Jesus commanded them to eat His flesh and drink His blood, said "This is a hard saying; who can listen to it?" (Jn 6:60). Jesus' disciples were scandalized at His words. They didn't even want to listen to them, much less try to understand them. But Jesus told them that they needed supernatural faith to understand His words. They could not understand the Eucharist by reason alone. So Jesus says, "It is the spirit that gives life, the flesh is of no avail" (Jn 6:63).

Some Protestants argue that this verse proves Jesus was only speaking symbolically about His flesh being real food. But it is obvious that Jesus, after repeatedly and graphically telling His disciples that they must eat His flesh to have eternal life, wasn't suddenly saying that His flesh now profited nothing. Jesus often used the "spirit versus flesh" comparison to teach about the need to have faith to understand His teachings.[227] Paul also compares the "spirit" to the "flesh" to explain that a lack of understanding is due to a lack of faith.[228]

Other Christians focus on Jesus' next statement, "the words that I have spoken are spirit and life"* to try to prove Jesus was speaking symbolically.*[229] But, again, Jesus is explaining that His words require faith. Jesus does not say, "My flesh is spirit." He says, "My *words* are spirit." The spiritual words that Jesus spoke, which are *life,* are that we must eat His flesh and drink His blood, or we have *no life* in us.[230]

In the next verse, Jesus says, "But there are some of you who do not believe" (Jn 6:64). This proves quite compellingly that Jesus' statements in John 6:63 (about the spirit versus flesh and His words being spirit and life) were about *believing* in Jesus' words in John 6:53-58, and not somehow repudiating the words He previously spoke. In fact, Jesus ties the disbelief in His Eucharistic words to Judas' betrayal in the very next verse. "For Jesus knew from the first who those were that did not believe, and who it was that should betray him" (Jn 6:64). Jesus again says, "Did I not choose you, the twelve, and one of you is a devil?" (Jn 6:70). Those who don't believe in Jesus' miracle betray Him as Judas betrayed Him.

What concretizes the Catholic position is what happens at the end of Jesus' Eucharistic discourse. We know the disciples understood Jesus literally, and, as a result, they left Jesus — and Jesus let them go! "After this, many of His disciples drew back and no longer went about with Him" (Jn 6:66).

If they had simply misunderstood His teaching on what it takes to gain eternal life, why didn't the Lord Jesus, the Savior of the world who became man to bring us eternal life, call back the wayward disciples? Why didn't Jesus say, "Hey people, come back here. You misunderstood me. I was only speaking symbolically!"? Jesus did not do this because they understood Him correctly.

Jesus would never drive anyone away from Him, especially over a misunderstanding of His teaching. A few minutes before the Eucharistic discourse in John 6:41-58, Jesus says, "All that the Father gives me will come to me; and him who comes to me I will not cast out" (Jn 6:37). Scripture also says that Jesus always explained to His disciples the real meaning of His teachings,[*] and demonstrates this by giving examples of when Jesus did correct wrong impressions of His teaching.[*231] In John 6, Jesus does not correct the disciples' impressions because their understanding was correct. After Jesus looks at His apostles and asks whether they too would go away, only Peter, the chief shepherd Jesus would choose to lead the Church, has the faith to say "Lord, to whom shall we go? You have the words of eternal life; and we have believed, and have come to know, that you are the Holy One of God" (Jn 6:68-69).

Elsewhere in Scripture, Jesus does speak about Himself using metaphors. For example, Jesus calls himself "the door of the sheep" (Jn 10:7) and "the true vine" (Jn 15:1,5). However, in each case His disciples understood that Jesus was speaking metaphorically. No one asked Jesus, "Are you really a door?" or "Are you really a vine?" In John 6, Jesus' disciples understand Him to be speaking literally, and even ask if their understanding was correct. Jesus confirms that they understood correctly. Moreover, Jesus' command to eat His flesh and drink His blood has precedent elsewhere in Scripture,[232] while His claims of being a "door" and a "vine" do not.

Some also argue that drinking blood and eating sacrificed meats were prohibited in the New Testament, so Jesus would never have commanded us to consume His body and blood. Drinking blood was prohibited in the Old Testament because blood was considered a source of life.[233] These prohibitions no longer apply in the New Testament. Paul taught that all foods, even meat offered to idols, strangled, or with blood could be consumed by the Christian if it didn't bother the brother's conscience and were consumed in thanksgiving to God.[234] Christ's blood, our source of eternal life in the New Covenant, must now be drunk.

Jesus' Passion is connected to the Passover sacrifice

Another argument against the Eucharist leads us into further proof that Jesus explicitly connected the Eucharistic sacrifice with His sacrifice on the cross to demonstrate that they are the same sacrifice. When Jesus instituted the Eucharist, in which He changed the bread into His body and the wine into His blood, He said, "Truly, I say to you, I shall not drink again of the fruit of the vine until that day when I drink it new in the kingdom of God."[235]

Some Protestants argue that, because Jesus said "fruit of the vine," the wine cannot be His blood. However, while Matthew and Mark record Jesus' statement that He would not "drink the fruit of the vine" as coming after His consecration of the bread and wine, Luke puts this statement of Jesus *before* His consecration (see Lk 22:18-20). This lends ambiguity to the timing of Jesus' statement. Perhaps Jesus was only explaining to His apostles that His time on earth was short, and He wouldn't eat or drink normally again until after His Resurrection.

The Greek word for "fruit" is *genneema*, which literally means, "that which is generated from the vine." In John 15:1,5, Jesus says, "I am the vine." Therefore, "fruit of the vine" can also mean Jesus' blood. There are other verses in Scripture that show that *genneema* means "birth" or "generation."[236] Paul also uses "bread" and "the body of the Lord" interchangeably in the same sentence to refer to Jesus' actual body,[237] so if Paul can do that Jesus can too. But Jesus' use of the phrase "fruit of the vine" is pointing to something more mystical.

When Jesus instituted the Eucharist, He was celebrating the Seder meal to commemorate the Jewish Passover. The Gospel writers expressly link Jesus' Passion to the Passover.[238] The Seder meal requires the participants to drink four cups of wine. But the Scriptures indicate that Jesus only presented the first three cups. He stops at the third cup, called the "Cup of Blessing." That is why Paul uses the phrase "Cup of Blessing" to describe the Eucharist (1 Cor 10:16). Jesus does not drink the fourth cup, called the "Cup of Consummation," which is the high point of the Seder meal when the Lamb is eaten. Instead, Jesus tells His disciples He will no longer drink the "fruit of the vine." Then they sang a hymn that traditionally followed the third cup,* and went out to the Mount of Olives.*[239]

Why did Jesus conspicuously omit the Cup of Consummation? Because Jesus was going to drink it while He was crucified, thereby connecting the Eucharistic sacrifice with His sacrifice on the cross. Jesus was instituting a new Passover meal, the Eucharist, where the true Lamb of God is slain and consumed.

The sacred writers teach this throughout the Scriptures. For example, after Jesus goes out to the Mount of Olives, He comes to the Garden of Gethsemane. In the garden, Luke says, Jesus' sweat became "like drops of blood" (Lk 22:44), indicating that His sacrifice had already begun. As Jesus agonizes in the garden, He acknowledges that He has one more cup to drink, and prays "My Father, if it be possible, let this cup pass from me; nevertheless, not as I will, but as thou wilt."[240] When Jesus is arrested, He is brought before Pilate who finds Him to be without blemish or fault.[241] This happens within the same period of time the Passover lambs were examined for blemishes prior to being killed. Jesus is the true Lamb of God without blemish who takes away the sins of the world.[242]

On His way to crucifixion, Jesus is offered wine, but refuses to drink it.[243] Matthew and Mark point this out to emphasize Jesus will drink the final Cup of Consummation on the cross. John also writes that Jesus had on a priestly tunic which had no seam, woven from top to bottom (Jn 19:23). This was the same *chiton* garment the Old Testament priests wore to offer sacrifices, and shows that Jesus is both Priest and Victim.[244]

From the cross Jesus says, "I thirst," and He is given wine to drink;* this was the fourth cup of the Seder meal, connecting the meal with the sacrifice.*[245] John notes that Jesus is provided the wine on a hyssop branch,* the same kind of branch used to sprinkle the Passover lambs' blood on the doorposts.*[246] Then, after Jesus drinks the Cup of Consummation, He says, "It is consummated!"[247]

John writes that Jesus was crucified at noon, just when the Passover lambs were sacrificed (Jn 19:14). Further, none of Jesus' bones were broken, just as the Passover lambs' bones could not be broken.[248] What does all this mean? Two things:

- It means that Jesus Christ's Calvary sacrifice and His Last Supper sacrifice are one and the same sacrifice.
- It means that we must now eat our New Covenant Passover Lamb, just as God commanded in the Old Covenant (Ex 12:8,11).

Just as the Old Covenant Passover was both a sacrifice and a meal, the New Covenant Passover of the Eucharist is also a sacrifice and a meal. Jesus tells us to "take and eat."[249] Paul likewise tells us that, because our paschal Lamb has been sacrificed, we must "celebrate the festival" (1 Cor 5:7-8).

Are there other scriptural proofs of the Real Presence of Christ in the Eucharist?

We have learned that Jesus instituted the Eucharist as a memorial sacrifice, and that this sacrifice makes present Jesus' actual body and blood. We have further evidence of this when we look again at the words Jesus used. In the Synoptic Gospels, Jesus says, "This is my body."[250] As we have seen, Jesus does not say, "This is a symbol of my body," or "This represents my body." In fact, Aramaic had literally two-dozen words for "represent," but Jesus did not use any of them.

Further, when we again examine the Greek (*touto estin to soma*), the word for "this" is a neuter adjective. Thus, it cannot refer to "bread" (in Greek, *artos*) because *artos* is a masculine noun. Rather, since the word "body" (in Greek, *soma*) is a neuter noun, the word "this" refers to "body," not "bread." Thus, Jesus actually said, "This is the body of me" (not, "This bread is my body"). In other words, the word "this" refers, not to the bread, but to the *new substance* that is now Jesus' body.

When non-Catholics limit the Eucharist to a "sign," it is important to remember that *a sign can also be the reality.*

- In Matthew 12:39, when Jesus says no "sign" will be given except the "sign of the prophet Jonah," He was speaking of the reality of His Resurrection (both sign and reality).
- In John 2:19-22, when Jesus says that He will raise the temple in three days (in reference to His body), He speaks literally, not just symbolically.
- In his letter to the Corinthians, Paul says of the Eucharist, "The cup of blessing which we bless, is it not a participation in the blood of Christ? The bread which we break, is it not a participation in the body of Christ?" (1 Cor 10:16).

Was Paul really asking the Corinthians because he, the divinely inspired writer, did not understand? Of course not. Paul's questions are obviously rhetorical; he is trying to convince the Corinthians of the Real Presence of Christ in the Eucharist. The word for "participation" (in Greek, *koinonia*) is also used to describe an actual, not symbolic participation in Christ's body and blood.

In the next chapter, also on the Eucharist, Paul emphasizes that he had received this teaching directly from the Lord Jesus (1 Cor 11:23). Paul wanted it to be clear that these were not his own ideas. Paul also writes, "For as often as you eat this bread and drink the cup, you proclaim the Lord's death until he comes" (v.26). This means that celebrating the Eucharist is proclaiming the gospel.

One of the most compelling Scripture passages for Christ's Real Presence comes in the next few verses. Paul says,

> Whoever, therefore, eats the bread or drinks the cup of the Lord in an unworthy manner will be guilty of profaning the body and blood of the Lord. Let a man examine himself, and so eat of the bread and drink of the cup. For any one who

eats and drinks without discerning the body eats and drinks judgment upon himself (1 Cor 11:27-29).

In other words, if we partake of the Eucharist unworthily (receiving Christ in mortal sin), we are guilty of profaning (literally, murdering) the body and blood of the Lord.

If the Eucharist were just a symbol, we could not be guilty of profaning it. It is impossible to murder a symbol. The New Testament records no such penalty for the failure to recognize the meaning of symbols. Either Paul, the divinely inspired apostle of God, is imposing an unjust penalty on us or the Eucharist is the actual body and blood of Christ. In fact, Paul says that the reason some in the Corinthian church had become ill and died was because they had received the Eucharist unworthily (see 1 Cor 11:30). Receiving the physical body and blood of Jesus unworthily resulted in physical consequences to their bodies.

This Scripture passage reminds me of a debate I had with a Protestant gentleman at work about the Real Presence of Christ in the Eucharist. I explained to him that in all three Synoptic Gospel accounts of the Last Supper, as well as in Paul's teaching, which he received directly from Christ, Jesus took bread, blessed and broke it, and said "This is my body." In the same manner, He took wine, gave thanks, and said, "This is my blood." I emphasized that Jesus did not say, "This represents my body and blood," or "This is a symbol of my body and blood." I further explained to him that God does not, and cannot, declare something to be without making it so. For example, when God said, "Let there be light," there was light! I challenged him to find a Scripture verse where God declares something without making it so, to prove me wrong. He could not.

Instead, the Protestant took down a picture of his wife, which he had pinned up in his cubicle, gave me the picture, and said, "This is my wife." Then he asked me, "But it is not really her, is it?" He thought he had me cold.

I first congratulated him on having such a beautiful wife. I then pretended to rip up the picture and, after it fell to the ground, pretended to stomp all over it. I made a bit of a scene. He looked at me with an expression of surprise and confusion. I then asked him "Am I now guilty of profaning your wife's body and blood?"

After quite a pause, he responded, "No."

"No," I repeated. "Of course not. The picture of your wife is just a symbol of her, and you can't profane a symbol, can you?" He agreed.

I then drove home my point. "Then why," I asked him, "does Paul in 1 Corinthians 11:27 declare us to be guilty of profaning Christ's body and blood if we receive the Eucharist unworthily? If the Eucharist were just a symbol, wouldn't that be an unjust penalty?"

My Protestant brother was at a loss for words. All he could do was ask me to give him back his wife's picture, and he promised he would read the verses in their proper context and get back to me. He never did.

Many of our non-Catholic brothers and sisters tell us that we need to have a personal relationship with Jesus. Catholics would agree. We cannot have a more personal relationship with Christ than consuming His body and blood. As Catholics, our relationship with Jesus is not only spiritual but physical as well. We truly come to know and love Jesus "in the breaking of the bread." Luke emphasizes this in the Emmaus Road story, when Jesus explains the Scriptures to the two disciples and then celebrates the Eucharist (which has been the order of the Holy Mass to the present day). The disciples did not recognize Jesus until "he took the bread and blessed, and broke it, and gave it to them. And their eyes were opened and they recognized him; and he vanished out of their sight."[251]

Jesus says that a husband and wife become one flesh in the life-giving union of the marital act.[252] This union of marital love, which reflects Christ's union with the Church, is physical, not just spiritual. Thus, when Paul says we are a part of Christ's body, the Church, he means that our union with Christ is physical, not just spiritual.[253] If not, Paul would have called us the soul of Christ, not the body of Christ (souls are invisible and spiritual, and bodies are visible and physical). Our union with Christ can only be physical if Christ is actually giving us something physical, that is, Himself. This self-giving and life-giving love is the Eucharist.

God coming to us under the appearance of elements He created (bread and wine) is an extension of the awesome mystery of the

Incarnation. If we can believe in the incredible reality of the Incarnation, that the almighty and ineffable God of the universe became a little helpless baby, we can certainly believe that the same God can give Himself to us under the appearance of bread and wine. Nothing is impossible with God (see Lk 1:37). Jesus promised that He would be with us always (see Mt 28:20). Jesus also says that we must become like children in order to enter into the kingdom of God (see Mt 18:2-5). We must believe Jesus' words with childlike faith, even though His words surpass our understanding. Our salvation depends upon it.

Confirmation

Jesus Christ instituted the sacrament of confirmation to more perfectly bind the baptized into the Church and enrich them with a special strength of the Holy Spirit.[254] In the western Church, a bishop generally administers this sacrament to teenagers, although it can be given later. The sacrament includes a renewal of baptismal promises, reading of Scripture, and anointing of chrism oil[255] on the forehead.

The sacrament of confirmation brings to completion the grace received at baptism, and strengthens those who receive it to spread and defend the faith by word and deed. Along with baptism and the Eucharist, the sacrament of confirmation completes the sacraments of Christian initiation. Those who are confirmed are "sealed"[256] with the fullness of the Holy Spirit.

Scripture mentions the sacrament of confirmation in several places. The author of Hebrews gives general instructions about confirmation when he writes about "the doctrine of baptisms and the laying on of hands, of the resurrection of the dead and of eternal judgment."[257] In this case, the phrase "laying on of hands," which was directed to the whole Hebrew community, refers to confirmation. This verse also refers to the cycle of life and its relationship to the sacraments — baptism (beginning of life), confirmation (perfection of baptismal graces), resurrection and judgment (end of life).

In the book of Acts, we read that the apostles at Jerusalem found out that the people of Samaria had not received the fullness of the Holy Spirit (Acts 8:14). In fact, the Scripture says the people of

Samaria "had only been baptized in the name of the Lord Jesus" (Acts 8:16). But as we have seen in the section on baptism, when a person is baptized, they do receive the Holy Spirit. This means the baptized people of Samaria did not receive the fullness of the Holy Spirit until they were confirmed. Then the apostles "laid their hands on them, and they received the Holy Spirit" (Acts 8:17). These verses are not about ordination because Luke is writing about the entire city of Samaria, and the apostles did not ordain entire cities. There is also nothing in theses verses suggesting the people of Samaria had any teaching or other capacities in the Church.

Later in Acts, Paul finds some disciples on his journey through Ephesus (Acts 19:1). When Paul discovers that these disciples believed in Jesus but were not yet baptized, Paul both baptizes them and lays hands on them to confer the sacrament of confirmation and to give them the Holy Spirit (see Acts 19:5-6). Baptism and confirmation were usually given together in the early Church, which is still the practice of the Eastern Catholic church today. Paul also tells the Ephesians that they "were sealed with the promised Holy Spirit" (Eph 1:13), and that they should "not grieve the Holy Spirit of God, in whom you were sealed for the day of redemption" (Eph 4:30). In confirmation, just as the Father set His seal on Christ,[*] so we are sealed with the Holy Spirit in Christ and protected from spiritual harm.[*258]

Holy Matrimony

From the very beginning of creation, God established the marital covenant as a sign of the absolute and unfailing love God has for man. The union of a man and a woman in marriage reflects the self-giving and life-giving love of the Creator. "Therefore a man leaves his father and his mother and cleaves to his wife, and they become one flesh" (Gen 2:24).

Jesus Christ elevated this marital covenant between baptized persons to the dignity of a sacrament. The sacrament occurs when one baptized male and one baptized female freely consent to give themselves to each other until death.[259]

The marital covenant between two baptized persons is indissoluble because God brings the couple together and makes them "one flesh." Jesus reiterates the Father's teaching on marriage: "So they are no longer two but one flesh."[260] Paul likewise teaches that, in marriage, "the two shall become one flesh."[261] Paul further teaches that the sacrament of matrimony signifies the very union of Christ and His Church.[262] This holy, mystical, supernatural union is covenantal and not merely a human institution.[263] Because God establishes the marital covenant, and this union is the image of Jesus and the Church, nothing can separate it. Christ the Bridegroom and His Church the Bride are one forever. "What therefore God has joined together, let not man put asunder" (Mt 19:6).

Divorce and remarriage

Although many Christian churches no longer recognize the indissolubility of Christian marriage, Jesus was clear that the sacrament of marriage is irrevocable. "Whoever divorces his wife and marries another, commits adultery against her; and if she divorces her husband and marries another, she commits adultery."[264] Paul taught the same thing to the Romans (see Rom 7:3). When the Pharisees reminded Jesus that Moses permitted divorce, Jesus said, "For your hardness of heart Moses allowed you to divorce your wives, but from the beginning it was not so" (Mt 19:8). God has told us in strong words, "I hate divorce" (Mal 2:16).

In Matthew's Gospel, Jesus seems to qualify His teaching on divorce and remarriage when He says, "And I say to you: whoever divorces his wife, except for unchastity, and marries another, commits adultery."[265] This is not a qualification. The Greek word for "unchastity," *porneia,* generally refers to unlawful sexual intercourse between blood relatives (or "incest"). *Porneia* would also encompass any type of non-sacramental union. However, in the case of *porneia,* a marriage bond is not broken, for it never existed in the first place.

In other words, the Lord was not permitting divorce, but allowing for the dissolution of an unlawful union. Notice also that that the Lord does not allow divorce and remarriage in cases of "adultery" (in Greek, *moicheia*), though many non-Catholic Christian churches allow a person to remarry in cases of adultery.

Besides the death of a spouse, which is the natural way a marital union dissolves, the Catholic Church permits disbanding a union only in two limited cases, and only when the union jeopardizes the Christian faith.

- *The Pauline privilege.* In his letter to the Corinthians, Paul addresses a situation in which two unbaptized people are married and, after the marriage, one of the persons is baptized. Paul teaches that, if the unbaptized person decides to leave the marriage, the Christian is free to remarry.[266] This marital union was not indissoluble because it was not ratified by God in the sacrament of matrimony.
- *The Petrine privilege.* In this case, a baptized person marries an unbaptized person. If this marriage jeopardizes the baptized person's faith, and hence his or her salvation, the pope may dissolve this marriage pursuant to his binding and loosing authority.[267]

Thus, the marital covenant between one man and one woman reflects Christ's union with the Church at the heavenly marriage supper of the Lamb.[268] Just as Jesus and His Church become one flesh through the Eucharist and this union brings forth spiritual life for God's children, a man and a woman become one flesh in the sacrament of marriage, and their union brings forth physical life for the Church.

Contraception

Most Christians do not realize that all Christian churches opposed contraception (which is intentionally trying to prevent the conception of a child) until the 1930 Lambeth Conference, when the Anglican church permitted contraception in very limited circumstances. Since this concession, most other Protestant churches have followed suit, leading to widespread and unprecedented decay in sexual morality. Only the Catholic Church has remained faithful to God's teaching: Contraception is an intrinsic evil that is not permissible under any circumstances. This is another sign that the Catholic Church is Christ's true Church.

The Church forbids contraception because it violates the marital covenant and thwarts God's ability to "join together" husband and wife in one flesh. True love is both self-giving and life-giving, because it comes from God Himself, the Author of life, who "is love" (1 Jn 4:16). When contraception is introduced into the marital act, it removes the life-giving aspect of marital love, reducing the act to one of selfish pleasure, and not selfless giving, and turning the expression of love into a lie. Contraception removes God from the very covenant He has established with the couple, and the couple says, "Not your will, God, but ours be done." Thus, contraception is mortally sinful. The Church has always taught that life and love can never be separated;[269] thus, every act of sexual intimacy between a husband and wife must be open to the transmission of human life.

From the very beginning of creation, God commanded us to be fruitful and to multiply.[270] Thus, about God the prophet Malachi says, "And what does he desire? Godly offspring" (Mal 2:15). The Scriptures always describe children as blessings from God, like the arrows in the hand of a warrior. "Happy is the man who has his quiver full of them!" (Ps 127:5). God's promises to faithful Israel include the blessings of many children with no miscarriages or barrenness.[271] Isaac's prayer over Jacob shows that fertility and procreation are God's blessings (Gen 28:3). Accordingly, the Church teaches that the marital covenant is primarily ordered to the procreation and education of children.

The Scriptures also teach that contraception is contrary to both God's moral and natural law. In the book of Genesis, when Onan had relations with his brother's wife to continue the family lineage (which was customary at this time in history), he terminated the sexual act by withdrawing because he did not wish to conceive a child. God killed Onan for his contraceptive act. "So when he went in to his brother's wife he spilled the semen on the ground, lest he should give offspring to his brother. And what he did was displeasing in the sight of the LORD, and he slew him also" (Gen 38:8-10).

Some say Onan was killed for disobedience, but not for contraception. But the penalty for refusing to keep up a family lineage was not death; it was public mockery with a good spit in the face (see Deut 25:7-10). Judah, who commanded Onan to go into his brother's wife, also refused to keep up the family lineage, but God did not kill Judah (see Gen 38:11-26). God killed Onan not for disobedience but for wasting seed. The author's graphic usage of the word "semen," which is uncharacteristic of Hebrew writing, also underscores the reason for Onan's death.

Before Tobit marries Sara, the angel Raphael warns him that the devil has power over those who contracept, engaging in the marital act for physical pleasure only. "Hear me, and I will shew thee who they are, over whom the devil can prevail. For they who in such manner receive matrimony, as to shut out God from themselves, and from their mind, and to give themselves to their lust, as the horse and mule, which have not understanding, over them the devil hath power."[272] After Raphael instructs Tobit to abstain from marital relations for the first three days of his marriage, Raphael says, "And when the third night is past, thou shalt take the virgin with the fear of the Lord, moved rather for love of children than for lust, that in the seed of Abraham thou mayst obtain a blessing in children."[273]

Elsewhere in Scripture God reveals His displeasure with nongenerative sexual acts, including expressly condemning homosexuality and bestiality.[274] Paul likewise condemns homosexual acts because they pervert the marital covenant.[275] God also condemns deliberate sterilization such as crushed testicles* and castration.*[276] This condemnation would also include vasectomies and tubal ligations. God punishes even those who inflict potential damage to private parts (Deut 25:11-12). God punishes Israel by preventing pregnancy, which shows that contraception is a curse.[277] God further condemns premarital intercourse (Deut 22:13-21). The Scriptures also condemn "sorcery" (in Greek, *pharmakeia*), which includes abortifacient potions such as birth-control pills and other chemicals that prevent conception.[278]

The marital act, at the depth of its mystery, is a reflection of the Blessed Trinity. The union seals the marital covenant because, fueled by God's grace, it becomes a supernatural exchange of persons. Just as God is three in one, so are a husband and wife, who become one flesh and bring forth new life, three in one. Marital love is, therefore, incarnational, just as God became incarnate in His ultimate expression of love for humanity.

Paul says, "Husbands, love your wives, as Christ loved the church and gave himself up for her" (Eph 5:25). When Christ gave up His body for His Bride, He held nothing back. Similarly, because the sacrament of marriage symbolizes the union of Christ and the Church, married couples must freely and completely give themselves to each other, including even their fertility. This expression of authentic marital love reintegrates our bodies and souls to God, and leads us on the way of perfection in Christ.

The husband as head of the family

The Holy Catholic Church has always taught through Scripture and Tradition that in the sacrament of holy matrimony, the husband is the head of his family and has God-given authority over his wife and children. The husband's headship over his bride reflects Christ's headship over His Bride, the Church. As the Apostle Paul writes:

> Wives, be subject to your husbands, as to the Lord. For the husband is the head of the wife as Christ is the head of the church, His body, and is himself its Savior. As the church is subject to Christ, so let wives also be subject in everything to their husbands (Eph 5:22-24).

Paul similarly tells the Colossians (3:18): "Wives, be subject to your husbands, as is fitting in the Lord." Paul also teaches Titus that wives should be "submissive to their husbands, that the word of God may not be discredited" (Titus 2:5). In his first epistle, Peter teaches, "Likewise you wives, be submissive to your husbands, so that some, though they do not obey the word, may be won without a word by the behavior of their wives, when they see your reverent and chaste behavior" (1 Pet 3:1-2).[279]

Just as a wife must submit to her husband, the husband must love his wife as Christ loves His Bride, the Church: "Husbands, love your wives, as Christ loved the church and gave himself up for her. . . husbands should love their wives as their own bodies" (Eph 5:25,28). Paul further says, "let each one of you love his wife as himself" (Eph 5:33). Paul also tells the Colossians: "Husbands, love your wives, and do not be harsh with them" (Col 3:19).

What does this mean? Husbands must love their wives sacrificially, and wives must be submissive to their husbands "in all things."[280] This includes submitting to the husband's judgment about those important family decisions that affect her and their children.

The husband must exercise this authority in the natural order, such as making family rules and disciplining his children. He must also exercise this authority in the supernatural order, teaching his children the Christian faith and leading the family in prayer. These are grave responsibilities, and God will judge both husbands and wives on how they fulfill them.

The husband's spiritual leadership is particularly important. After all, a husband's principal duty is to lead his wife and children to heaven. Just as mothers give natural life to their families, fathers must give their families supernatural life. Hence, the father is the head priest of his domestic church (his family), just as Christ is the High Priest of His Catholic Church (the family of God). As we will see in the next section on holy orders, fatherhood and priesthood have always been identified together.[281] This is why Catholics call their ministerial priests "father."

Further, just as Christ our High Priest is the human family's one mediator before God, the husband, as royal priest, should view himself as a mediator before God on behalf of his family. His responsibilities not only include teaching the faith and ensuring the frequent reception of the sacraments, but must also include making spiritual sacrifices for his family (see 1 Pet 2:5). These include prayer, fasting and other self-mortifications which, when united to Christ's sacrifice, bring about his family's sanctification.

This does not mean that the wife has no responsibility in these matters; she clearly does, and her contribution is significant. Husbands must be humble and unselfish enough to know when the wife is in the best position to make a family decision. She is often the person running the home and raising the children, and may be more intimately familiar with all the facts that are relevant to a family decision (for example, understanding the children's needs and personalities, the daily finances, and so on). In fact, a husband's decision may be to let his wife make the decision. Thus, as the wife is submissive to her husband, he learns to yield to his wife; as the husband loves his wife, she also becomes loving toward him.

In His infinite wisdom, God blessed the marital covenant with this order of authority so that peace and harmony in families would prevail. Without a final authority, there would be chaos, which is all too often seen in families where the father is weak, uninvolved, or absent altogether. This order reflects the divine order between God, Christ, and man. Paul says, "But I want you to understand that the head of every man is Christ, the head of a woman is her husband, and the head of Christ is God" (1 Cor 11:3).

This gift of authority does not give a husband greater dignity than his wife. Both are equal members of the marital covenant, as is reflected by God's creating woman from the side of man (as opposed to, for example, his head or feet).[282] Christianity, more than any other religion, recognizes the equality of the sexes. In fact, the Blessed Virgin Mary, a woman, is God's greatest creation, higher than not only every human being, but also higher than all the angels combined. Even so, Mary was under the headship of Joseph during their earthly life together.

Some people believe that God imposed the submission requirement upon wives as a punishment for the original sin. This is not true. Just as God from the beginning commanded husbands and wives to procreate as part of their indivisible union, from the beginning He also designated the husband as the head of his family in the order of creation.[283]

In fact, God revealed that wives would desire to usurp their husband's authority as a *result* of the original sin. Right after the sin, God told Eve, "Yet your desire shall be for your husband, and he shall rule over you" (Gen 3:16). As a result of sin and concupiscence, Eve would desire to rule over Adam, but God ensured that Adam would continue to have authority over Eve. The Hebrew word for "desire" (*teshuqah*) refers, not to a hunger for affection, but a yearning to rule over someone. We see the same word when God tells Cain, "And if you do not do well, sin is couching at the door; its *desire* is for you, but you must *master* it" (Gen 4:7). In other words, sin would desire to rule over Cain, but God tells Cain to rule over sin.

Unfortunately, many men fail to exercise this divinely appointed authority in the manner intended by God. This happens when a father does not put his wife and children ahead of his own interests. Instead, he relinquishes his responsibilities to his wife while he chases selfish pleasures. This often leads to separation and divorce, forcing women to raise children alone, attempting to fulfill the role of both mother and father.

We cannot, however, overlook the part that women have played in this breakdown. Many women today try to assume the role of men, just as Isaiah lamented about in the time of Israel (see Is 3:12). They deny their motherhood through contraception and abortion. What children they do have are often raised by other people, while the mothers pursue careers and seek leadership positions outside the home, and often with the consent and encouragement of their husbands. While many women must work outside the home because of necessity, others choose to do so for selfish reasons, at the expense of their children.

The children are the ones who suffer. They lose the inimitable maternal care that is so essential for a child's formation, and often turn to drugs, alcohol, sex (including homosexuality), and other harmful outlets as antidotes for their resulting loneliness and depression. Some even commit suicide. Those children who go on to have families of their own often repeat the errors of their parents, and the vicious cycle continues. Both men and women are responsible for the breakdown in family life, and this is largely due to their failure in executing their God-given roles.

To reconstitute the family in accord with the divine plan, men and women must recognize and faithfully perform their respective duties as husbands and wives, fathers and mothers. In this way, holy matrimony will not only bring about stable, loving families and well-adjusted children, but also be a channel of grace and a vehicle for salvation as God intends.

Holy Orders

Jesus Christ instituted the sacrament of holy orders for baptized males in order to continue His mission through the Church until the end of time. Thus, it is the sacrament of apostolic ministry, and, as we have seen in the chapter on the Church, includes three degrees: episcopate (bishops), presbyterate (priests), and diaconate (deacons). Unlike the common priesthood of believers, this ministerial priesthood participates in the most intimate way with the one priesthood of Christ, most especially through the Eucharist and the forgiveness of sins. Like baptism and confirmation, the sacrament of holy orders confers an indelible spiritual mark on the soul of the man who receives it.

We have already seen in the Scriptures how the early Church conferred this sacrament by "the laying on of hands."[284] Rather than repeat what we have already learned regarding apostolic succession, this section will instead address some of the common misconceptions non-Catholics have of the priesthood.

Call no man "Father"?

Non-Catholics often say the priesthood is unbiblical because Catholics call their priests "Father." In the Gospel of Matthew, when Jesus is teaching His disciples not to be like the Pharisees, He says, "And call no man your father on earth, for you have one Father, who is in heaven" (Mt 23:9). However, as we consider this passage, it is important not to confuse *eisegesis* (imposing one's view upon a passage) with *exegesis* (drawing out the meaning of the passage from its context). Here, Jesus was simply discouraging His followers from ascribing titles like "father" and "rabbi" to the scribes and Pharisees who were hypocrites. In the previous verse, Jesus tells the disciples not to call anyone teacher (Mt 23:8), but how many Christians call themselves "teachers"? For that matter, how many call their paternal parent, "Father"?

As previously mentioned, priesthood and fatherhood have always been identified together.[285]

- In the book of Acts, the priests of the early Church were called "father."[286]
- John also calls the priests of the Church "father."[287]
- Paul calls himself a father when he writes, "I became your father in Christ Jesus" (1 Cor 4:15). Paul also says he has become the father of Onesimus (see Philem 10).
- Paul describes Timothy's service to him as a son serves a father (Phil 2:22). Paul also compares the ministerial priesthood's ministry to God's people like a father with His children (1 Thess 2:11).

The priests of the early Church always viewed those to whom they ministered "children."

- Paul calls Timothy a beloved and faithful child in the Lord.[288]
- Paul calls Titus his true child in the common faith (see Titus 1:4).
- Paul also describes his role as a parent over his children to the Corinthians.[289]
- Peter refers to himself as a father by calling Mark his son (1 Pet 5:13).
- John also calls members of the Church "children."[290]

Jesus also calls spiritual leaders "father." For example:

- Jesus refers to Abraham as our "father."[291]
- Jesus refers to the spiritual fathers who gave the Jews the practice of circumcision.[292]
- Jesus also uses "father" when He teaches God's commandment to "honor your father and mother,"* as does Paul.*[293]

There are many other examples in Scripture where the sacred writers use the word "father" to address spiritual leaders. The Holy Spirit, the angels, the Virgin Mary, and others also call spiritual leaders "father."

- The Holy Spirit says, "your fathers put me to the test" (Heb 3:9).
- The angel Gabriel says that Jesus will be given the throne of His "father" David (Lk 1:32).
- Mary says that God spoke to "our fathers" (Lk 1:55).
- Stephen refers to our "fathers" in the faith.[294]
- Ananias refers to the God of our "fathers" (Acts 22:14).
- Zechariah refers to the oath God swore to our "father" Abraham (Lk 1:73).
- The Samaritan woman asks Jesus if He is greater than our "father" Jacob (Jn 4:12).

Call no man father? Catholics should ask non-Catholic Christians why they don't call their pastors "Father."

Priestly celibacy

In the Catholic Church's Western (Latin) rite, celibacy is a requirement for the priesthood, with very few exceptions. In the Eastern rite, married men may enter seminary and be ordained as priests (but no longer bishops). The celibacy requirement is not Church dogma, but a discipline; therefore, the practice could theoretically be changed in the future. However, priestly celibacy has been practiced since the time of Christ, and became a universal practice around the beginning of the second millennium.

Jesus, who Himself was celibate, praises and recommends celibacy for full-time ministers of the Church. "There are eunuchs who have made themselves eunuchs for the sake of the kingdom of heaven. He who is able to receive this, let him receive it" (Mt 19:12). Jesus also says that whoever gives up children for the sake of His name will receive a hundred times more and will inherit eternal life (see Mt 19:29). Isaiah says that eunuchs who keep God's Covenant will have a special place in the kingdom of heaven,* and Jeremiah is told by God not to take a wife or children in order to seek the greater spiritual good.*[295] Celibacy is a gift from God, and those who criticize the Church's practice of celibacy are criticizing God and the wonderful gift He gives to His chosen ones.

In heaven there are no marriages (see Mt 22:30).[296] To bring about Jesus' kingdom on earth, priests live out a heavenly consecration to God by not taking a wife in marriage. In this way, priests are able to focus on the spiritual family, without the additional pressures of a biological family, which is reserved for the vocation of holy matrimony. Priests are free to go where they are most needed, without having to worry about the impact their transfer would have on their wives and children.

Paul also encouraged celibacy. In his letter to the Corinthians, Paul says it is well for a man not to touch a woman, and wishes that all were celibate like him.[297] Paul teaches that marriage can introduce worldly temptations, which can interfere with one's relationship with God (see 1 Cor 7:28). Paul recommends the practice of celibacy for men of God so they can focus entirely on God to build up His kingdom. "So that he who marries his betrothed does well; and he who refrains from marriage will do better" (1 Cor 7:32-38). Referring to priestly celibacy, Paul tells Timothy that no soldier on service gets entangled in "civilian pursuits," since his aim is to satisfy the One who enlisted him (see 2 Tim 2:3-4). Paul also recommended that older widows take a vow of celibacy, and this was the beginning of religious orders for women (see 1 Tim 5:9-12).

In an effort to denounce the Church's practice of celibacy, some non-Catholics argue that bishops were required to be married. They refer to Paul's letter to Timothy where Paul instructs bishops to be married only once (see 1 Tim 3:2). However, this verse is intended to impose a marriage *limitation,* not a marriage requirement: Bishops who were widowed could not remarry.

Non-Catholics may also point to Paul's letter to Timothy, where he condemns deceitful doctrines that forbid marriage (see 1 Tim 4:3). However, the Catholic Church, unlike most other Christian churches, elevates marriage to a sacrament.[298] In this verse, Paul was referring to teachings that declare marriage and other goods created by God to be bad. In this passage, Paul is emphasizing that while all God created is good, those who give up marriage for the sake of Christ are giving up one good for an even greater good.

Some people attribute the sexual scandals in the Church to priestly celibacy. Such criticisms are very misguided. The scandals are not because of celibacy, but a loss of faith. God's gifts, including celibacy, do not cause scandal when accepted and lived in faith. There are thousands of holy priests who are living a chaste and celibate life. In our world where sexual promiscuity is pervasive, priestly celibacy is yet another sign of Christ's presence within His Church.

Women and the priesthood

Many people, even some Catholics, believe that women should have the opportunity to become priests. The Church, however, has definitively taught that she has no authority to ordain women to the priesthood. Those who hold a view contrary to the Church's teaching demonstrate a profound misunderstanding of the priesthood instituted by Jesus Christ.

When Jesus instituted the Eucharist and established the priesthood by His commandment, "Do this in memory of me," He was conferring the priesthood only upon His twelve male apostles. The language "the twelve" and "apostles" in Mark and Luke's accounts of the Last Supper confirms this fact.[299] Jesus also only breathed on His male apostles, giving them the priestly authority to forgive and retain sins (see Jn 20:22). Because the priest acts *in persona Christi* (in the person of Christ) in offering the Eucharistic sacrifice to the Father and forgiving sins, the priest cannot be a woman. Jesus, the Son of God, is both Priest and King after the priest-king Melchizedek, and so His priesthood embodies both kingship and sonship.[300]

In choosing His apostles, Jesus "called to Him those whom He desired" (Mk 3:13). This verse reveals that Jesus chose male apostles according to His will, and not according to the demands of His culture. Because Jesus acted according to His will, which was perfectly united to the will of the Father, we cannot criticize Jesus for selecting only men to the priesthood without criticizing God Himself.

Jesus' decision to institute a male priesthood had nothing to do with the culture of His times. Jesus allowed women to uniquely join in His mission, even exalting women above cultural norms. We see this in many Gospel accounts, including the woman who anointed Jesus' feet,* the woman caught in adultery,* and even Jesus' post-Resurrection appearance to Mary Magdalene before He appeared to His apostles.*[301] The Gospels are clear that women had an important role in Jesus' ministry and, unlike men, didn't betray Jesus.

The Church has always held women in the highest regard; the Church's greatest saint is a woman. The Church has also passionately taught about and vigorously defended the dignity of motherhood, and the Church has always understood humanity as being the bride of Christ.

And yet, as we have seen, priesthood and fatherhood have always been inseparable. "Stay with me, and be to me a father and a priest."[302] The account of Abraham's sacrifice of Isaac foreshadowed how God would secure our redemption by the sacrificial love that the son gives to his father. This, of course, reflects the inner life of the Trinity, where the eternally begotten Son pours Himself out to the eternal Father in the Spirit of love. God chose only men to be priests to reflect the complementarity of the sexes. Just as women bring forth natural life, men (as priests) bring forth supernatural life through the sacraments of the Church. Women also participate in giving supernatural life by bringing forth priests from their wombs.

In opposition to the male priesthood and diaconate, some non-Catholics point out that Paul called Phoebe, a woman in the early Church, a helper and a deaconess (see Rom 16:1-2). These females assisted the priests, especially in their ministrations to women.[303] However, there is nothing in Scripture that remotely suggests that they were ever ordained. Similarly, prophetesses like Anna were women consecrated to religious life, but they were not ordained.[304]

Paul was clear about women and teaching authority in the Church. Paul says a woman is not permitted to preach the Word of God in Church.[305] Hence, it has always been the practice of the Church for the priest or deacon to read the gospel and preach the homily at the Holy Mass (the Church's law precludes anyone not ordained, male or female, from doing so). Can you imagine how much Mary, the mother of Jesus, would have been able to teach Christians about her Son in the churches? Surely, Mary had a profound influence on the Gospel writers' accounts of the life of Jesus. Yet Mary, God's greatest creation and the person closest to Jesus, was not permitted to preach the gospel in the same way as a priest or deacon would in the Church.

The movement to blur the distinction between the priesthood and the laity is rooted in rebellion against authority. This is not new to the Catholic Church. Korah incited a similar rebellion against Moses and the Levitical priests in the Old Testament.[306] As a result, Korah and over fourteen thousand people perished by being swallowed up by the earth.[307] Isaiah also complained that the priests of ancient Israel were having their authority usurped by women, and this was at the height of Israel's covenant apostasy (see Is 3:12). The male priesthood of Christianity was a clear distinction from the priestesses of paganism that existed during the age of the early Church. A female priesthood would have been a reversion to non-Christian practices. The sacred Tradition of the male priesthood is another sign of the presence of Christ in His Catholic Church.

Anointing of the Sick

Jesus Christ instituted the sacrament of the anointing of the sick (also called "Extreme Unction") to commend those who are seriously ill to God, so that He may raise them up and save them. The sacrament is given to those who are in danger of death by anointing them on the forehead and hands with blessed oil, accompanied by readings from Scripture. Only priests (not deacons) can administer this sacrament because the sacrament also brings about the forgiveness of sins. Christ, the Divine Physician, heals the sick, both body and soul, and prepares them for their journey to heaven. "And they cast out many demons, and anointed with oil many that were sick and healed them" (Mk 6:13).

James sets forth the scriptural basis for the sacrament of the sick in James 5:14-15:

> Is any among you sick? Let him call for the elders of the church, and let them pray over him, anointing him with oil in the name of the Lord; and the prayer of faith will save the sick man, and the Lord will raise him up; and if he has committed sins, he will be forgiven.

While some Christian groups believe in healing prayer, and even "call for the elders" (often a pastor) as a means to attain physical healing, they do not (and cannot) administer this sacrament because it results in the priestly forgiveness of sins. They must disregard the last nine words of James' teaching: "if he has committed sins, he will be forgiven." We thus see a dual purpose to the sacrament: physical *and* spiritual healing.

By Jesus' own example, we see that the greatest possible healing is not physical, but spiritual. When presented with the paralytic who was let down through the roof, Jesus first declared, "Man, your sins are forgiven you" (Lk 5:20). When the scribes and Pharisees began to question Jesus in their hearts, Jesus said, "But that you may know that the Son of man has authority on earth to forgive sins" — and he said to the man who was paralyzed — "I say to you, rise, take up your bed and go home" (Lk 5:24).

This does not mean that only Catholic priests are able to intercede for the sick. As we will see in the chapters on the Blessed Virgin Mary and the Saints, God calls each of us to intercede for those who are ill. However, those who are ordained with apostolic authority are also entrusted with the binding and loosing power of Jesus Christ. And so, according to the Apostle James, if someone is sick, we must invoke Christ's power by calling for the priests of the Church — men who have been specially ordained to do the job — to anoint the sick person (see James 5:14). James says the priest will pray over the sick man, anointing him with oil, and the priest's prayer of faith will save the sick man and the Lord will raise him up (v.15). By virtue of the actions and prayers of the priest, the sick man's sins are forgiven (v.15). This is what saves the sick man's soul.

Non-Catholic Christians have great difficulty with this verse, particularly because it provides another powerful proof that priests have the authority to forgive sins. Nowhere in its theology or practice does Protestantism provide for priestly forgiveness of sins. Also, nowhere in Scripture does it say that this authority ended in the apostolic age.

This is more scriptural evidence that the Church's priests act *in persona Christi* in furthering Christ's work of salvation. Jesus is our only Savior, but He has called certain men to participate in a very intimate way in His saving mission through the ministerial priesthood described, among other places, in James 5:14-15.

In this chapter, we have seen how God uses material things to confer grace and unite Himself to us. God created our five senses, and He has us use them in the sacraments. He knows what is best for us. When we worship God the way He wants us to worship Him, we don't just see our Bibles and prayer books and touch the pages. We also hear the words of absolution in the sacrament of confession; we smell the incense offered at the Holy Mass; and we taste the bread from heaven in the Eucharist. We worship God with everything He gave us. God wants to use all of our senses because He wants us to give our entire selves to Him, just as He has given all of Himself to us. This self-giving and life-giving love is the essence of "sacrament."

CHAPTER FOUR

The Blessed Virgin Mary

From the very beginning of creation, God revealed the importance of the Blessed Virgin Mary's role in our redemption. After Adam sinned, God declared how He would destroy the devil in what is called the Protoevangelium (or "first gospel"):

> I will put enmity between you and the woman, and between your seed and her seed; he shall bruise your head, and you shall bruise his heel (Gen 3:15).

The "enmity" is Jesus and the "woman" is Mary, the mother of Jesus. In the Douay-Rheims translation of the Latin Vulgate, Genesis 3:15 even says it is the woman who will crush the serpent's skull. The odd phrase "her seed" (in Greek, *spermatos*) does not appear elsewhere in Scripture, which underscores the uniqueness of Mary's role as mother of the Savior.

Just as Paul calls Jesus Christ the new Adam (see 1 Cor 15:45), the Church has always called Mary the new Eve. Hence, the Scriptures begin and end with Eve battling Satan.[308] However, there is a radical difference between the two women: Unlike the old Eve, who was disobedient to the Father, the new Eve restored motherly obedience to the Father by her fiat, "Let it be done to me according to your word" (Lk 1:38).[309]

Mary is a stumbling block for many non-Catholics, for two reasons: First, they misunderstand what the Church teaches about Mary. Second, most non-Catholics do not understand the scriptural basis for the Church's teaching on Mary. We now address the most common issues regarding Mary.

"Full of Grace" and "Most Blessed Among Women"

When the angel Gabriel appears to Mary at the Annunciation, he does not call her Mary. Instead, he says "Hail, full of grace" (Lk 1:28). We have already seen in Scripture how conferring a title on someone changes their spiritual status. The phrase "full of grace" (in Greek, *kecharitomene*) means that Mary received a complete and perfect endowment of grace from God. Only one other person in Scripture is described as "full of grace," and that person is Jesus Christ (see Jn 1:14). Remember also that it was God who first gave this title to Mary, since the angel is a messenger of God.

This perfection of grace that Mary had already received is called the Immaculate Conception. The Church has always taught that Mary was redeemed from the moment of her conception, that she might fulfill the unique role of bearing God's Word in her womb.[310] Mary's sinless conception was solely due to the merits of Jesus Christ's future death and Resurrection. God applied the merits of Christ in advance to Mary. Many often analogize this to preventing a child from stepping into a pit filled with mud. God allowed us to step into the pit and get dirty, and then cleaned us off in the waters of baptism. God did not allow Mary to step into the pit. But in both cases, we and Mary have been spared from the pit of sin by Jesus Christ and Him alone. Thus, like us, Mary says, "My spirit rejoices in God my Savior!" (Lk 1:47).

The Scriptures provide other examples where God has sanctified certain people in the womb to perform important spiritual tasks:

- Of the prophet Jeremiah, God said: "Before I formed you in the womb I knew you, and before you were born I consecrated you; I appointed you a prophet to the nations" (Jer 1:5).
- John the Baptist was consecrated in the womb when he leaped for joy before Mary, and his mother Elizabeth was filled with the Holy Spirit (Lk 1:41).
- God also distinguished between Jacob and Esau in the womb (see Rom 9:9-12).
- God likewise set apart Mary from the rest of His children at the moment of her conception for the greatest task ever per-

formed by a human being — to bring forth to the world the Word of God made flesh. This is because, as Job says, "Who can bring a clean thing out of an unclean? There is not one" (Job 14:4).

Mary's visitation of her kinswoman Elizabeth after the Annunciation also gives us insights into Mary's uniqueness. When Mary arrives at Elizabeth's house, Elizabeth says, "Blessed are you among women, and blessed is the fruit of your womb" (Lk 1:42). The literal translation of Elizabeth's statement in Greek is "you are most blessed of all women."[311] Mary is the most blessed of all God's creatures.

Mary declares to Elizabeth, "My soul magnifies the Lord" (Lk 1:46). This is a bold statement from a young Jewish girl from Nazareth, and unlike any other statement made by holy people in Scripture. Mary also prophesies, "For behold, henceforth all generations will call me blessed" (v.48). Only the Catholic Church, which calls Mary blessed with special prayers and devotions, has existed in all generations.

We also note that Elizabeth calls Mary the "mother of my Lord."[312] This is the equivalent of the title "Mother of God" (in Greek, *Theotokos*), which the Church has formally given to Mary since the fifth century.[313] Some non-Catholics feel this title exalts Mary too much. But why? The formula is simple: Although Jesus has two natures — human and divine — He is one person, a divine person, and this person is God (see Lk 1:35). Because Mary is Jesus' mother, she is the mother of God. (Mothers give birth to persons, not natures.) Moreover, the title "Mother of God," while rightly exalting Mary, more specifically points to the divinity of Jesus Christ.

Immaculate Ark of the New Covenant

Why was it necessary for Mary to be conceived without original sin, and why is it so important to believe that she remained a holy virgin throughout her life? The sacred writers considered Mary the Ark of the New Covenant. In the Old Testament, the Ark of the Covenant was for the Jews the holiest article of religious worship; it contained the stone tablets of the Ten Commandments, Aaron's rod that budded, and the manna from heaven. To put this in proper context, the Ark of the Covenant was for the Jews what the sacred tabernacle is for Catholics.[314]

The Ark was made of the purest gold (see Ex 25:11-21). The Jews reverenced the Ark by celebrating its presence with veneration, vestments, and songs, including the playing of harps, lyres, cymbals and trumpets (see 1 Chron 15-16). In fact, the Ark was considered so holy that when Uzzah put his hand on the Ark to prevent it from tipping over during a journey, God killed Uzzah for touching it.[315] God even slew some of the men of Beth-shemesh because they looked into the Ark (see 1 Sam 6:19). God would not let anything defiled come into contact with the undefiled Ark of His Word.

In the New Testament, the Scriptures make a clear and direct connection between the Ark of the Covenant and Mary. For example, the word "overshadow," which the angel Gabriel used to describe Mary's conception of Jesus, is the same word (in Greek, *episkiasei*) used to describe God's glory cloud overshadowing the Ark of the Old Covenant.[316] Mary was overshadowed by God's *shekinah* (glory cloud), and became the "Holy of Holies" of the New Covenant.

Luke also makes specific comparisons between Elizabeth's greeting of Mary and David's greeting of the Ark of the Old Covenant as described in the book of Samuel.

- In 2 Samuel 6:2, David "arose and went" to bring out the Ark of the Covenant; in Luke 1:39, Mary "arose and went" to greet Elizabeth.
- In 2 Samuel 6:9, David says, "How can the ark of the Lord come to me?" and in Luke 1:43, Elizabeth says, "And why is this granted me, that the mother of my Lord should come to me?"
- The Ark of the Covenant remains in the house for three months;[317] in Luke 1:43, Mary remains in the house for three months.
- In 2 Samuel 6:16, David leaps for joy before the Ark; in Luke 1:41, John the Baptist leaps for joy before Mary.

In the book of Revelation, John also teaches that Mary is the Ark of the New Covenant. When John received his Revelation, the Jews had not seen the Ark of the Old Covenant, their center of worship, for six centuries (see 2 Mac 2:7). In Revelation 11:19, John says, "Then God's temple in heaven was opened, and the ark of his covenant was seen within his temple." The Jewish people would have been absolutely amazed at John's discovery, and would have begged John to tell them more.

Instead, John ignores the details of the old Ark and, in the very next verse, says, "And a great portent appeared in heaven, a woman clothed with the sun, with the moon under her feet, and on her head a crown of twelve stars"(Rev 12:1). John ignores the details of the old Ark and immediately describes the "woman clothed with the sun." Why? Because John is emphasizing that Mary is the Ark of the New Covenant and that, like the old Ark, she is worthy of veneration and praise.[318] The woman, Mary, has the moon under her feet and is crowned with twelve stars, representing both the twelve apostles and the twelve tribes of Israel (which symbolize the Church). Just as the moon reflects the light of the sun, so Mary, with the moon under her feet, reflects the glory of the Sun of Justice, Jesus Christ (see Mal 4:2).

Some Christians contend that because the "woman" (Mary) "cried out in her pangs of birth, in anguish for delivery" in reference to the birth of Jesus, Mary was a woman with sin.[319] We have already seen that Mary, being full of grace, was without sin. In the Virgin Mary, God prepared a perfect and immaculate dwelling place for His Son and preserved Mary, the Ark of the New Covenant, from all stain and defilement.

Moreover, when Christians read the book of Revelation, they must remember that it is apocalyptic literature unique to the first century; as such, it contains varied symbolism and multiple meanings. The birth pangs describe both the birth of the Church and Mary's offspring being formed in Christ as the devil wages war on them, which is seen at the end of the chapter in Revelation 12:17.

The Scriptures generally describe birth pangs in connection with being formed as disciples of Jesus (in the New Testament) and followers of God (in the Old Testament). For example,

- Paul tells the Galatians, "My little children, with whom I am again in travail until Christ be formed in you!" (Gal 4:19);

- Paul also says, "The whole creation has been groaning in travail together until now" (Rom 8:22).
- Jeremiah describes the birth pangs of Israel like a woman in travail.[320]
- Ephraim is described as travailing in childbirth for his sins (Hos 13:12-13).
- Micah describes Jerusalem as being seized by birth pangs like a woman in travail (Mic 4:9-10).

Isaiah also prophesies about the virgin birth of Jesus Christ when he says, "Before she was in labor she gave birth; before her pain came upon her she was delivered of a son. Who has heard such a thing? Who has seen such things?" (Is 66:7-8). This is the same woman about whom Isaiah prophesies elsewhere in Scripture: "Behold, a virgin shall conceive, and bear a son, and his name shall be called Emmanuel."[321]

But doesn't Paul say that "all have sinned"?

To prove that Mary was a sinner, some refer to Paul's teaching in Romans that "all have sinned and fall short of the glory of God" (Rom 3:23). But this verse simply means that all people, including Mary, are subject to original sin. Mary was spared from original sin by a direct intervention of God through the merits of Christ. In addition, while Paul writes, ". . .all have sinned," he does not mean that all commit sin. Some are incapable of sin; for example, infants, the mentally retarded, and the severely senile cannot sin. Jesus must also be an exception to this rule, and Mary is an exception as well.

In his letter to the Corinthians, Paul says, "For as in Adam all die, so also in Christ shall all be made alive" (1 Cor 15:22). The word for "all" (in Greek, *pantes*), which is the same word used for "all" in Romans 3:23, does not necessarily mean "every single one." Not all have died (Enoch and Elijah were bodily assumed into heaven)[322] and not all shall live (because Jesus said some people will choose hell). Elsewhere in his letter to the Romans, Paul says, "So death spread to all men because all men sinned" (Rom 5:12). Once again, this proves that "all" does not mean "everyone" because death did not spread to Enoch and Elijah. Paul also says to the Romans, "For as by one man's disobedience *many* were made sinners, so by one man's obedience many will be made righteous" (v.19). In this verse, Paul says "many" (in Greek, *polloi*) and not "all" (*pantes*), which proves that when Paul says "all," he really means "many."

What about Paul's statement to the Romans, "None is righteous, no, not one" (Rom 3:10)? The basis of Paul's statement is Psalm 14, which does not teach that all are sinners. Instead, the psalm teaches that, among the wicked, all are sinners, but the righteous continue to seek God. Similarly, in Psalm 53, the phrase "there is none that does good" expressly refers to those who have fallen away from God. Those who remain faithful do good.

If there are some who do good, then why does Jesus say, "No one is good but God alone" (Lk 18:19)? He is not speaking absolutely, but trying to emphasize the infinite distance between God's goodness and our goodness. Elsewhere in Scripture, Jesus *does* call people good, such as "the good man out of his good treasure ..." (Mt 12:35).

Some may also ask, if Mary was not sinful, why does she call herself "lowly" (Lk 1:48)? This has nothing to do with the presence of sin. All creatures are lowly compared to God, and lowliness is a sign of humility, not sinfulness. Jesus also describes Himself as "gentle and lowly in heart" (Mt 11:29). Hence, none of these verses prove that Mary was a sinner.

The "New Eve" and "Suffering Woman with the Redeemer"

Just because Mary was without sin does not mean that she did not suffer as the Mother of Christ. To the contrary, God reveals to us in Scripture that Mary did suffer with Jesus in a very unique way, and He reveals this to emphasize that Mary played an important role in our redemption. Of course, Jesus' suffering and death was perfectly efficacious for our redemption. But God desired Mary to participate on an intimate, though subordinate, level in her Son's suffering, just as He allows us to participate through our own sufferings.

This is why Paul says, "Now I rejoice in my sufferings for your sake, and in my flesh I complete what is lacking in Christ's afflictions for the sake of His body, that is, the church" (Col 1:24). Was anything lacking in Christ's sufferings? Of course not. But Paul is teaching us that Jesus leaves room in His body, the Church, for us to unite our sufferings with His, to further the work of salvation in the world. We participate in Christ's work by virtue of our royal priesthood received in baptism. This is a mystery, but it is as true as God's love for us, and it is precisely *because* of God's love for us. Through her sufferings, Mary participated in our redemption in a very special way, particularly at the foot of her Son's cross.

God reveals to the Old Testament prophets the sufferings of Mary. Lamentations says, "The Lord has trodden as in a wine press the virgin daughter of Judah" (Lam 1:15). It also says, "What can I say for you, to what compare you, O daughter of Jerusalem? What can I liken to you, that I may comfort you, O virgin daughter of Zion? For vast as the sea is your ruin; who can restore you?" (Lam 2:13). Micah also prophesies about Mary sufferings when he writes, "Writhe and groan, O daughter of Zion, like a woman in travail" (Mic 4:10).

When the angel Gabriel greets Mary with the phrase "Hail, full of grace," the word "hail" (in Greek, *chaire*) is the same word used in the prophecies of Zephaniah and Zechariah about the "daughter of Zion" and the "daughter of Jerusalem."[323] This connects these Old Testament prophecies to Mary. At the presentation of Jesus in the Temple, God reveals to Simeon that Mary would suffer along with her Son, as he tells Mary "(and a sword will pierce through your own soul also), that thoughts out of many hearts may be revealed" (Lk 2:35). Just as Christ's heart was pierced on the cross with a lance, so was Mary's heart pierced as she participated in her Son's redemption of the world. Why does God reveal Mary's sufferings to us? To teach us about her significant role in our redemption, and about how we also participate by "completing what is lacking in the sufferings of Christ for the sake of his body, that is, the Church" (Col 1:24).

Many non-Catholics cringe when Mary is called "co-redemptrix." I must admit that even I was startled when I first heard the term. But the term co-redemptrix simply means "with the redeemer." This is because "co" is from the Latin word *cum* which means "with," and "redemptrix" means redeemer. God sent His Son, "born of a woman," to redeem us (Gal 4:4). Mary was with Jesus the Redeemer from the moment of His conception to the moment of His

Ascension and is now with Him in heaven for all eternity. Mary is therefore the woman "with the redeemer," which is most poignantly understood as she suffered at the foot of the cross. In no way does this term mitigate the absolute exclusivity of Christ as our Redeemer. Jesus is the one and only Redeemer. Instead, the term gives even more glory to Jesus because even though He did it all on His own, He invites us, like Mary, to share in His divine mission.

"Mother of All Christians" and "Queen of the New Covenant Kingdom"

We have seen how Jesus came to fulfill the Old Covenant kingdom of David in His New Covenant kingdom of the Catholic Church. In the Old Covenant kingdom, the king's mother was called the "queen mother" (in Hebrew, *Gebirah*) of the kingdom, and sat at the king's right hand.[324] The queen mother had a powerful position in Israel's royal monarchy.[325] Because of her importance, the king would venerate the queen by bowing down to her (see 1 Kings 2:19). The queen mother also interceded on behalf of the people by making requests to the king, and the king did not refuse her. "Then she said, 'I have one small request to make of you; do not refuse me.' And the king said to her, 'Make your request, my mother; for I will not refuse you'" (1 Kings 2:20). The queen was the principal intercessor before the king.

Mary is our eternal *Gebirah* and Queen of the New Covenant Kingdom of Jesus Christ. She is at the right hand of Christ the King, crowned in heaven with twelve stars,* which refers to the crown of righteousness,* the crown of glory,* and the crown of life.*[326] Jesus made Mary the spiritual mother of us all as He hung on the cross when he said to her, "Woman, behold your son," and then to the disciple, "Behold your mother!" (Jn 19:26-27). Jesus did not say "*John*, behold your mother" because Jesus was giving Mary to all of us. Jesus was also not just telling Mary and John to take care of each other. Every precious word Jesus spoke in agony on the cross had a redemptive purpose.

Why does Jesus call Mary "woman"?

Jesus does so to reveal that Mary is the "woman" God promises in Genesis 3:15,[327] whose seed will crush the devil's head, which Jesus does from the cross.[328] This woman is the new Eve, the mother of the new creation in Christ, and our mother. Mary's spiritual motherhood is also confirmed in the book of Revelation, after Mary is seen in heaven. John writes,

> Then the dragon was angry with the woman, and went off to make war on the rest of her offspring, *on those who keep the commandments of God and bear testimony to Jesus.*[329]

This is Mary, the woman, whose offspring obey Jesus Christ. This makes Mary the mother of all Christians. The master plan of God's covenant love for us is family, just as God in His essence embodies and perfects the characteristics of family (Fatherhood, Sonship, and Divine Love). However, we cannot be a complete family with the Fatherhood of God and the brotherhood of Christ without the motherhood of Mary.

We therefore imitate Christ the King and pay homage to His mother. We also praise Christ through Mary as Elizabeth praised Christ through Mary, by first calling Mary most blessed among women and then praising Jesus (see Lk 1:42). We further make our requests to Jesus through our mother Mary because she is our most powerful intercessor before the King in the New Covenant kingdom.

In John's Gospel we see that Mary was the one who triggered Jesus' earthly ministry, at the wedding feast in Cana. When the wedding guests ran out of wine, Mary told Jesus, "They have no wine" (Jn 2:3). Jesus invites Mary's intercession by replying, "Woman, what is that to me and to thee? My hour is not yet come."[330] These words of Jesus were not a rebuke; He was actually inviting Mary to make her request.[331] Otherwise, Mary would have ceased and desisted at this point. Instead, Mary responds to Jesus by going to the servants and saying, "Do whatever he tells you" (Jn 2:5), and the servants obey her. Jesus responds to His mother's intercession by performing His first miracle of changing water into wine, a miracle that foreshadows the Eucharistic celebration of the wedding feast of the Lamb in heaven.

Thus, when Jesus says, "What have you to do with me?" (Jn 2:4), He is actually acknowledging Mary's intercessory power and her role in His kingdom. For example, when a demon similarly asks Jesus, "What have you to do with me, Jesus, Son of the Most High God?" (Lk 8:28), the demon is not rebuking Jesus, for God would never allow Satan to rebuke His Son. Instead, the demon is acknowledging the power of Jesus.

We need never be afraid that honoring Mary and asking for her intercession will somehow take glory away from God. Mary always leads us to Jesus, and tells us to do whatever He asks of us. Mary is indeed our loving mother and most powerful intercessor before Christ.

Why does Jesus seem to diminish Mary's importance?

There are some verses, particularly in the Synoptic Gospels, that some Christians use in an attempt to prove that Jesus diminished Mary's significance after He started His earthly ministry. For example, in the account where Jesus is told that His mother and relatives are waiting to speak with Him, Jesus answers:

> "Who is my mother, and who is my brothers?" And stretching out his hand toward his disciples, he said, 'Here are my mother and my brothers! For whoever does the will of my Father in heaven is my brother, and sister, and mother'"[332]

Was Jesus' response a rebuke? Not at all. Jesus was simply emphasizing the spiritual family's importance over that of the biological family. Jesus was also fulfilling the prophecy of Psalm 69:8-9, which predicted that those closest to Jesus would betray Him. Finally, when Jesus' response is read in light of Luke 8:5-15 and the parable of the sower, which Jesus taught right before this, we see that Jesus is actually implying that Mary had already received the Word as the sower of good ground and is bearing fruit. Jesus is teaching that others must, like Mary, also receive the Word and bear fruit.

What about the account in Luke's Gospel, where a woman in the crowd says to Jesus, "Blessed is the womb that bore you, and the breasts that you sucked!" (11:27). Jesus responds by saying, "Blessed rather are those who hear the word of God and keep it!" (v.28). The word for "rather" (in Greek, *menounge*) actually means, "Yes, but in addition to," or "Further." Paul uses the same word in his letter to the Philippians: "But whatever gain I had, I counted as loss for the sake of Christ. *Indeed* I count everything as loss because of the surpassing worth of knowing Christ Jesus my Lord" (Phil 3:7-8). In verse eight, the word "indeed" (*menounge*) means "Yes, and in addition to" the losses Paul describes in verse seven.

In Luke 11:28, Jesus is saying, "Yes, my mother is blessed indeed, but further blessed are those who hear the word of God and keep it." Once again, Jesus is emphasizing the spiritual role over the biological role. Also, note that the woman in the crowd is complimenting Jesus, not Mary. Therefore, Jesus is refocusing the attention from Himself to those who obey the Word of God. If Jesus is shifting the attention away from Himself to others, His response cannot be a rebuke of His mother.

Ever-Virgin

Did Mary have other children? Some Christians seem to think so, based on texts describing Jesus' "brothers."[333] However, after seeing how the Scriptures describe Mary as the sinless, undefiled and immaculate new Eve and Ark of the New Covenant, such an assertion is ridiculous. The Scriptures also *never* say that the "brothers" of Jesus are the Virgin Mary's children. So, what do we do with verses such as Matthew 13:55 and Mark 6:3, in which people ask about Jesus, "And are not his brethren James and Joseph and Simon and Judas?" There are simple answers to this contention.

For example, the Scriptures prove that James and Joseph are Jesus' cousins, not His biological brothers. In John's Gospel, Mary of Clopas is the Virgin Mary's sister[334] (see Jn 19:25). Matthew refers to Mary of Clopas as "the other Mary."[335] In Matthew and Mark's Gospels, we learn that Mary of Clopas (not the Virgin Mary), is the mother of James and Joseph.[336] In fact, it seems as though Matthew and Mark identified James and Joseph as the sons of Mary of Clopas at the crucifixion scene so that there would be no mistaking the identity of their mother. Thus, when the Gospels say James and Joseph are Jesus' brothers, they are really Jesus' cousins.

Throughout Scripture, cousins are called "brothers" (in Greek, *adelphoi*) because there is no word for "cousin" in Hebrew or Aramaic.

For example, in the book of Genesis we see that Lot is Abraham's nephew (in Greek, *anepsios*).[337] But later we see that Lot is also described as Abraham's brother (in Greek, *adelphos*).[338] Laban calls Jacob his brother even though Jacob is his nephew (Gen 29:15). Scripture also shows that "brethren" can even refer to those who are not related by blood, such as a friend[339] or an ally (Amos 1:9).

There are many other examples in the Old Testament where "brethren" means kinsmen.[340] There are also many examples in the New Testament where the word "brethren" does not necessarily mean biological relations:[341]

- Jesus tells Peter to strengthen his brethren in reference to the other apostles, not all of whom were Peter's biological brothers (see Lk 22:32).
- In the book of Acts, the gathering of Jesus' brothers was about 120 (see Acts 1:12-15).
- Paul also uses "brethren" and "kinsmen" interchangeably (see Rom 9:3).

The Annunciation demonstrates further proof of Mary's lifelong virginity. The angel Gabriel tells Mary, "And behold, you will conceive in your womb and bear a son, and you shall call his name Jesus" (Lk 1:31). Mary was already betrothed to Joseph at this time. If Mary had any intentions of starting a family with Joseph in the future, she would not have responded, "How shall this happen, since I do not know man?"[342] We can assume that Mary knew how children were conceived. Thus, Mary's response shows she had taken a vow of lifelong virginity; otherwise, her question would not make any sense.

Jesus is also referred to as "the" son of Mary, not "a" son of Mary (see Mk 6:3). When Mary and Joseph search for Jesus and find Him in the Temple, there is no mention of other siblings (see Lk 2:41-51). As devout Jews, had they been Jesus' younger blood brothers they would not have tried to advise Jesus, as it would have been considered extremely disrespectful.[343] It would have also been unthinkable for Jesus, as a devout Jew, to commit the care of His mother to a friend if Jesus had biological brothers or sisters (see Jn 19:26-27).

Scriptures used to "prove" Mary did not remain a virgin

- *Luke 2:7.* Why does this verse refer to Mary's "first-born son," if she had no other children?

The term "first-born" is a common Jewish expression meaning the first child to open the womb (Ex 13:2,12). Under the Mosaic Law, the "first-born" son had to be sanctified (Ex 34:20). "First-born" status does not require a "second-born" because the term has nothing to do with the mother having other children. As Ezekiel prophesied about the Virgin Mary, "This gate shall remain shut; it shall not be opened, and no one shall enter by it; for the LORD, the God of Israel, has entered by it; therefore it shall remain shut" (Ez 44:2). Mary remained a virgin before, during, and after the birth of Jesus Christ.

- *Matthew 1:24-25.* "Joseph... took his wife, but knew her not until she had borne a son; and he called his name Jesus." Doesn't the "until" imply that Joseph had relations with Mary after the birth of Jesus?

No. When the Scriptures use the phrase "not until" (in Greek, *heos hou*), it is an action that only describes the past, and not the future. He knew her "not until" she bore a son means he knew her "not up to the point that" she bore a son. It has nothing to do with Joseph's relationship with Mary after she bore a son. This also confirms that Mary was a virgin when she bore Jesus Christ.

For example, Jesus says, "For truly, I say to you, till heaven and earth pass away, not an iota, not a dot, will pass from the law *until* all is accomplished" (Mt 5:18). This does not mean that after heaven and earth pass away, all will no longer be accomplished. When Jesus said He would be with us always, *until* the end of the world (see Mt 28:19), He did not mean that He would no longer be with us after the end of the world. Luke says that Anna was a widow *until* she was eighty-four (see Lk 2:37). This does not mean that she was not a widow after age eighty-four.

Examples may be found in the Old Testament as well. In Genesis, we see that the raven "went to and fro *until* the waters dried up from the earth" (Gen 8:7). This does not mean the raven didn't fly after the waters dried. The Lord says to Jacob, "I will not leave you *until* I have done that of which I have spoken to you" (Gen 28:15). This does not mean the Lord will leave Jacob afterward. "And Michal the daughter of Saul had no child *to* the day of her death" (2 Sam 6:23). This does not mean Michal was with child after her death. There are many other examples in Scripture where "not until" describes only the past, and not the future.

Assumed into Heaven

The Church has always taught that Mary, after she completed her earthly life, was assumed, body and soul, into heaven. This means that God took Mary up into heaven (she did not rise on her own power, as Jesus did). Mary could be bodily assumed into heaven because she was without sin. The Scriptures teach us that sin led to bodily decay and death.[344] If Mary did not have sin, she would not be subject to decay and death.

Scripture does not explicitly teach that Mary was assumed into heaven, but it is strongly implied:

- When John sees the "woman clothed with the sun" in the book of Revelation, the evidence demonstrates that this woman is Mary.[345]
- In the book of Revelation, while John sees the disembodied souls of the martyrs in heaven,[*] he sees Mary, body and soul, as he describes the crown on her "head" and the moon under her "feet."[*][346]
- As we have seen, John also associates Mary with the Ark of the Old Covenant, which was taken up into heaven (Rev 11:19).
- Psalm 132:8 also prophesies about Mary's bodily assumption into heaven with the Lord: "Arise, O LORD, and go to thy resting place, thou and the ark of thy might."

The Scriptures also teach that other people were assumed into heaven. As we have mentioned, Enoch was bodily assumed into heaven.[347] Elijah was also assumed into heaven in a fiery chariot.[348] Would Jesus do any less for His blessed mother? Paul speaks of a man (himself) who was caught up to the third heaven (see 2 Cor 12:2). Paul also says that we will be caught up in the clouds to meet the Lord in the air and so we shall always be with the Lord (see 1 Thess 4:17). Nothing in Scripture precludes Mary's assumption into heaven. Hopefully, when they read in the light of faith, non-Catholic Christians can see how Mary's assumption into heaven can be, and is, true. For Catholics, we know it is true because the Church has revealed the Assumption of Mary as a dogma of faith.

CHAPTER FIVE

The Saints

For two thousand years the Church has taught that Christians are one family in heaven and on earth, united together as children of the Father through the one mystical body of Jesus Christ.[349] Our brothers and sisters who have gone to heaven before us are not part of a different family. Through baptism, we are one and the same family. We are fellow citizens with the saints in heaven and members of the one household of God (see Eph 2:19). Death does not divide the family of God or separate us from the love of Christ.[350] This is why the Apostles' Creed professes a belief in the "communion of saints."

Communion of Saints: One Family in Christ

The communion of saints refers to the union of Christians living and deceased, whether on earth (the "Church Militant"), in heaven (the "Church Triumphant"), or in purgatory (the "Church Suffering"), over which Jesus Christ is the Head.[351] The apostles call it the "communion" of saints because we are all in communion with each other in a mystical way. The word "saint" (in Hebrew, *qaddiysh*) means "holy one," and the Scriptures refer to both living and deceased humans as saints who partake of this communion.[352] The Scriptures also refer to angels as saints.[353] Hence, the communion of saints includes angel saints in heaven as well as human saints in heaven, on earth, and in purgatory (this will be discussed further in the last chapter).

The author of Hebrews describes the communion of saints in heaven with those on earth when he says, "...we are surrounded by so great a cloud of witnesses" (Heb 12:1). The "cloud of witnesses" (in Greek, *nephos marturon*) refers to a great amphitheatre with an arena for the runners (us on earth) and many tiers of seats occupied by the saints (in heaven), which rise up like a cloud.

The *martyrs* are not merely spectators, but witnesses who testify to God's promises and cheer us on in our race to heaven. This means that the saints in heaven are concerned for our welfare on earth. This also means that they express their concern for us through prayers to God, which is the spiritual way of expressing love for another. Thus, Jesus says the angels and saints in heaven rejoice over our repentance (see Lk 15:7,10). Paul also says we can become spectacles, not only to men, but to angels as well (see 1 Cor 4:9). This is because we are in communion with each other in the one body of Christ.[354] As a result, Paul says, "If one member suffers, all suffer together; if one member is honored, all rejoice together" (see 1 Cor 12:26).

God's Fellow Workers and Subordinate Mediators in Christ

Christians who do not believe that the saints in heaven help those on earth generally decry praying to saints because they confuse praying to a saint with worshiping God. Praying to a saint in heaven simply means asking the saint to pray to God for us. It has absolutely nothing to do with worshiping the saint, which would be idolatry. Asking the saints in heaven for prayers is just like asking our family and friends on earth to pray for us. Because the saints in heaven behold the face of God and are living the very life of the risen Christ, they are infinitely closer to Jesus than we are, and their prayers can be more effective than ours on earth. In fact, they are more alive than we are! Our God in heaven is the God of the living, not the dead.[355] Thus, we ask the righteous saints in heaven for their intercessory prayers, because the prayers of the righteous have powerful effects.[356]

We should also point out that praying to the saints is different from necromancy (trying to communicate with the dead through a medium). For example, Saul practiced necromancy by using a woman medium to contact the dead, and was therefore condemned.[357] When we pray to the saints, we acknowledge that God is the source and channel of all communication, and know that it is God (not the saint) who permits a prayer to be heard and answered.

Isn't Jesus the "one mediator between God and men"?

In his first letter to Timothy, Paul writes, "For there is one God, and there is one mediator between God and men, the man Christ Jesus" (1 Tim 2:5). Because Jesus is the only mediator between God and man, some Christians argue, we can't seek the mediation of anyone else. Right?

Let's look at the context. Right before he teaches about Christ's role as our one mediator, the Apostle Paul says, "I urge that supplications, prayers, intercessions, and thanksgivings be made for all men" (1 Tim 2:1). Paul is therefore appealing for mediation from others besides Christ right before he says that Christ is the one mediator. Why? Because, Paul says, "This is good, and it is acceptable in the sight of God our Savior, who desires all men to be saved and to come to the knowledge of the truth" (1 Tim 2:3-4). Therefore, although Jesus Christ is the one mediator between God and man, God invites us to be intercessors, or "subordinate mediators" with Christ, to help save all men by bringing them to the knowledge of the truth. Remember, we are able to do this work by virtue of our baptismal priesthood. God finds our mediation with Christ "good and acceptable" in His sight.

How can imperfect humans add anything to the perfect work of Christ?

As we have seen with Paul's teaching about how we complete "what is lacking in Christ's sufferings" (Col 1:24), the Scriptures continually teach us that God invites us to participate in the work of the Lord Jesus. We do this through the ministerial priesthood (by forgiving sins, celebrating the Eucharist, and so on) and the royal priesthood (by raising children, praying for others). This is what a loving Father does for His children.

God does not need our help. Jesus Christ has already redeemed us through His death and Resurrection. However, God raises us up with Christ to continue His mission of saving the world. God is not threatened by the glory He gives His children! This Catholic and scriptural understanding of God also gives Jesus Christ the most glory, because even though He does not need us, He wants us to be His fellow workers in the world.

Paul describes this role in his letter to the Corinthians when he says, "For we are God's fellow workers" (1 Cor 3:9). The phrase "fellow workers" (in Greek, *sunergoi*) literally means "synergists," or cooperators with God in matters of salvation. God wants us to be fellow workers because He wants to transform us into the image of His Son (see Rom 8:29). To become the righteousness of God in Christ, Paul says, "Working together with him, then, we entreat you not to accept the grace of God in vain" (2 Cor 6:1). The phrase "working together" (in Greek, *sunergountes*) with God means we participate in God's plan of salvation through our actions.

Paul further says, "We know that in everything God works for good with those who love him, who are called according to his purpose" (Rom 8:28). The phrase "works for good with" (in Greek, *sunergei eis agathon*) again shows that we synergize with God in His work. Mark also says, "And they went forth and preached everywhere, while the Lord worked with them and confirmed the message by the signs that attended it" (Mk 16:20). The phrase "worked with them" (in Greek, *sunergountos*) is another example of God allowing our participation in His work to effect the salvation of the world.

Examples of Saintly Mediation

The Scriptures are full of examples of saintly mediation and intercessory prayer to help those on earth. During His Passion, Jesus says, "Do you think that I cannot appeal to my Father, and he will at once send me more than twelve legions of angels?" (Mt 26:53). If Jesus says He could ask for the assistance of angel saints — and He obviously would not have been worshiping them in so doing — then so can we, who need their help infinitely more than Jesus, and without engaging in idolatry.

Jesus also says that when we get to heaven, we will be "like the angels" (Mt 22:30). This means the human saints in heaven, like the angel saints in heaven, are able to assist people on earth. These angels did in fact minister to Jesus after His temptations in the desert.[358] God has given us the angels precisely to assist us on our journey to heaven as the author of Hebrews says, "Are they not all ministering spirits sent forth to serve, for the sake of those who are to obtain salvation?" (Heb 1:14). God sends forth His angels to assist us, who participate in God's work by giving us grace and peace (see Rev 1:4).

At the Transfiguration of Jesus, Moses and Elijah appear and converse with Jesus in the presence of Peter, James and John.[359] This is another example of communication with the saints in heaven. This also shows that the saints in heaven have capabilities that far surpass our limitations on earth. We see a similar event when the deceased prophet Samuel converses with Saul.[360] In the book of Maccabees, we also see the high priest Onias and the prophet Jeremiah, who were dead for centuries, interact with the living Judas Maccabeus and pray for the holy people on earth (see 2 Mac 15:12-16).[361]

When Jesus cried out from the cross, the people thought that Jesus was calling on Elijah for intercessory assistance, and they waited to see if Elijah would come to save Jesus.[362] When Jesus died on the cross, many saints were raised up out of their graves and went into the city to appear, and presumably interact with the people, just as Jesus did after His Resurrection (see Mt 27:52-53). Far from abhorring or cutting off communication with the deceased, the Scriptures clearly teach that God allows the saints in heaven to assist and communicate through Christ's mystical body with those on earth.

In the book of Revelation, the martyred saints in heaven cry out to God to avenge their blood by judging those on the earth:

> When he opened the fifth seal, I saw under the altar the souls of those who had been slain for the word of God and for the witness they had borne; they cried out with a loud voice, "O Sovereign Lord, holy and true, how long before thou wilt judge and avenge our blood on those who dwell upon the earth?" Then they were each given a white robe and told to rest a little longer, until the number of their fellow servants and their brethren should be complete, who were to be killed as they themselves had been (Rev 6:9-11).

These are called "imprecatory prayers," which are pleas for God's judgment.[363] This means that the saints in heaven are praying for those on earth. These prayers are presented to God as golden bowls of incense,[364] and God answers these prayers by avenging the saints' blood and initiating all kinds of earthly activity such as thunder, lightning, earthquakes, hail and fire (see Rev 8:3-5). God responds to His children's requests, whether from His children on earth or in heaven.

Jesus instructs us to pray for (to mediate on behalf of) those who persecute us,* and tells us that whatever we ask in prayer, we will receive it.*365 We have also seen how Jesus responded to the intercession of the Virgin Mary at the wedding feast in Cana.

Paul gives many examples of subordinate mediation:

- He says the earthly saints* and the priests*366 pray for the Corinthians, that they may do right and improve.
- He acknowledges the power of the Philippians' earthly intercession, which will deliver him (Phil 1:19).
- Paul says that he and the elders pray for the Colossians, that they may gain wisdom.367
- He tells the Thessalonians that he prays for them (2 Thess 1:11).
- Paul also hopes that through Philemon's intercession he may be able to be with him (Philem 22).

John also gives us examples of subordinate mediation. He expresses confidence that God will grant us anything we ask of Him according to His will (see 1 Jn 5:14-15). John further says that our prayers for others call God to give them life and keep them from sinning (see 1 Jn 5:16). Finally, John prays for Gaius' health, acting as a subordinate mediator (see 3 Jn 2).

We are often commanded in the Scriptures to be intercessors for others.

- James 5:16-17 instructs us to "pray for one another, that you may be healed," and reminds us how Elijah's effective intercession moved God to prevent rainfall.
- Paul appeals to the Romans* and the Ephesians* to pray for him, and asks the Thessalonians* to pray for him, Silvanus and Timothy, so that they may be delivered.368

- Paul also instructs the faithful to pray for the priests of the Church,* as does the author of Hebrews.* [369]
- Paul also charges the communion of saints to bear one another's burdens and to build each other up. [370]
- Paul tells the Romans and Timothy "without ceasing I mention you always in my prayers,"* and tells us to "pray constantly."* [371]
- Paul even suggests that the more prayers there are, and the more who pray, the better (2 Corinthians 1:11)!

The Old Testament is also filled with examples of intercessory prayer:

- God responds to Abraham's intercession and heals Abimelech, his wife and slaves (Gen 20:17);
- God responds to Moses' intercession; [372]
- God responds to the Levite priests' prayers before the holy habitation (2 Chron 30:27);
- Samuel says he would be sinning against God if he didn't continue to intercede for the people of Israel (1 Sam 12:23);
- Job prays for three friends in sin and God responds (Job 42:7-9);
- David asks that his prayer be counted as incense before God (Ps 141:2);
- King Zedekiah sends messengers to ask Jeremiah to intercede for the people, that he might pray to God for them,* and all the people come before Jeremiah asking for his intercession;* [373]
- Baruch asks the Lord to hear the prayers of the dead of Israel (Bar 3:4);
- Daniel intercedes on behalf of the people of Israel, confessing both his sins and the sins of the people (Dan 9:20-23); and,
- God's angels also intercede by bringing Tobit and Sarah's prayers before the Lord,* touching Isaiah's lips and declaring the forgiveness of his sins,* and interceding for the people of Judea.* [374]

On Vain and Repetitious Prayer

Some Christians criticize Catholics (and other Christians) not only for praying to the saints but for the manner in which they offer these intercessory prayers. For example, when Catholics pray the Rosary,[375] or recite one of the Church's ancient litanies,[376] some non-Catholics call them "vain and repetitious." They point to Jesus' statement in Matthew 6:7 where He says, "And in praying do not heap up empty phrases as the Gentiles do; for they think that they will be heard for their many words." However, when Jesus instructed His disciples not to "heap up empty phrases," He was focusing on the "vain," and not on the "repetition." In other words, Jesus was referring to redundant babbling without thinking, or prayer that seeks the praise of men and not God (see Jn 12:43). This is because God judges our prayers by looking into our hearts, not necessarily at our words.

For example, the tax collector, who would not even lift up his eyes to heaven, kept beating his breast and saying, "God, be merciful to me a sinner" (Lk 18:13). Jesus said the tax collector was justified because of his sincerity and humility, while the arrogant Pharisee was not (v.14). Cornelius likewise feared the Lord "and prayed constantly to God" (Acts 10:2), and his prayers "ascended as a memorial before God" (v.4). These Scriptures show that God responds to repetitious prayers when they are offered with a sincere and repentant heart. Jesus Himself offered a repetitious prayer to the Father when He was suffering in the garden of Gethsemane: "So, leaving them again, he went away and prayed for the third time, *saying the same words*" (Mt 26:44).

If God is offended by repetitious prayers, then why did He inspire the psalmist to repetitiously praise Him with the phrase "for his steadfast love endures for ever" in Psalm 136? Why also did He inspire Azariah to repeatedly chant, "Bless the Lord" in the fiery furnace?[377] God inspired such prayers because they move Him when they are offered in faith, hope and love. Even the angels in heaven offer repetitious prayers incessantly before the throne of God. "...and day and night they never cease to sing, "Holy, holy, holy, is the Lord God Almighty, who was and is and is to come!" (Rev 4:8). Far from being offended by them, God is moved by repetitious prayers when they are offered to Him "in spirit and in truth" (see Jn 4:24).

Veneration and Imitation of the Saints

As we mentioned, Catholics view the saints in heaven as our brothers and sisters in Christ, and our heroes in the faith. Because the saints in heaven are part of our family and are now with Christ for all eternity, Catholics not only ask them for their intercessory assistance, but also venerate and attempt to imitate the saints.

The Scriptures teach us to venerate (honor) those worthy of veneration (honor). Paul tells us to pay honor to whom honor is due (see Rom 13:7). Peter teaches us to honor all men (see 1 Pet 2:17). Those living with Christ deserve such honor, and we venerate them for their great dignity and union with God. Paul tells the Philippians to honor Epaphroditus, who almost died for the faith (see Phil 2:25-29). How much more honor is owed to those who died in and for the faith of Christ! The author of Hebrews says Jesus is worthy of "more glory than Moses," but this does not mean that the saints are worthy of no glory and honor (see Heb 3:3).

To the contrary, the saints are also entitled to glory. Thus, we honor those in heaven with Jesus because they share in Jesus' glory. This is why the Catholic Church universally celebrates, almost daily, special feast days of the saints in heaven at the Holy Mass. We remember them on their special day, just like we remember our relatives and friends, living and dead, on their birthdays and anniversaries. We are one family in Christ.

Why do we venerate the saints? Because we want to imitate them. The goal of veneration is imitation. We wish to imitate their holy lives and ask for their assistance so that we, like they, will live with Jesus forever. Paul urges the Corinthians to be imitators of him (see 1 Cor 4:16). Paul tells them "Be imitators of me, as I am of Christ" (1 Cor 11:1). Paul repeatedly exhorts the faithful to be imitators of Christ and of his saints.[378] The author of Hebrews also instructs the faithful to be imitators of those who through faith and patience inherit the promises.[379] James further teaches us to take heart in the examples of the prophets and Job, who endured suffering

(James 5:10-11). These instructions to imitate saintly people, far from distracting us from God, give us more direction to God through their witness and example.

We see examples of venerating the saints and other holy people in the Old Testament as well. For example, religious leaders were adorned with sacred garments to give them dignity and honor (see Ex 28:2). Hezekiah was honored by all of Judah and the inhabitants of Jerusalem at his death (see 2 Chron 32:33). God also tells us to "honor the face of an old man" (Lev 19:32). In the book of Sirach, we read, "Let us now praise famous men, and our fathers in their generations. The Lord apportioned to them great glory, his majesty from the beginning" (Sir 44:1-2). God shares His glory with His children, and we honor both God and His children for these great gifts.

Expressions of Veneration for the Saints

We also see in Scripture many examples where people venerate others by bowing down to them. This is veneration and not worship. God's command "You shall not bow down to them" means "Do not worship them" (Deut 5:9). Catholics express veneration for the saints by bowing, for example, to a statue or other image of the saint, and making other gestures of reverence. Even Jesus said that people would bow down in reverence before the faithful members of the church of Philadelphia (Rev 3:9). We see examples of this type of veneration throughout the Scriptures:

- Lot venerates two angels in Sodom by bowing himself with his face to the ground (see Gen 19:1);
- Joseph's brothers bow before Joseph with their face to the ground (see Gen 42:6);
- Joshua falls to the ground prostrate to venerate an angel (see Josh 5:14);
- Saul bows down before Samuel with his face to the ground (see 1 Sam 28:14);
- the prophet Nathan bows down before king David (see 1 Kings 1:23);
- the sons of the prophets bow down to Elisha at Jericho (see 2 Kings 2:15);

- Ornan the Jebusite does obeisance to king David with his face to the ground (see 1 Chron 21:21);
- the Israelites bow down to give honor to the king (see 1 Chron 29:20);
- King Hezekiah and the assembly venerate the altar by bowing down before the sin offerings (see 2 Chron 29:29-30);
- Tobiah and Tobit fall down to the ground to venerate the angel Raphael (see Tobit 12:16);
- Achior the Ammonite kneels before Judith venerating her and praising God (see Judith 14:7);
- David bows down before God's holy temple (see Ps 138:2);
- the king falls down on his face paying homage to Daniel (see Dan 2:46); and,
- Daniel falls down prostrate to venerate the angel Gabriel (see Dan 8:17).

These and many other examples in the Scriptures demonstrate that bowing and other forms of veneration are not forms of worship.

Why are there images and statues in Catholic churches?

Catholics and other Christians use images, statues other items to help them honor the saints and call to mind their heroic virtues. These items are often called "sacramentals."[380] The Church's use of images and statutes of the saints is no different than a person who keeps pictures of his or her loved ones. These are expressions of love and veneration we have for the person represented by the image or statute, not worship. Further, the reverence we give to the saints is ultimately directed to God, for God is the source of all the holiness of the saint we are venerating.

Some Christians condemn the use of statues and other images to honor God and the saints because God has told us, "Thou shall not make a graven image" (Deut 5:8). However, God's commandment proscribed the worship of false gods. In early history, Israel was forbidden to make images of God because God had not yet revealed Himself in physical form (see Deut 4:16). If the Israelites had been allowed to make images, they might have been tempted to worship Him in the form of a beast, bird, reptile, or fish (see vv.17-19).

However, God did command Israel to make images to facilitate worship. For example:

- God commands the making of the bronze serpent (see Num 21:8-9);
- God also commands the making of golden cherubim;[381]
- Solomon's temple contained statues of cherubim and images of cherubim, oxen and lions;[382]
- David also gave Solomon a plan for the altar made of refined gold with golden cherubim;[383]
- the place of worship was lined with gold and elaborate cherubim carved in wood and overlaid with gold;[384] and,
- Ezekiel describes the graven images in the temple consisting of carved likenesses of cherubim (see Ez 41:18).

These images and statues of angels are similar to those seen in Catholic churches. It was only when the people began to worship these statues and images that they incurred God's wrath and the king destroyed them (see 2 Kings 18:4).

What are relics?

Some Catholics also use relics in their devotions to the saints. Relics are parts of the body of a saint (typically a piece of bone), or the clothing of a saint, or something that a saint had used or touched. They are used to facilitate devotion to the saints and the worship of God. Catholic churches around the world usually keep relics beneath the altar on which the Holy Sacrifice of the Mass is offered. This is to honor the saints and martyrs whose souls John saw beneath the heavenly altar in Revelation 6:9.

Relics are not good-luck charms. The Church prohibits superstition. Catholics use relics to honor and imitate the heroic faith of those who have gone before us to be with Christ. This is like keeping articles of deceased loved ones, which help us remember and honor them.

There is also scriptural evidence for the use of relics:

- Elisha's bones brought a man back to life;[385]

- Paul's handkerchiefs healed the sick and those with unclean spirits;[386]
- Peter's shadow healed the sick;[387] and,
- the woman with the hemorrhage sought just the hem of Jesus' cloak and was cured.[388]

Jesus' dead body was also venerated. The women of Jerusalem came to anoint Jesus' body even though it had been sealed in the tomb.[389] Nicodemus also donated over one hundred pounds of spices to accompany Jesus' body (see Jn 19:39).

How can created things (such as water, bread, or oil) be sources of supernatural grace?

Just as Jesus chose to be incarnate and possess a physical body, God chooses the physical things He created to effect the supernatural (like water, bread and wine). We have already seen this with baptism (water), the Eucharist (bread and wine) and anointing of the sick (oil).

Catholics also use holy water[390] in their worship and devotions. For Jews and Christians, water has always been considered a sign of God's life. For the Christian, water has its ultimate expression of God's life in the sacrament of baptism. Holy water fonts are located at the entrance of Catholic churches, and Catholics dip their fingers into the water and sign themselves with the sign of the cross. Priests also use holy water to bless people and things.

Even in the Old Testament, water was used for the sacred.

- Aaron and his sons were washed in holy water in their consecration to the priesthood.[391]
- The Lord also required Aaron and his sons to wash their hands and feet in water before they offered sacrifices to Him.[392]
- The Old Testament priests would use "holy water" in their priestly duties (see Num 5:17).
- In King Solomon's temple, there were ten large basins of holy water (see 1 Kings 7:38-39).

In the New Testament, Jesus used water to wash the apostles' feet on the night they were consecrated to the New Testament priesthood (see Jn 13:4-10). Jesus also used clay and spittle to heal the blind man's eyes, and ordered him to wash in the Pool of Siloam to affect the cure (see Jn 9:6-7). Of course, Jesus did not need to use clay, spittle and water, but He does so to demonstrate that God uses the material things He created to meet our spiritual needs. The Lord uses physical properties to convey His supernatural property of grace. The greatest sign of life-giving water is the water that flowed from Jesus' pierced side as He hung dead on the cross.[393] This water, along with the blood that accompanied it, symbolizes our new life in Christ through baptism and the Eucharist.

CHAPTER SIX

Justification

How does a person attain the purity of soul necessary to gain heaven and attain the Beatific Vision? Is it by faith alone, as Martin Luther and other Protestant Reformers insisted, or are works also necessary? This issue has divided Catholics and Protestants for nearly five centuries, and is the focus of this chapter called "justification."

Justification is the process by which man, moved by grace, turns toward God and away from sin, and accepts God's forgiveness and righteousness. Through justification, God both remits sin and infuses sanctifying grace into the soul by the power of the Holy Spirit. Sanctifying grace is the gratuitous gift of God's own divine life, which makes us pleasing to God. If we die in the state of justification, we go to heaven.

Justification, which puts us into a right relationship with God, has been merited for us by the Passion of Jesus Christ. Through Christ, God freely decided to associate man with the work of His grace. Man, therefore, cannot achieve justification by his own natural efforts.

As we have seen, God justifies us in baptism. Baptism regenerates and renews the inner man and purifies the conscience[*] by the working of the Holy Spirit.[*394] Faith, hope and love are poured into our hearts, and obedience to the divine will is granted to us (see Rom 5:1-5). Baptism also sanctifies the person[*] so that we, like Christ, are "begotten from above"[*395] and made pleasing to the Father.

As we have also seen, many Christians do not believe baptism brings about our justification; they believe instead that God justifies us when, at a specific point in time, we choose by our own free will to renounce sin, and to accept Jesus as our personal Lord and Savior. These same Christians argue that this justification comes about only

157

by faith in Jesus Christ, and not by works. This is called *sola fide* (faith alone).

Like *sola Scriptura, sola fide* is a novel theological invention that was introduced by the Protestant Reformers. It is especially dangerous because those who subscribe to the doctrine of *sola fide* also generally believe that, once a person is justified, he cannot lose his justification. In other words, he is assured of his place in heaven.

Since we have already demonstrated that the Scriptures teach baptism justifies, sanctifies and saves us, we will not discuss this further. Instead, we will address the Protestant contentions that justification happens by faith alone, at one specific point in time, and cannot be lost. Because these are such contentious issues between Catholics and Protestants, we will spend an adequate time addressing them. In the end, we will demonstrate the truth of the Catholic view of justification, and that the view of Luther and the other Protestant Reformers has no basis in Scripture.

Works of Law vs. Good Works

Most Protestants believe that Christians are justified by faith alone, and generally attribute this teaching to Paul. The obvious problem with this view is that neither Paul nor any other New Testament writer *ever says we are justified by faith alone*. In fact, Paul uses the word "faith" over two hundred times in the New Testament, and he never qualifies "faith" with the words "alone" or "only." Since Paul uses the word "alone" more than any other New Testament writer, one would think that he would have modified the word "faith" with the qualifier "alone" at least once if he were teaching justification by faith alone. In fact, the only time the phrase "faith alone" (in Greek, *pistis monon*) occurs in the Scriptures is when James says, "A man is justified by works and *not by faith alone*" (James 2:24).

System of grace (faith) / system of law (works)
So why do so many Christians believe we are justified by faith alone? There are a couple of verses in Scripture where Paul teaches we are justified by faith and not "works of the law." For example, Paul teaches the Romans that "a man is justified by faith apart from works

of law" (Rom 3:28). Similarly, Paul teaches the Galatians that "a man is not justified by works of the law but through faith in Jesus Christ" (Gal 2:16).

How do we reconcile Paul's teaching, that we are *not* justified by "works of the law," with James' teaching, that we *are* justified by "works and not by faith alone?" James 2:24 appears to be entirely inconsistent with Romans 3:28 and Galatians 2:16, until we remember that the Word of God can never contradict itself. This must mean that the "works" (in Greek, *ergois agathois*) in James 2:24 are different from the "works of the law" (in Greek, *ergon nomou*) in Romans 3:28 and Galatians 2:16 (which the Greek language demonstrates).

Before addressing this difference, we should reiterate that Paul's teaching does not say we are justified by faith alone. He says only that we are not justified by "works of law." Thus, on a purely grammatical level, the faith that justifies excludes "works of law," but not necessarily other things such as love, or hope, or obedience, or repentance. In fact, Paul often qualifies justifying faith with the phrases "work of faith"* and "obedient faith."*[396] Paul says the faith that we need must increase as a result of our obedience (see 2 Cor 10:15). This is why Paul admonishes us to examine ourselves, to see whether or not we are holding to our faith (see 2 Cor 13:5). Paul also connects love with faith such that they must act together.[397] Scripture also teaches us that we need a "repentant" faith, not just an intellectual faith that believes in God.[398] Thus, Scripture teaches us that we need a certain *kind* of faith to be justified, and this is a faith that is accompanied by obedience, repentance and love.

Paul also introduces another apparent inconsistency in his teaching on justification. Paul tells the Romans, "For it is not the hearers of the law who are righteous before God, but the *doers of the law who will be justified*" (Rom 2:13). In this verse, Paul expressly teaches that the law *does* justify, while Paul says elsewhere that works of law *do not* justify.[399] Thus, not only does James seem to be contradicting Paul, but Paul also seems to be contradicting himself.

While these passages seem contradictory and confusing, they are not. As we will see, *Paul and James are teaching the critical difference between works performed in a system of law versus works performed in a system of grace.* Works done in a system of law do *not* justify, and works done in a system of grace *do* justify. This is the *key* paradigm in the biblical teaching of justification.

Paul emphasizes the grace versus law paradigm more than any of the other sacred writers. In fact, this teaching is at the heart of Paul's theology on justification. Thus, it is critical to understand this distinction if we are to understand Paul's teaching.

In a system of law, we view God as one who is obligated to pay us for our works. We therefore take a very impersonal view of God and approach Him, not as a loving Father, but as an employer who owes us by legal obligation. Since, in this system, we view our works as based on law and legal contract, they cannot be a part of God's benevolence in the system of grace. We can never establish a legitimate relationship with God in this way.

Because God is a personal being, He wants us to relate to Him on a personal level. In the system of grace, we come to God in faith, seeking a personal relationship with Him, and acknowledging that He owes us nothing. But in the system of grace, we also know that God will reward us according to His kindness and mercy. *The system we choose, whether law or grace, is based upon the personal relationship that we establish with God.*

Paul introduces the principle of obligation to the Romans by saying, "Now to one who works, his wages are not reckoned as a gift but as his due" (Rom 4:4). In distinguishing works based on law versus works based on grace, Paul explains, "But if it is by grace, it is no longer on the basis of works; otherwise grace would no longer be grace" (Rom 11:6). Paul points out the folly of viewing God in a system of law by saying, "Or who has given a gift to him that he might be repaid? For from him and through him and to him are all things" (Rom 11:35-36). God is not obligated to pay anyone for his work because no one can do anything for God that is deserving of repayment. God already has everything. In fact, Paul teaches that eternal life is a free gift from God, and those who "work" for it in a system of law will die. "For the *wages* of sin is death, but the *free gift* of God is eternal life in Christ Jesus our Lord" (Rom 6:23).

Thus, in the system of grace, we approach God *with faith in Him.* God requires faith because it was precisely a *lack* of faith that caused the fall of man. God requires us to pass the test that Adam failed, and this faith comes from God's grace through the second Adam, Jesus Christ. Paul explains that it is faith in Christ that allows us to move out of the system of law and into the system of grace. "Therefore, since we are justified by faith, we have peace with God through our Lord Jesus Christ. Through him we have *obtained access to this grace* in which we stand, and rejoice in our hope of sharing the glory of God" (Rom 5:1-2). We "obtain access" to the system of grace by faith in Jesus Christ, not works of law.

Paul says to the Galatians, "A man is not justified by works of the law but through *faith in Jesus Christ,* even we have believed in Christ Jesus, in order to be justified by *faith in Christ,* and not by works of the law" (Gal 2:16). Paul also tells the Romans that "the righteousness of God has been manifested apart from law," and that we now receive "the righteousness of God through *faith in Jesus Christ* for all who believe" (Rom 3:22-23). Paul further says, "You are not under law but *under grace*" (Rom 6:14) and says, "That is why it depends on *faith,* in order that the promise may rest on *grace*" (Rom 4:16). Paul describes himself to the Philippians by saying, "...not having a righteousness of my own based on law, but that which is through *faith in Christ*" (Phil 3:9). Paul further tells the Ephesians, "For by *grace* you have been saved *through faith*...not because of works, lest any man should boast" (Eph 2:8-9).

Unlike the system of grace, in the system of law we approach God *with faith in ourselves.* We therefore seek the praise of men, and not God. Jesus points this out to the Pharisees who were trying to obligate God by works when He says, "You are those who justify yourselves *before men,* but God knows your hearts" (Lk 16:15).

While, in the system of grace, we attribute our good works to God, in the system of law we attribute them to ourselves. Paul points this out when he teaches about those who "boast" before God about their works:

- "You rely upon the law and boast of your relation to God" (Rom 2:17);
- "You who boast in the law, do you dishonor God by breaking the law?" (Rom 2:23);

- "Then what becomes of our boasting? It is excluded. On what principle? On the principle of works? No, but on the principle of faith" (Rom 3:27); and,
- "What have you that you did not receive? If then you received it, why do you boast as if it were not a gift?" (1 Cor 4:7).

Paul tells the Ephesians they are saved by grace through faith and not by works, "so that no one can *boast*" (Eph 2:8-9). But notice how Paul says in the very next verse that we are "...created in Christ Jesus for *good works*" (v.10). These are good works done in the system of grace. In the system of law, we seek to please ourselves, and in the system of grace, we seek to *please God*.

The sacred writers emphasize the importance of pleasing God in our relationship with Him:

- Paul says, "So whether we are at home or away, we make it our aim to please him" (2 Cor 5:9);
- Paul also says we must "lead a life worthy of the Lord, fully pleasing to him" (Col 1:10);
- Paul further says, "we speak not to please men, but to please God who tests our hearts" (1 Thess 2:4);
- Paul also warns, "Those who are in the flesh cannot please God" (Rom 8:8);
- John says, "We receive from him whatever we ask because we keep his commandments and do what pleases him" (1 Jn 3:22);
- the author of Hebrews says we must do "that which is pleasing in his sight" (Heb 13:21); and
- the author of Hebrews also says, "Without faith, it is impossible to please [God]" (Heb 11:6).

Thus, we must establish our relationship with God based on faith in Him and His goodness, and not on ourselves.

Let me provide an illustration of law versus grace in action. Let's say my daughter Anna approaches me in love and asks me if she can take out the garbage. I am pleased with her request and kindly oblige. I also tell her that I will reward her with a piece of candy for her works. Thus, my daughter approaches me in love, not motivated by seeking payment, but by pleasing me, while also knowing that I, as her loving Father, will reward her in love for her good works (with at least a hug and kiss). If she drops a soda can on the driveway, I will overlook this and still reward her. I am pleased with her faith, hope, and love, and will reward her out of the goodness of my heart.

Now let's say that I overhear Anna brag to her younger sisters Mia and Mara that I will give her a piece of candy if she takes out the garbage. After boasting about her works to her sisters, she asks me if she can take out the garbage, and I oblige. In this situation, my daughter approaches me with the motivation of obligating me to pay her for her works, and not pleasing me out of love, with faith that I will love her in return. This does not please me. Now if she drops a soda can on the driveway, I will not overlook it. I will hold her to the strict standard of the law, and will not reward her for her work. This is because she based her relationship with me upon obligation, and not grace. She, in a sense, has fallen out of my good graces (see Gal 5:4).

God's grace was already operative in the Old Testament, based upon the anticipated sacrifice of Jesus Christ. Thus, even before Christ formally inaugurated the system of grace by His death and Resurrection, those who approached God personally in faith were justified by God through His grace.

For example, the author of Hebrews says, "*By faith* Abel offered to God a more acceptable sacrifice than Cain" (Heb 11:4). Thus, "the Lord looked *with grace* on Abel and his offering, but on Cain and his offering he did not look *with grace*.[400] Similarly, the letter to the Hebrews says, "*By faith* Noah, being warned by God concerning events as yet unseen, took heed and constructed an ark for the saving of his household" (Heb 11:7). Thus, "Noah *found grace* in the eyes of the Lord."[401] Paul also explains that Abraham was justified as a Gentile *through faith*, which came before his "work" of circumcision.

> We say that faith was reckoned to Abraham as righteousness. How then was it reckoned to him? Was it before or after he had been circumcised? It was not after, but before he was circumcised (Rom 4:9-10).

Similarly, the author of Hebrews says, "*By faith* Moses, when he was grown up... considered abuse suffered for the Christ greater wealth than the treasures of Egypt, for he looked to the reward" (Heb 11:25-26).

Speaking of circumcision, we note that Paul uses the Mosaic Law as the primary example in Scripture of works that are done in a "system of law." Because the Jews had the Law of God in writing and the Gentiles did not, the Jews viewed themselves as having a superior relationship with God. But this led the prideful Jews to base their relationship with God upon the works they performed under the Mosaic Law, and not on faith.

Paul says, "Israel who pursued the righteousness which is based on law did not succeed in fulfilling that law. Why? Because they did not pursue it *through faith*, but as if it were based on works" (Rom 9:31-32). We see that, after Paul tells the Romans that a man is justified by faith apart from works of law, he says, "Or is God the God of the Jews only? Is he not the God of the Gentiles also? Yes, of Gentiles also, since God is one; and he will justify the circumcised on the ground of their faith, and the uncircumcised through their faith" (Rom 3:29-30). Paul is saying that both Jew and Gentile are justified by faith, irrespective of the law. In fact, Paul says that, through Christ, we have now been freed from the Law of Moses (see Acts 13:39).

In Galatians 3, Paul gives other evidence that works under the Mosaic Law are part of the "system of law." For example, after saying that the law does not rest on faith (v.12) and all who rely on works of law are under a curse (v.10) from which Christ freed us (v.13), Paul says that this law came 430 years after Abraham (v.17). This refers to the *written* law that God gave to Moses. In describing this law, Paul says that "the *written* code kills" and that the written code was "the dispensation of death, carved in letters on stone" (2 Cor 3:6-7). Christ has now opened up for us the system of grace by "abolishing in his flesh the [*written*] law of commandments and ordinances" (Eph 2:15). Paul also says "He forgave us all our sins, having canceled the *written* code, with its regulations, that was against us and that stood opposed to us; he took it away, nailing it to the cross" (Col 2:13-14). Paul further says, "But now we are discharged from the law, dead to that which held us captive, so that we serve not under the old *written* code but in the new life of the Spirit" (Rom 7:6). Therefore, when Paul uses the phrase "works of law," he is often referring to the Mosaic Law, *but not exclusively.*

Paul taught about "works of law" to the Gentiles (e.g., Corinthians, Ephesians) as well, who were never under the Law of Moses. Paul applies "works of law" to the Gentiles because they, like the Jews, were falling into the sin of pride and boasting about their religion. They began to think that, because of their own natural powers, they were earning what they received. For example, Paul addresses the Gentile Ephesians as "Gentiles in the flesh, called the uncircumcision" (Eph 2:11). Paul notices their boasting and reminds them that they were saved by grace through faith in Christ, so that none of them *would boast* (vv.8-9). Paul also reminds the Gentile Corinthians, "For who sees anything different in you? What have you that you did not receive? If then you received it, why do you *boast* as if it were not a gift?" (1 Cor 4:7). Paul also says to them "So let no one *boast* of men. For all things are yours" (1 Cor 3:21). Christians of today, if they do not establish a personal relationship with God, can likewise risk approaching God in a system of law versus a system of grace. God will judge us by the system we choose.

Works of law — ceremonial laws only?

When discussing the Mosaic Law in the context of justification, many people believe that "works of law" refer only to the Jewish ceremonial laws, and not to the legal and moral laws of Moses as well. Many Catholic apologists even take this view to prove that, when Paul says we are not justified by works, he does not mean all works. He only means the ceremonial works of Israel, thereby preserving non-ceremonial works as a basis for justification. This argument, however, distorts the Catholic Church's teaching on justification.

First, it is true that "works of law" include Israel's ceremonial laws. Ceremonial laws deal with our relationship with and worship of God (based on the first Three Commandments). One of the most prominent examples of the ceremonial law is circumcision.[402] Moral laws, on the other hand, deal with our relationship with one another (based on the last Seven Commandments).

Those who exclude the moral Law of Moses from "works of law" assume that the Jews and Gentiles had only the moral law in common (for example, "Thou shalt not kill," "Thou shalt not steal," "Thou shalt not covet"). They may even cite Romans 2:15 to impute the moral law to the Gentiles, as it says the law "is written on their hearts." Consequently, they assume that the Jews and Gentiles did not have the ceremonial, or worship laws, in common. Since Jews and Gentiles are one in the New Covenant, and the Church no longer requires the ceremonial law of circumcision, the apologist concludes that "works of law" must only refer to Israel's ceremonial laws.

The apologist making this argument fails to recognize that the Gentiles also had worship laws, not just moral laws, written on their hearts. For example, Paul says that even though the Gentiles knew God through His eternal power and divine nature, "...they did not honor him as God or give thanks to him" (Rom 1:20-21). Thus, just as the Jews had the first three worship laws written on tablets of stone, the Gentiles had the worship law (the obligation to give God honor and thanks) written on their hearts. These were the same laws that Adam and Eve had written on their hearts.

Therefore, when Paul says "works of law" in the context of the Mosaic Law, he is referring to the *entire* Law of Moses (legal, moral and ceremonial laws). For example, when Paul points out that the Romans "boast in the law" (Rom 2:23), he identifies the law as including stealing (v.21) and adultery (v.22). These are *moral* laws — specifically, the Fifth and Sixth Commandments. When Paul says, "I should not have known what it is to covet if the law had not said, 'You shall not covet'"(Rom 7:7), he is referring to the *moral* laws of the Ninth and Tenth Commandments. When Paul says "Cursed be everyone who does not abide by all things written in the book of the law, and do them," (Gal 3:10) he is quoting from Deuteronomy 27:26 and Leviticus 18:5, which include *all* the religious laws of Israel.

Paul gives another great example in his letter to Titus, written mainly for Gentiles, when he says:

> He saved us, not because of deeds done by us in righteous-
> ness, but in virtue of his own mercy, by the washing of

regeneration and renewal in the Holy Spirit, which he poured out upon us richly through Jesus Christ our Savior, so that we might be justified by his grace and become heirs in hope of eternal life (Titus 3:5-7).

Paul's use of "deeds of righteousness" refers to works done in a system of law before baptism. Further, "deeds of righteousness" refer to moral works, not ceremonial works. While Paul uses circumcision in Scripture as perhaps the most prominent example of "works of law," he never uses it at the exclusion of the legal and moral laws.

This brings us to a critical point: If both the Jews and Gentiles had moral and worship laws in common (though the Jews alone had them in writing), then Paul is not attempting to create a Jew/Gentile, or a circumcision/uncircumcision distinction. Instead, *Paul is creating a grace/law distinction*. This is the foundation of Paul's whole theology on justification and works of law. Paul makes this even clearer when he writes about how the Jews of his time are seeking God through their works, just as the Jews were doing during the time of Elijah.[403] Because there were no Gentiles around in Elijah's time, Paul is not making a Jew/Gentile distinction. Paul says at the present time, just like in Elijah's time, there is only a remnant of the Jews being saved *by grace* (Rom 11:5). This means that the Jews of the past, like the Jews of the present, were basing their relationship with God on works, not faith in grace.

Paul concludes this passage by reminding the Jews, "If it is by grace, it is no longer on the basis of works" (v.6). This is why Paul teaches that if either Jewish or Gentile Christians seek God by the ceremonial law of circumcision, they put themselves under the *whole* law. "I testify again to *every man* who receives circumcision that he is bound to keep the *whole* law. You are severed from Christ, you who would be justified by the law; you have fallen away from grace" (Gal 5:3-4). In other words, law versus grace applies to *both* Jews and Gentiles, and is an *all or nothing* proposition. God wants a personal relationship, based totally on faith in Him, as a Father who loves us, and not an employer who owes us. God wants our whole hearts.

Why is this issue important? Because if you argue that "works of law" only refer to ceremonial laws, then you are arguing that only a *part* of Old Covenant has been set aside. As we have seen, this means that we would still be under the curse of the law.[404] We would still be in a system of law, not grace, and would stand condemned. This view cannot be reconciled with our dignified place as children of the New Covenant, established by Jesus Christ, who "is the end of the law" (Rom 10:4).

Why did God give us laws if we are only justified in a system of grace? God originally gave His law to lead people to love Him and their neighbor as themselves. But, as we have seen, people began to use God's law, not as a means to an end, but as an end in itself. They began to focus on the letter of the law, and not the principle of the law. This also led people to view their salvation as theirs to earn, and not God's to give.

When we abuse God's good gifts, we anger God, and He punishes us by giving us more of what we seek, but always with our own good in mind. When God's people began to approach Him in a "system of law," God gave them more laws. God says through Ezekiel: "I gave them statutes that were not good and ordinances by which they could not have life; and I defiled them through their very gifts" (Ez 20:25-26). Thus, God gave man more laws to show man how sinful he was, "since through the law comes knowledge of sin" (Rom 3:20). But God did this for the purpose of moving him from a system of law to a system of grace. If we refuse to approach God through grace by faith and establish a personal relationship with Him, God will judge us under the system of law, and this means we will be condemned. God shows no mercy in a system of law, and we cannot live up to the law's exacting standards:

- "For whoever keeps the whole law but fails in one point has become guilty of all of it" (James 2:10).
- "Cursed be everyone who does not abide by all things written in the book of the law" (Gal 3:10).
- "For the law brings wrath" (Rom 4:15).
- "Law came in, to increase the trespass; but where sin increased, grace abounded all the more, so that as sin reigned in death, grace also might reign through righteousness to eternal life through Jesus Christ our Lord" (Rom 5:20-21).

If we come to God with faith in Jesus Christ, we uphold God's law as He originally intended. That is, we uphold the principle of the law, not the letter of the law. What is the principle of the law? Paul sums it up: "For the whole law is fulfilled in one word, 'You shall love your neighbor as yourself'"[405] Elsewhere, he says, "For he who loves his neighbor has fulfilled the law" (Rom 13:8). James calls this the "royal law according to the scripture, 'You shall love your neighbor as yourself'" (James 2:8). Thus, Paul says, "...love is the fulfilling of the law" (Rom 13:10). Loving God and neighbor fulfills "the law of Christ" (Gal 6:2). This is why Jesus says "all the law" depends on these two commandments (Mt 22:40). This is also why Paul says, "the law is holy,"* and can say, in the system of grace, "the doers of the law will be justified."*[406]

Thus, even though we are no longer under the Old Covenant laws, we must still obey their principles. In fact, the New Covenant of grace goes beyond the Old Covenant of laws by perfecting them in love. Jesus says, "You have heard that it was said to the men of old, 'You shall not kill; and whoever kills shall be liable to judgment.' But I say to you that everyone who is angry with his brother shall be liable to judgment" (Mt 5:21-22). Jesus also says "You have heard that it was said, 'You shall not commit adultery.' But I say to you that every-one who looks at a woman lustfully has already committed adultery with her in his heart" (vv.27-28).

In the New Covenant, then, Jesus exalts the law to its original purpose, which is to lead us to love God and our neighbor. While the Old Covenant dealt with the exterior, the New Covenant deals with the interior. God now peers into our hearts and can see our most secret motives. In the system of law, God was obligated to us. In the system of grace, we are obligated to God. Through the grace of the sacraments, which are the New Covenant worship laws, we can purify our hearts and fulfill the heart of the law as God had always intended.

But while the New Covenant is more merciful than the Old Covenant, it is also more demanding. Christ holds us more account-able than Moses ever could. Jesus is our "one lawgiver and judge, he who is able to save and to destroy" (James 4:12). Thus, the sacred writer says, "A man who has violated the Law of Moses dies without mercy at the testimony of two or three witnesses. How much worse punishment do you think will be deserved by the man who has spurned the Son of God, and profaned the blood of the covenant by which he was sanctified, and outraged the Spirit of grace?" (Heb 10:28-29).

Justified by Faith Alone?

Now that we understand the paradigm of law versus grace, we can understand how James can say, "...a man is justified by works and not by faith alone" (James 2:24). James is referring to good works performed in the system of grace to which we gain access by faith in Christ (see Rom 5:1-2). James says these good works are summed up in the royal law of loving your neighbor as yourself (see James 2:8).

It is critical to understand that James is teaching that these good works *cause* our salvific justification, not that good works just flow from someone who is *already* justified and saved. James says, "What does it profit, my brethren, if a man says he has faith but has not works? Can his faith *save* him?" (James 2:14). James' follows his question with a description of a person who is ill-clad and lacking daily food (v.15). If we don't respond to the person's needs, then the answer to James' rhetorical question is a resounding, "No." Faith alone cannot save him. James then says, "So faith by itself, if it has no works, is dead."[407]

Notice also that James doesn't say, "Can his faith demonstrate that he is already saved?" Unlike what many Protestants contend, Scripture never distinguishes between genuine faith and false faith. Scripture also never says that works qualify faith into saving faith, or demonstrate that a person was already saved. Faith is faith and works are works (James 2:18). They are separate and distinct entities, and yet must act *together* in order to achieve justification.

Faith (a mental process) and works of love (actions) are never separated in the Scriptures.[408] Paul summarizes this beautifully when he says we need "faith working through love" (Gal 5:6). Paul further says that if our faith moves mountains, but we have not love, we are nothing (1 Corinthians 13:2), and that the greatest of the theological virtues[409] is love (v.13). Faith in Christ gives access to grace and puts us on the road to justification, but once we are in the system of grace, we must add works to our faith to be justified. Faith alone never obtains the grace of justification.

Justification "before men"?

Because James' teaching on the necessity of works for salvific justification is so clear, non-Catholic Christians have gone to great lengths to twist the plain meaning of his words. Since Protestants believe we are justified by faith alone, they argue that the justification James is teaching about is not really justification at all. They must so argue, for if James is really speaking of salvific justification before God, the Protestant view of justification by faith alone collapses.

For example, because James says, "*You see* that a man is justified by works and not by faith alone" (James 2:24), Protestants argue that James is teaching about a justification before men, and not God (because of the phrase "you see"). If it is a justification before men, there can be no salvific component to the good works.

A problem with this argument is that James says Abraham was justified by his works when he offered his son Isaac on the altar (see James 2:21). No human beings witnessed Abraham's attempted sacrifice of Isaac. The two young men who accompanied Abraham and Isaac to Mount Moriah, "stayed with the ass" at the base of the mountain (Gen 22:5). Only the angel, who ordered Abraham to cease from sacrificing Isaac, was present (vv.11-12). The focus of the account of Abraham's sacrifice in Genesis 22 is between Abraham and God, who chose to test Abraham's faith (Gen 22:1), and not between Abraham and men.

Moreover, the word "justified" (in Greek, *dikaioo*) that James uses in James 2:24 is the same word that Paul uses in Romans 4:2, which describes Abraham's justification. Thus, if Paul is talking about Abraham's justification before God in Romans 4:2 (which Protestants believe), then that means James is talking about justification before God in James 2:24.

James underscores the extreme importance of adding works to faith by saying, "Even the demons believe — and shudder" (James 2:19). This also demonstrates that James is addressing justification before God and not men, since demons, like God, are in the spiritual realm. Some dismiss this passage, saying that James is only teaching that we cannot have faith like the demons. But that is the point. The demons believe God exists. But the demons will not "draw near to God and believe that He rewards those who seek him" (Heb 11:6). James is using the most extreme example of beings with faith in God who will never do good works, to emphasize that good works are absolutely essential to salvific justification.

Are works a "by-product" of faith?

Some Christians argue that good works only demonstrate the type of faith that one has. As such, works are only a qualifier of faith, and not something that needs to be added to faith in order to achieve justification. While those who make this argument may acknowledge that works are a separate entity from faith (see James 2:18), they view works as simply a by-product of faith which reveals the sanctity of the person, but does not justify and save the person. Therefore, they contend, good works are classified in the category of non-salvific sanctification, and not salvific justification.

However, Scripture never says that works qualify faith, or are a by-product of faith, or only sanctify a person who already has saving faith. In fact, James' epistle rejects these views. James is speaking to genuine Christian believers who already "hold the faith of our Lord Jesus Christ, the Lord of glory" (James 2:1). James, therefore, continually refers to these believers as "my brethren" (James 2:1,5,14). But even though James is speaking to true Christian believers, he repeatedly warns them about doing good and avoiding sin.

- He tells them to avoid anger,* slander,* and worldly things.*[410]
- He exhorts them to have patience,* humility,* and endure to achieve salvation.*[411]
- He warns them not to engage in sins of commission such as murder and adultery (James 2:11).
- He also warns them not to fall into the sin of omission by failing to help the poor man in shabby clothing (James 2:2) or the person lacking daily food (v.15).

James specifically says that the failure to do good works is a sin (see James 4:17). Thus, James admonishes them to make a *conscious decision* to add works to their faith. It is obvious that good works are not just flowing naturally out of these believers.

Can justification be separated from sanctification?

While Protestants want to make sanctification a separate, non-salvific category, Scripture never separates justification from sanctification. For example, we saw in baptism that justification and sanctification occur simultaneously (1 Cor 6:11). This is because, in baptism, we receive God's sanctifying grace that makes us holy, and this holiness is what justifies us before God. In fact, justification never chronologically precedes sanctification in Scripture. Instead, Scripture subsumes sanctification into justification. For example, Paul says, "Those whom he predestined he also called; and those whom he called he also justified; and those whom he justified he also glorified" (Rom 8:30). Paul does not mention sanctification in the salvation process because it is automatically a part of justification. Similarly, Paul tells the Galatians that they are trying to be "justified by the law; you have fallen away from grace" (Gal 5:4). Paul uses "justification," and not "sanctification," to describe the Galatians' ongoing relationship with God. Because Scripture fuses sanctification and justification together, and justification is salvific, sanctification cannot be a separate, non-salvific category.

"Actual" vs. "declared" justification?

Because Protestants believe that justification is a one-time event by faith alone, they are forced to create two stages of justification: actual justification (which refers to the one-time event that comes by faith alone), and declared justification (which refers to subsequent events like good works which vindicate the person's previously received, one-time justification). By creating these two stages, they can argue that James is not really teaching about justification by works, but a "vindication" by works (even though James never once uses the word "vindication"). Again this attempts to divest good works of their salvific attributes, and distorts the plain meaning of Scripture.

Those who define justification in this manner use Abraham as their primary example of an actual justification followed by a declared justification: Abraham received his one-time, actual justification by faith alone in Genesis 15:6 when God said, "And he believed the Lord; and he reckoned it to him as righteousness." In Romans 4:3, Paul confirms that Abraham was justified in Genesis 15:6. Therefore, in James 2:21 when James speaks about Abraham's justification by works in Genesis 22, the Protestant argues, these works only vindicated Abraham's previous justification by faith in Genesis 15:6. These works, therefore, fall into the category of declared (not actual) justification.

The problem with this argument is that James describes Abraham's justification by works in Genesis 22 with the *same* language that describes Abraham's justification in Genesis 15:6 (see James 2:23). This is significant because the author of Genesis does not use the "reckoned to him as righteousness" language in Genesis 15:6 to describe how God viewed Abraham for his works in Genesis 22. James does. Therefore, James is saying that *God viewed Abraham's works in Genesis 22 in the same way that He viewed Abraham's faith in Genesis 15:6.*

Since Genesis 15:6 has nothing to do with vindication, James is connecting the events of Genesis 15:6 and Genesis 22 in the context of justification. Thus, if Abraham's justification by faith was actual and salvific in Genesis 15:6 (which all Christians believe), his justification by works was also actual and salvific in Genesis 22.

This can *only* be true, however, if Abraham had *both* faith *and* works in Genesis 15:6 and Genesis 22. Why? A man is not justified by faith alone (James 2:24). In fact, Scripture demonstrates that Abraham had both faith and works long before Genesis 15:6.

In Genesis 12:1-3, for example, God calls Abram out of Haran and embarks on his journey to the Promised Land of Canaan. Hebrews 11:8 says that Abram had justifying faith at this moment. But Abram added works to his faith because he "obeyed and went, even though he did not know where he was going" (Heb 11:8). Abram's faith and works acted together.

Abraham also added works to his faith in Genesis 15:6. When God promises Abram a natural son to be his heir, Abram was one hundred years old (see Rom 4:19). His wife Sarai was also aged and barren. Yet Abram believes that God will do what He promises, and he is justified. We must recognize that Abram and Sarai's subsequent intimate relations, in light of their obvious obstacles of agedness and infertility, was an act of obedience that was added to their faith, and that faith in God's promise alone didn't justify.

Finally, while James speaks of Abraham's offering of Isaac as a justification by works, it was also a supreme act of faith. Hebrews 11:17 confirms that faith was present along with Abraham's works.

James explains this synergism of Abraham's faith and works when he says, "You see that faith was active along with his works, and faith was completed by works" (James 2:22). Both faith and works always accompany salvific justification. These works of faith, hope, love and obedience are the same works that James requires in his epistle. We also mention that God swears a covenant oath in Genesis 22:16, but not in Genesis 15:6, which suggests that Abraham's obedience in Genesis 22 was necessary to maintain the justification he acquired in Genesis 15.

The justification language used in Genesis 15:6 to describe Abraham is also used to describe a man named Phineas. Psalm 106:30-31 says, "Then Phineas stood up and interposed, and the plague was stayed. And that has been reckoned to him as righteousness from generation to generation for ever." This is important because this justification language *is being used to describe a "work."* Let's see how Phineas was justified.

In Numbers 25, Israelite men were having sexual intercourse with Moabite and Midianite women. This enraged God, who inflicted a plague on them and ordered Moses to kill them. To defy Moses, one of the Israelite men took a Midianite woman into the tent of meeting, in front of Moses and the people. When Phineas saw this act of defiance, he took a spear, went into the tent, and killed them both (Num 25:7-8). This act propitiated God, who stopped the plague, made a covenant of peace with Phineas and his descendants, and "reckoned Phineas with righteousness."[412] Only Abraham and Phineas are described this way in Scripture. Of course, Phineas had strong faith in God and was zealous for God's honor. Based on this faith, God could accept Phineas' work of justice. But this passage is more evidence that the "credited with righteousness" language of Genesis 15:6 does not describe a justification by faith alone, and that works must be added to faith for justification to occur.

James says that Rahab was also justified "in the same way" as Abraham (James 2:25). While Protestants try to divide Abraham's justification between actual (see Gen 15:6) and declared (see Gen 22), they cannot do so with Rahab. Rahab's initial faith was demonstrated by her works. When Joshua sends spies out to the land of Jericho and they come to Rahab's house, she cooperates with God's plan by hiding and protecting them (see Josh 2:4). Only later does Rahab acknowledge that God has given the land to the Israelites (v.9). James says that Rahab was justified by her works (see James 2:25). Before this encounter, however, Rahab was a harlot. Thus, her justification came about immediately upon helping the spies. This means Rahab's justification described in James 2:25 was an actual justification, not a declared justification or a vindication of a prior justification. Because James says Rahab was justified "in the same manner" as Abraham, this means that Abraham's justification in Genesis 22 was also an actual (not declared) justification. James' example of Rahab once again speaks to the inseparability of faith and works to achieve salvific justification. Works are a *cause*, not just an effect, of our justification.

Does Jesus Require Good Works?

Jesus continually teaches that faithful disciples must perform good works to be forgiven of sins and grow in their relationship with God. Jesus' teaching of the all-important beatitudes goes beyond faith — being pure, merciful, and peacemakers are all good works.[413] Jesus confirms this by teaching, "Let your light shine before men, that they may see your *good works* and give glory to your Father who is in heaven" (Mt 5:16). Jesus is talking about good works when He:

- teaches us to give our striker the other cheek, give away our cloak, and go with someone for two miles instead of one (see Mt 5:39-42);
- teaches us to sell what we have and give it to the poor (see Mt 19:16-22); and,
- commands us to love our enemies and pray for those who persecute us.[414]

Jesus wants us to go beyond faith, because faith alone does not justify. This is why Jesus says "I tell you, on the day of judgment men will render account for every careless word they utter; for by your words you will be justified, and by your words you will be condemned" (Mt 12:36-37).

Matthew's Gospel records the story of the rich young man, who asks Jesus what he must do to gain eternal life. "Keep the commandments," Jesus replies, upholding the principles of the law. When the rich man claims to have done that, and asks what he still lacks, Jesus says, "If you would be perfect, go, sell what you possess and give to the poor, and you will have treasure in heaven; and come follow me" (Mt 19:16-22). The rich man had to add works to his faith to have eternal life; his faith alone was not sufficient. Jesus' teaching also highlights the fact that strict observance of the law will not justify the rich man, unless he observes the law in the system of grace. Jesus invites the rich man to have faith in Him, which will give him access to this grace. If the man would only have faith in Jesus, he would have treasure in heaven by his performance of works.

In the parable of the Pharisee and the tax collector, Jesus emphasizes that the Pharisee observed the letter of the law, but the tax collector observed the heart of the law (see Lk 18:9-14). Paul describes himself before his conversion like the Pharisee when he says he was blameless as to righteousness under the law (see Phil 3:6). While the Pharisee prayed, fasted, and tithed, he was full of self-righteous pride before God and contempt for his fellow man. The tax collector, on the other hand, beat his breast and said, "God, be merciful to me, a sinner" (Lk 18:13). The Pharisee was trying to justify himself before men in the system of law. The tax collector was seeking justification before God through faith in the system of grace. While the parable does not mention faith and works expressly, we know they were present in the tax collector because of his act of repentance (which is always accompanied by faith and works). Accordingly, about the tax collector, Jesus says, "I tell you, this man went down to his house justified rather than the other" (Lk 18:14).

Luke gives another example of how repentance justifies. When Jesus is dining at the home of a Pharisee, a sinful woman comes in and anoints Jesus' feet with oil, kissing them and weeping at His feet (see Lk 7:37-38). The Pharisee, a strict observer of the law, scoffs at this display of affection. Jesus, however, is pleased with her repentance, and forgives her many sins (see Lk 7:44-48). Although Jesus tells the woman, "...your faith has saved you," He explains that her works of love were the real basis for her forgiveness (see Lk 7:45-46). Jesus is teaching us that we need to act on our faith in order to be forgiven of sins and gain eternal life. This woman acted on her faith, and this is how she was saved by her faith.

Luke's account of the woman with the hemorrhage (see Lk 9:20-22) is another example of how we must add works to our faith to be healed. While Jesus was teaching, a woman who suffered with a hemorrhage of blood for twelve years approached Jesus. Convinced that she would be healed if she just touched Jesus, she came up behind Jesus and touched the fringe of His garment. Seeing her, Jesus said, "'Take heart, daughter, your faith has made you well.' And instantly the woman was made well" (Lk 9:22). Certainly, the woman had faith in Jesus *before* she touched His garment. But Jesus does not heal her until *after* she touches His garment. Again, Jesus is teaching us that we must act on our faith to be healed by Him.

When we pray the Lord's Prayer, asking God to forgive our sins, we ask for His forgiveness, not based on how much faith we have, but as we forgive those who trespass against us (see Mt 6:12). Forgiving others is a good work done in faith. Simply saying, "Lord, Lord" is not enough to gain life eternal.[415] We must add good works to our faith to be accepted by the Father. Jesus also says, "No one who does a mighty work in my name will be able soon after to speak evil of me" (Mk 9:39). Good works transform us because good works justify us. Jesus even says that His good works testify to who He is.[416] Our works will also testify to who we really are.

Therefore, believing in Jesus is not enough if we do not persevere in His Word.[417] Knowing the Scriptures is not enough if we do not have love in our hearts.[418] Believing in God is not enough if we deny Him by our deeds (see Titus 1:16). As we have seen in the teachings of Paul and James, Jesus tells us that the law of the New Covenant is love. Jesus says, "A new commandment I give to you, that you love one another; even as I have loved you, that you also love one another,"* and "If you love me, you will keep my commandments.'"*[419] John also continually tells us to keep Jesus' commandments of love.[420] Love is a work because it is an act of the will. Jesus tells us to demonstrate our love by bearing the fruit of good works (see Jn 15:5,8). Faith in Christ and works of love must act together.

The Church's theology of grace as taught by Scripture, which brings about justification through faith and works, underscores our filial relationship with God. We are not in a debtor/creditor relationship with God, for He owes us nothing. We do not obligate God to give us payment like an employee obligates his employer to pay wages. We are also not in a courtroom where we are defendants and God is our merciless judge. Instead, we are in a familial, covenant relationship with God, and He will reward us for being faithful. The sacred writers use this filial imagery throughout Scripture.[421] Thus, Paul teaches us that we are "sons of God" who have received the spirit of divine sonship and cry, "Abba! Father!" (Rom 8:14-15). Because we are children of God, we are also heirs of God and fellow heirs with Jesus Christ.[422]

Justification — Change or Declaration?

Many non-Catholic churches teach that when God declares a person justified, there is no real interior change in the justified person. In other words, God's declaration is not followed by the reality of what He actually declares. God instead "covers" the person in the righteousness of Christ (often called "imputing" Christ's righteousness to us). This is based on the notion that we are so depraved that even God cannot change our inner selves.

Like *sola Scriptura* and *sola fide*, this view of justification is also unbiblical, introduced to Christianity by the Protestant Reformers. The Catholic and scriptural view is that God is powerful enough to blot out our sins and renew our inner selves through the ongoing sacrifice of Jesus Christ. The righteousness of Christ's eternal sacrifice satisfies God's wrath, and God responds by restoring our relationship with Him in a system of grace. In so doing, He forgives our sins and infuses grace into our souls, so that we become His righteous sons and daughters.

We become righteous in Christ

We have already seen how God changes our interior lives through baptism. When God declares us righteous, *He actually makes us righteous*. The declaration is followed by the reality. As we have seen with the Eucharist, God does not declare something without making it happen. To say that God only declares us righteous even though we are not really righteous infringes upon God's integrity. It also denigrates the role of the Holy Spirit in our lives, who continues the work of Christ through the Church.

Proponents of "imputed righteousness" generally base their beliefs on Romans 1:17: "For in it the righteousness of God is revealed through faith for faith; as it is written, 'He who through faith is righteous shall live.'" Paul, however, does not say that God's righteousness is "imputed" to us. In fact, Paul says that we *are* righteous through faith. James also says, "Let every man be quick to hear, slow to speak, slow to anger, for the anger of man does not *produce* the righteousness of God" (James 1:19-20). This verse demonstrates that the "righteousness of God" is a quality that God wants men *to produce.*

In Paul's letter to the Corinthians, the apostle says, "For our sake he made him to be sin who knew no sin, so that in him we might become the righteousness of God" (2 Cor 5:21).[423] Protestants argue that this verse describes imputed righteousness, for we become righteous only by being "in him" (Christ). Since we are not really Christ, they conclude, God imputes Christ's righteousness to us.

However, the verse can also be interpreted to mean just the opposite, that being "in Christ" is to share the very righteousness that He possesses. This is how Paul can say we "*become* the righteousness of God." In the previous verse, Paul also says, "We beseech you on behalf of Christ, be reconciled to God" (v.20). If being imputed Christ's righteousness is a one-time event and is something we can never lose, then why is Paul begging the Corinthians to be reconciled to God? After all, this was the second letter Paul wrote to the Corinthians, so their faith in Christ was already well-established.

The Scriptures are clear that, through God's grace, we actually become righteous because God shares Christ's righteousness with us. For example, Jesus warns us not to practice our *own* righteousness before men (see Mt 6:1). He was referring to the Pharisees who appeared outwardly righteous to men, but inside they were filled with hypocrisy.[424] The Pharisees cleansed the outside of the cup, but inside they were full of wickedness.[425] Jesus tells us that we must have real, interior righteousness that exceeds the external righteousness of the Pharisees in order to enter the kingdom of heaven (see Mt 5:20). This is our *own* righteousness, not Christ's righteousness imputed to us (which would be impossible to receive). Zechariah and Elizabeth were righteous because the obeyed the commandments of God (see Lk 1:6). Jesus says that in heaven, "...the fine linen is the righteous deeds of the saints" (Rev 19:8). The saints do righteous deeds and are not just declared righteous. John also says, "He who does right *is righteous*, as he [God] is righteous" (1 Jn 3:7).

Paul also teaches about how God makes us righteous through faith. Paul says that "Abraham believed God, and it was reckoned to him as righteousness" (Rom 4:3). The word "reckoned," which is literally translated as "credited," (in Greek, *elogisthe*) means to make a book entry. God records what there actually is; He does not make a phony entry on the books. Paul says that we "*receive* the abundance of grace and the free gift of righteousness" in Christ (Rom 5:17). What we receive, we possess. "For as by one man's disobedience many were *made* sinners, so by one man's obedience many will be *made* righteous" (Rom 5:19). Because we are sinners in reality and not just appearance, we are also righteous in reality and not just appearance. The word "made" (in Greek, *katestathesan*) refers to a real, actual, ontological change in the person's soul. This requires an objective change in our nature, not just a relational change in our status.

Paul tells us to put off our old nature, and put on the new nature, created after the likeness of God in true righteousness and holiness.[426] This means we are a new creation in Christ, not the old creation covered up with Christ's righteousness. Paul says, "... for God is at work in you" (Phil 2:13). God is so powerful; He can transform us by working *within us*. Paul also says, "Do you not realize that Jesus Christ is in you?" (2 Cor 13:5). This indwelling of Christ in our souls brings about an internal transformation for those who cooperate with His grace. "Therefore, if any one is in Christ, he is a new creation; the old has passed away, behold, the new has come" (2 Cor 5:17). God loves us so much in Christ that He makes our righteousness a reality.

As we have alluded to, when we are justified, we, through God's grace, receive an infusion of faith, hope, and love into our souls. This is what makes us righteous. This first occurs at baptism. Paul explains this to the Romans:

> Therefore, since we are justified by *faith*, we have peace with God through our Lord Jesus Christ. Through him we have obtained access to this *grace* in which we stand, and we rejoice in our *hope* of sharing the glory of God... because God's *love* has been *poured* into our hearts through the Holy Spirit which has been given to us.[427]

This passage affirms the Catholic view that, through God's grace, faith, hope, and love are simultaneously infused into us upon justification. God continues to draw these virtues out of us in the system of grace throughout our lives.

The Old Testament also shows how God forgave sins and changed the interior of the lives of those who approached Him in faith. David cries out to God in the beautiful Psalm 51:

> *Wash* me thoroughly from my iniquity, and *cleanse* me from my sin!... Behold, thou desirest truth in the *inward being*; therefore teach me wisdom *in my secret heart*. *Purge* me with hyssop, and I shall be *clean*; *wash* me, and I shall be whiter than snow.... Hide thy face from my sins, and *blot* out all my iniquities. Create in me a *clean heart*, O God, and put a *new and right spirit within me*.[428]

God reveals through the psalm that He washes, cleanses, purges, blots, and creates a new heart and spirit in those who approach Him in faith. There is nothing about God declaring us clean or covering us in righteousness in a legal or forensic sense. God doesn't just cover up our sins; He removes them by the power of the Holy Spirit, as we read in the words of these prophets:

- "Though your sins are like scarlet, they shall be as white as snow; though they are red like crimson, they shall become like wool" (Is 1:18).
- "I, I am He who blots out your transgressions for my own sake, and I will not remember your sins" (Is 43:25).

- "I have swept away your transgressions like a cloud, and your sins like mist; return to me, for I have redeemed you" (Is 44:22).
- "A new heart I will give you, and a new spirit I will put within you; and I will take out of your flesh the heart of stone and give you a heart of flesh. And I will put my spirit within you, and cause you to walk in my statutes and be careful to observe my ordinances."[429]

Over and over, God teaches us that He will actually change our hearts and put His Spirit within us. If God is giving us a new heart (interior life) and putting His Spirit within us (interior life), He is bringing about a change in our interior life. This shows how much our Father loves us and wants us to be like His Son.

This reminds me of one of my favorite passages in the Old Testament, when God reveals to Moses, "And the LORD your God will *circumcise* your heart and the heart of your offspring, so that you will love the LORD your God with all your heart and with all your soul, that you may live" (Deut 30:6). What strong language! God could have chosen a lesser verb, but He chose "circumcise" to describe what He does to our hearts. Christ, the Divine Physician, performs a spiritual open-heart surgery on us. This shows the radical love God has for us, and the radical change we must undergo to love Him in return. God doesn't just cover us up and declare us good. He changes our hearts so that we become good.

In the New Testament, Peter tells the infant Church, "Repent therefore, and turn again, that your sins may be blotted out, that times of refreshing may come from the presence of the Lord" (Acts 3:19). The word "blotted" (in Greek, *exalipho*) means to wipe away or remove sin, and not cover up sin. Ananias tells Paul, "Rise and be baptized, and wash away your sins, calling on his name."[430] Again, the phrase "wash away" (in Greek, *apolouo*) means to remove sin, not cover it up. John also says Jesus "cleanses" us from all sin.[431] The word "cleanse" (in Greek, *katharizo*) refers to an actual infused cleansing, not an imputed covering. God cleanses us by changing our interior lives (primarily through the sacraments).

Paul says we must "cleanse ourselves from every defilement of body and spirit, and make holiness perfect in the fear of God" (2 Cor

7:1). Holiness deals with "being" because its source is God, who is perfect being. Holiness does not deal with what appears to be. The author of Hebrews says, "Strive for peace with all men, and for the holiness without which no one will see the Lord" (Heb 12:14). We can only grow in the holiness of Christ through prayer, service and self-sacrifice, which are all works of faith and come from the interior life of the person. Without holiness, we will not see God.

When Jesus blesses the poor in spirit, the meek, and the pure of heart, He is speaking about the interior life of the person.[432] When Jesus says those who hunger for righteousness are "filled," they are changed interiorly, not covered.[433] When Jesus teaches that just looking at a woman lustfully is adultery, He is talking about changing our interior lives (see Mt 5:28). Jesus teaches that the interior disposition is what defiles a person.[434] Because the interior of a person is what defiles, God changes the interior. He doesn't just cover up the exterior. This is why, when Jesus affected a physical cure (exterior), He also forgave sins (interior).[435] Jesus is the Lamb of God who "takes away" the sins of the world (Jn 1:29). Jesus does not just cover up the sins of the world.

Can human actions have any "merit" with God?

Non-Catholics generally do not like to talk about "merit" before God. But as we have seen throughout this book, God invites us to participate in His own divine work through our faith *and actions*. This means that God views our actions, when done with faith in Christ, as worthy of merit in His eyes.

In Catholic theology, we speak about "strict" merit versus "condign" or "congruent" merit. Strict merit means that God pays us for our works based on contractual obligation (system of law). As we have learned, we have no strict merit in the eyes of God. With condign merit, God rewards us based on non-contractual gratuity (system of grace). God rewards us, not because He is obligated to do so, but because it is His very nature to do so. Just as we are free to act, so God is free to respond. If we have faith in God, He will be faithful to us.

Thus, Paul teaches the Philippians, "I seek the fruit which increases to your credit" (Phil 4:17). These "credits," which are merits, bring forth more graces from God, increasing our justification as we are so disposed. Jesus also continually teaches about the need to bear good fruit.[436] These fruits, which are good works, increase our justification before God. In the system of grace, both fruits and merits are God's gifts to us.

Justification — Ongoing Process or One-Time Event?

As we have already mentioned, many Protestant churches believe that justification is a one-time event, which occurs when person accepts Jesus as his or her personal Lord and Savior. Once the person is justified, they argue, Christ's righteousness is imputed to them and they can never lose their justification. But if justification is a one-time event that occurs when we accept Jesus as personal Lord and Savior, then why does Christ continue to intercede for us in heaven as High Priest? As we have seen, Scripture describes Jesus as our intercessor before God for the purpose of *saving us*.[437] But if we already have salvific justification, isn't Christ's intercession superfluous?

Non-Catholic Christians have difficulty with this question. They generally say that Christ intercedes for us to maintain God's promise that He will not deal with us in the way He would have before Christ. This response, however, begs the question. If Christ's sacrifice is sufficient to make us justified once-for-all, why isn't God's promise secure? Why would the Father still require Christ's intercession? The Catholic and scriptural answer to this is simple: We are *not* justified "once-for-all." Scripture teaches that justification is an ongoing process that starts with baptism and continues until the moment we die.

Scripture also teaches that justification can be increased, decreased or even lost. For example, Paul says, "Though our outer nature is wasting away, our inner nature is being renewed every day" (2 Cor 4:16). This shows that not only is our interior life being changed by Christ but the change is ongoing. It continues every day. Paul says that we "are being changed into his likeness from one degree of glory to another; for this comes from the Lord who is the Spirit"

(2 Corinthians 3:18). Again, our inner nature is being changed in degrees throughout life. It does not happen all at once.

Is it possible to lose God's gift of justification?

The Scriptures give many examples that teach justification as an on-going process, and that we can even lose our justification. We have already seen this with Abraham. Abraham is justified when God sends him out from his home town, and promises to bless him, make his name great, and by him bless all the families of the earth (see Gen 12:1-4). The author of Hebrews confirms that Abraham's justification occurs at this point (see Heb 11:8-10). Paul also confirms Abraham's justification in Genesis 12 in his letter to the Galatians. Paul says that God would "justify the Gentiles by faith" (Gal 3:8), and records that God said to Abraham, "In you shall all the nations be blessed" (v.8).[438]

Abraham is also justified when he is blessed by the priest-king Melchizedek,[439] and further justified when God promises him that his descendants will be as numerous as the stars (see Gen 15:5). "And he believed the Lord; and he reckoned it to him as righteousness" (v.6).[440] While it is true that Abraham was justified in Genesis 15:6, he was also justified twenty-five years earlier in Genesis 12:1-4, as Hebrews 11:8-10 and Galatians 3:8-9 prove. Moreover, Abraham is further justified in Genesis 22:1-18 when he offers his son Isaac as a sacrifice to God. Since Genesis 22 says Abraham was "blessed," and Paul's letter to the Galatians shows that "blessed" means "justified," this means that Abraham was justified in Genesis 22, just as he was in Genesis 12 and 15. James confirms this when he attributes the "reckoned to him as righteousness" language to Abraham's offering of Isaac in Genesis 22 (see James 2:23). These verses prove that justification is an ongoing process and can increase as we persevere in faith and works.

In 1 Samuel 13:14, God describes David as "a man after his own heart; and the Lord has appointed him to be prince over his people." David is also justified in 1 Samuel 16:13, where it says, "the Spirit of the LORD came mightily upon David from that day forward"; in 1 Samuel 17:37-54, when God delivers David from the hand of Goliath the Philistine; and again in 2 Samuel 6:9,14, as

David expresses fear of the Lord in the presence of His Ark, and dances before the Ark of the Lord with all his might.

However, after David's ongoing justification before God, David loses his justification by committing adultery with Bathsheba and slaying Uriah the Hittite.[441] Afterward, David repents of his sins and is justified again by God, prompting him to write the beautiful Psalm 32 and Psalm 51 about God's mercy and forgiveness.[442] Of himself, he writes, "Blessed is he whose transgression is forgiven, whose sin is covered up."[443] David was justified, lost his justification, and is justified again by God.

To support their "once-for-all" theory of justification, some argue that David was justified for the first time when he wrote Psalm 32. But this would be absurd, since David, before his sins of murder and adultery, is described as "a man after God's own heart." If Psalm 32 recorded David's first and only justification, then he would have written the earlier psalms under divine inspiration as a pagan, with no personal relationship with God. Moreover, such a position would maintain that David never confessed his sins to God before Psalm 32. But Psalm 25:7 and Psalm 25:18 prove them wrong.

Simon is also justified in Matthew 16:18-19 when Jesus blesses him for receiving and professing a revelation from God. Jesus then changes Simon's name to Peter, and gives him the keys to the kingdom of heaven. In Luke 22:31-32, Jesus also prays for Peter that his faith may not fail and charges him to strengthen the rest of the apostles. In these and many other examples, Peter is justified before God.

We all know that Peter later denied that he even knew our Lord and lost his justification.[444] But Peter is justified again before God as he negates his three-fold denial of Jesus with a three-fold confirmation of his love for Jesus, who then charges Peter to feed the Lord's sheep.[445] Like David, Peter was justified, lost his justification, and is justified again through repentance and love. David, Peter, and all of us are like the Prodigal Son in Luke 15:3-32, who is "restored to life" through repentance and sorrow.[446]

Also, don't forget Paul. Most Protestants would say that Paul was instantly justified the moment he encountered Christ on the road to Damascus.[447] Paul obeys Jesus' command to enter the city and is moved by the Holy Spirit.[448] As we have seen, however, Ananias commands Paul to stand up and be baptized to wash away his sins.[449] Why? Because justification is not a one-time event. It is ongoing, from the moment of baptism until the moment we die. This is the teaching of Sacred Scripture and the Holy Catholic Church.

Chapter Seven

Salvation

"Are you saved?"

Many of us have been asked this question by good, God-fearing "Bible Christians" who know they are going to heaven and want to take us with them. Having professed their belief in Jesus Christ, they believe they are "once saved, always saved." This means that they can never lose the salvation they have found in Christ.

Heaven, of course, is where we all should want to be; it is the destiny for which God created us. We were meant to share in the very life Jesus has with the Father from all eternity. Salvation is thus "divine sonship" in Christ.

The Catholic response to the question "Are you saved?" should be, "I am redeemed by the blood of Jesus, and, as Paul says, I am 'working out my salvation in fear and trembling'" (see Phil 2:12).

Salvation is different from redemption. Christ has secured our redemption by His death and Resurrection (see Heb 9:12). By the merits of Jesus Christ, the doors of salvation are now open to us. But we decide, by our faith and works, whether to apply the merits of Christ to our own lives. We decide whether or not we will accept the salvation Jesus has won for us.

Therefore, salvation, like justification, is a lifelong process that, through perseverance, will be actualized in eternity. This happens when God, the Supreme Judge, makes His ultimate evaluation of an individual's life after death.[450] If that individual was faithful to God during his lifetime, he will receive his *final* justification and live with God forever in heaven. If he lost the grace that God infused into his soul when he was justified during his lifetime, and failed to repent of his sins, he will be eternally condemned. Therefore, salvation is not a one-time event. The Scriptures clearly teach that we can lose our salvation if we do not persevere in faith and works to the end of our lives. This, of course, contradicts the non-Catholic and unbiblical belief "once saved, always saved."

Salvation Is a Lifelong Process, Not a One-Time Event

Paul speaks of salvation as a past event:

- "For in this hope we were saved" (Rom 8:24).
- "...by grace you have been saved" (Eph 2:5)
- "For by grace you have been saved through faith" (Eph 2:8).
- The power of God "who saved us" (2 Tim 1:9).
- "He saved us...by the washing of regeneration and renewal in the Holy Spirit" (Titus 3:5).

However, Paul also speaks of salvation as an ongoing process, or a present event:

- "...but to us who are being saved it is the power of God" (1 Cor 1:18).
- "For we are the aroma of Christ to God among those who are being saved" (2 Cor 2:15).
- "...work out your own salvation with fear and trembling; for God is at work in you" (Phil 2:12-13).
- Peter also says, "As the outcome of your faith you obtain the salvation of your souls" (1 Pet 1:9).

Finally, the Scriptures also teach that salvation is a future event:

- Jesus says "But he who endures to the end will be saved."[451]
- Jesus also says, "He who believes and is baptized will be saved" (Mk 16:16).
- At the council of Jerusalem, Peter says "But we believe that we shall be saved through the grace of the Lord Jesus, just as they will" (Acts 15:11).
- Paul says, "Since, therefore, we are now justified by his blood, much more shall we be saved by him from the wrath of God. For if while we were enemies we were reconciled to God by

the death of His Son, much more, now that we are reconciled, shall we be saved by his life" (Rom 5:9-10).

- In his letter to the Corinthians, Paul says, "If any man's work is burned up, he will suffer loss, though he himself will be saved" (1 Cor 3:15).
- Exercising his binding authority, Paul says, "You are to deliver this man to Satan for the destruction of the flesh, that his spirit may be saved in the day of the Lord Jesus (1 Cor 5:5).
- In the sacrament of the sick, James says, "...the prayer of faith will save the sick man" (James 5:15).

The Scriptures also teach that we participate in saving others:

- Paul says, "I magnify my ministry in order to make my fellow Jews jealous, and thus save some of them" (Rom 11:13-14).
- To the Corinthians, he says, "I have become all things to all men, that I might by all means save some" (1 Cor 9:22).
- Paul says to Timothy, "Take heed to yourself and to your teaching: hold to that, for by so doing you will save both yourself and your hearers" (1 Tim 4:16).
- Paul also says a wife can save her husband (and a husband his wife) through the graces of the sacrament of marriage (see 1 Cor 7:16).
- Paul further says that a woman can be saved through bearing children if she continues in faith and love and holiness (see 1 Tim 2:15).
- James says, "Let him know that whoever brings back a sinner from the error of his way will save his soul from death and will cover a multitude of sins" (James 5:20).
- Jude also says, "And convince some, who doubt; save some, by snatching them out of the fire" (Jude 22-23).

We participate in Christ's work of salvation because we are priests in our High Priest by virtue of our baptism.

Scripture also teaches that God holds our future justification in abeyance until the final judgment. Jesus says, "...for by your words you will be justified, and by your words you will be condemned" (Mt 12:37). Paul also says, "But the doers of the law who will be justified"

(Rom 2:13). Paul's statement is in the context of our final judgment, when God "will render to every man according to his works" (Rom 2:6).

If salvation is a past, present, and future event, this means salvation is a process and not a one-time event. This also means we cannot be "once saved, always saved."

We Are Saved by Works, Not by Faith Alone

As with justification, good works done with faith in the grace of Christ are a cause of our salvation. Scripture never says that good works flow from those who are saved. Scripture also never teaches that good works distinguish those who are eternally saved from those who are not saved. Nevertheless, Protestants generally say that one only has to "believe" in Jesus to be saved. They so conclude based on certain passages in Scripture:

- "For God so loved the world that he gave his only Son, that whoever believes in him should not perish but have eternal life" (Jn 3:16).[452]
- "Truly, truly, I say to you, he who hears my word and believes him who sent me, has eternal life" (Jn 5:24).
- John says, "I write this to you who believe in the name of the Son of God, that you may know that you have eternal life" (1 Jn 5:13).
- Paul says, "It will be reckoned to us who believe in him that raised from the dead Jesus our Lord" (Rom 4:24).
- Paul also says, "...if you confess with your lips that Jesus is Lord and believe in your heart that God raised him from the dead, you will be saved" (Rom 10:9-10).

However, those who use these verses to prove "salvation by faith alone," fail to acknowledge that the word "believes" in these verses (from the Greek, *pisteo*) is a word that also includes "obedience." As we have seen in the chapter on justification, obedience is separate from faith, and something that must be added to faith in order to achieve salvific justification. Therefore, when these verses say that we have to "believe" in Jesus, they are not referring to accepting Jesus as

Lord and Savior by "faith alone." Here are a few scriptural examples, to support this:

- 1 Peter 2:7-8 uses the same words *pisteo* (to obey) and *apeitheo* (to disobey): "He who believes in him will not be put to shame. To you therefore who *believe*, he is precious, but for those who do not *believe*, 'The very stone which the builders rejected has become the head of the corner,' and 'A stone that will make men stumble, a rock that will make them fall'; for they stumble because they *disobey* the word as they were destined to do."
- John 3:36. "He who *believes* in the Son has eternal life; he who *does not obey* the Son shall not see life, but the wrath of God rests upon him."
- Hebrews 5:9. "He became the source of eternal salvation to all who *obey him*."

Believing in Jesus means obeying Jesus, and obeying Jesus means doing the good works He commands us to do. Belief includes works of obedience, and not faith alone. If our belief in Jesus is expressed in obedience to Him by doing His works of love, we will inherit eternal life.

The Old Testament teaches that God judges our eternal destiny based on the deeds we have done during our lives, whether good or bad:

- "According to their deeds, so will he repay, wrath to his adversaries, requital to his enemies" (Ps 59:18).
- God tells Jeremiah, "I will recompense them according to their deeds and the work of their hands."[453]
- God tells Ezekiel, "As for me, my eye will not spare, nor will I have pity, but I will requite their deeds upon their heads."[454]
- God tells Hosea "I will punish them for their ways, and requite them for their deeds."[455]
- Sirach also says, "He judges a man according to his deeds . . . every one will receive in accordance with his deeds."[456]

If salvation were based on faith alone, God would not judge our deeds to determine that salvation.

To maintain their "faith alone" theology, Protestants argue that God's judgment of our works is limited to determining our level of rewards. In other words, salvation is determined by faith, and rewards are determined by works. However, Jesus is clear that our salvation depends upon the works we perform during our lives. The works do not just determine the level of rewards we will receive in heaven; they determine *whether or not we will go to heaven*.

In the parable of the ten maidens, the five maidens who prepared for the bridegroom during their lives were allowed to enter the marriage feast of heaven when the bridegroom came (see Mt 25:1-10). The five maidens who did not do good works of preparation during their lives were not permitted to enter the heavenly feast. Because the door was shut and they could not enter, these maidens were denied not only rewards but also salvation (see vv.10-12).

In the parable of the servants and talents, the servants who increased their talents with good works were rewarded with eternal life (see Mt 25:14-30). The servant who buried his talent in the ground was declared "wicked and slothful," and was cast into eternal darkness where men weep and gnash their teeth.[457]

At the end of the world, Jesus says that He will come in glory with His angels and separate the sheep from the goats based upon what *we have done*, not how much faith we had in Him (see Mt 25:31-46). "Truly, I say to you, as you did it to one of the least of these my brethren, you did it to me."[458] Then Jesus says, based upon the works they have done, "And they will go away into eternal punishment, but the righteous into eternal life."[459] Jesus also says, "For the Son of man is to come with his angels in the glory of his Father, and then he will repay every man for what he has done" (Mt 16:27). Jesus explicitly teaches that God will judge the works of an individual *to determine his eternal destiny*.

After Jesus says "he who believes in me has eternal life" (Jn 5:25), He again describes the final judgment and says,

> Do not marvel at this; for the hour is coming when all who are in the tombs will hear his voice and come forth, those who have done good, to the resurrection of life, and those who have done evil to the resurrection of judgment (Jn 5:28-29).

Jesus tells us that He is judging our works from heaven, to determine our final destiny. "And all the churches shall know that I am he who searches mind and heart, and I will give to each of you *as your works deserve.*"[460] Jesus tells the church at Ephesus that they were doing good works but then abandoned the love they had at first. "Remember then from what you have fallen, repent and do the works you did at first. If not, I will come to you and *remove* your lamp stand from its place, unless you repent" (Rev 2:5). As this verse clearly reveals, Jesus is teaching that our repentance and good works determine whether or not we will *keep* our place in heaven.

God's angel affirms this: "Blessed indeed...that they may rest from their labors, for their deeds follow them!" (Rev 14:13). The Apostle John also sees that "...the dead were judged by what was written in the books, by what they had done" (Rev 20:12). Jesus completes His written revelation by saying, "Behold, I am coming soon, bringing my recompense, to repay every one for what he has done" (Rev 22:12). Our works, whether good or evil, determine our eternal destiny.

How was the "good thief" saved?

If works are necessary to attain heaven, on what basis did Jesus give salvation to the good thief on the cross, who did not even receive a water baptism (see Lk 23:43)? We have already discussed that salvation can be achieved by a baptism of blood or desire. However, it is also incorrect to say the good thief did not do any good works. In Luke 23:40-42, we see that the good thief:

- rebuked the bad thief who reviled Jesus (see Lk 23:40);
- feared the judgment of God and repented over his sins (see Lk 23:40-41); and,
- professed his faith in Jesus and expressed to Jesus his desire to be with Him in heaven (see Lk 23:42).

Thus, the good thief showed sorrow and repentance for his sins, and desired salvation. In other words, the good thief persevered in both faith and works to his death, and Jesus rewarded him with eternal life (see Lk 23:43).

"Be faithful to the end..."

This teaches us that we too must persevere in faith and works to the *end* of our lives in order to be saved. Jesus often says, "He who endures *to the end* will be saved."[461] If salvation occurred when we accepted Jesus as Savior, there would be no need to endure to the end to be saved. We would already be saved. However, Jesus tells the church at Smyrna, "Be faithful unto death, and I will give you the crown of life" (Rev 2:10). Jesus also says, "He who conquers and who keeps my works *until the end*, I will give him power over the nations" (Rev 2:26). If "once saved, always saved" were true, perseverance to the end would not be necessary.

Paul echoes Jesus' teaching about the final judgment throughout his epistles:

- Paul tells the Romans, "But by your hard and impenitent heart you are storing up wrath for yourself on the day of wrath when God's righteous judgment will be revealed. For he will render to every man according to his works; to those who by patience in well-doing seek for glory and honor and immortality, he will give eternal life; but for those who are factious and do not obey the truth, but obey wickedness, there will be wrath and fury" (Rom 2:5-8).
- Again, he says to them, "For we shall all stand before the judgment seat of God... So each of us shall give account of himself to God" (Rom 14:10,12).
- To the Corinthians, Paul preaches, "For we must all appear before the judgment seat of Christ, so that each one may receive good or evil, according to what he has done in the body" (2 Corinthians 5:10).

In these passages, there is a definite polarity between good deeds (which lead to eternal life), and bad deeds (which lead to eternal death, not less rewards). Thus, like Jesus, Paul teaches that our works (not just faith) determine our heaven or hell (not just rewards): "Their end will correspond to their deeds."[462]

Romans 2:5-8 is particularly troubling to non-Catholic Christians who claim to be saved by faith alone. Despite his teaching the Romans that no one can be saved by works of law, Paul unmistakably teaches that salvation (and not just rewards) depends on the works each person does. This, once again, underscores Paul's distinction between the system of law and the system of grace. Good works in the system of grace lead to eternal life, and bad works lead to "wrath and fury," which is eternal death.

To skirt the problems posed by Romans 2:5-8, non-Catholic Christians will often argue that Paul is just posing a hypothetical scenario of salvation (even though nothing in these passages suggests Paul is speaking hypothetically). They base their argument on Paul's teaching that we are not justified by works of law in Romans 3:28. This, of course, demonstrates the error of their premise; they do not understand the law-versus-grace paradigm. According to the *sola fide* argument, Paul is saying that if a man could do works to inherit eternal life, God would allow it. But, because Paul says we are not justified by works of law, Paul is actually teaching that we are *not* saved by works (even though Paul expressly says that we are).

As we now know, Paul is talking about works performed in the system of grace. In fact, in the verses preceding Romans 2:6-8, Paul says, "Or do you presume upon the riches of his kindness and forbearance and patience? Do you not know that God's kindness is meant to lead you to repentance?" (Rom 2:4). Kindness, forbearance and patience are qualities that God provides us *only* in the system of grace. Further, repentance occurs *only* in a system of grace. Therefore, Paul is talking about God judging our works in the system of grace. If we refuse to repent, God will judge our works according to the system of law, and we will be condemned (see Rom 2:5).

Our works judged "through fire" will determine our final end

In his letter to the Corinthians, Paul teaches that a man is saved (not just rewarded) "through fire" by a judgment of his works:

> Now if any one builds on the foundation with gold, silver, precious stones, wood, hay, stubble - each man's work will become manifest; for the Day will disclose it, because it will be revealed with fire, and the fire will test what sort of work each one has done. If the work which any man has built on the foundation survives, he will receive a reward. If any

man's work is burned up, he will suffer loss, though he himself will be saved, but only as through fire. Do you not know
that you are God's temple and that God's Spirit dwells in
you? If any one destroys God's temple, God will destroy
him (1 Cor 3:12-17)

The plain language of 1 Corinthians 3:12-17, properly understood, is devastating to the position that God's judgment is limited
to rewards, and not salvation proper.[463] At first glance, this may not
be readily apparent — after all, the man whose work is burned up
"will be saved, but only as through fire." What does this mean?

Using a string of metaphors, Paul demonstrates that God is judging our works to determine our salvation or damnation. Paul says that
we are God's building* and God's temple,* then explains that we build
up ourselves (the temple) in Christ with either good materials (gold,
silver, precious stones) or bad materials (wood, hay, stubble).* [464] In
1 Corinthians 3:14-17, Paul teaches that, at the last judgment, God
will test our works with His refining fire and will reveal three types
of people:

- Those who built with only good materials will receive a
  reward (v.14);
- Those who built with both good and bad materials will have
  to pass through fire, along with their works; the bad works
  will be burned up, but they will still be saved (v.15); and,
- Those who built with only bad materials will have destroyed
  God's temple, and God will destroy them (v.17).

Paul's teaching here contradicts the major premise of "faith
alone" theology — that works do not serve as a basis for determining salvation. Whether one builds with good or bad materials (a
metaphor for their conduct in life) determines both their final destiny *and* the manner in which they receive it. In other words, their
salvation *is affected by their works.*

If a man has done both good and bad works, his bad works are
burned up by fire. After his works are burned up, he must also pass
through the same fire.[465] This means that his bad works caused a *delay*
in his salvation. Paul underscores this by telling us that, in spite of this

fiery trial, the person is "*still* saved." This attaining salvation by degrees (as opposed to level of rewards) is antithetical to the doctrine of salvation by faith alone.

What about the person who has built his temple with only bad materials? Paul says that God will destroy him (1 Cor 3:17). This means that the person will be condemned. We thus see a continuum in Paul's metaphor: the person who did good works in his life was rewarded with salvation; the person who did both good and bad works suffered a delay, but ultimately received salvation; and, the person who did only bad works lost his salvation.

Because the man who built with both good and bad materials "suffered loss" for his bad works, he destroyed his temple *to some degree*. But the mixture of his good and bad works only retarded, and not prevented, his salvation. However, the man who built with only bad materials destroyed his temple *completely*, and he lost his salvation. Because the man who built with both good and bad materials "suffered loss," this opened up the possibility for this final scenario of ultimate loss — the total, eternal destruction of a person who built with only bad materials (that is, lived an evil life). Based on Paul's teaching, we can only conclude that our salvation is determined on the basis of faith and works, and not faith alone.

Those with a reward-only view of the final judgment, must conclude that God's judgment of a saved person's bad works is not a judgment of sin, for that person was already forgiven of sins by his faith alone acceptance of Jesus Christ as Savior. The problem with this position is that *Scripture never makes a distinction between bad works and sins*. It simply isn't there.

It's a real dilemma for non-Catholic Christians: If God judges and punishes a saved person's sins, then faith alone didn't save the person. (His sins would have already been washed away.)

This also proves that there is a state of forgiveness *after* death, which the Church calls "purgatory" (more on this in the next chapter).

In light of Paul's teaching, proponents of "faith alone" salvation will attempt to distinguish between a saved person's bad works from sins, calling them "bad motives." This is problematic for two reasons:

- It imposes an arbitrary dichotomy upon how God judges people — for the saved, He judges motives (interior); for the unsaved, He judges sinful acts (exterior).
- Scripture never says that bad motives are not sins. To the contrary, Scripture says that *bad motives can be among the worst kind of sins*. For example, James says, "Whoever knows what is right to do and fails to do it, for him it is sin" (James 4:17). James is teaching that the person who does not act on his faith when he knows he should *commits sin in his motives*. James also says, "Then desire when it has conceived gives birth to sin; and sin when it is full-grown brings forth death" (James 1:15). In other words, as soon as the person decides to act on his desire, he has committed sin in his motives, even before acting.

When Paul says that each of us will have to give an account of himself before the judgment seat of Christ,* he repeatedly focuses on the sinful, interior motive of passing judgment on others.*[466] Jesus also says we commit the mortal sin of adultery in our motives by looking lustfully at a woman (see Mt 5:28). Thus, Scripture teaches that our bad motives (interior) are sinful, even if we do not act out on them (exterior). As Paul reveals, God will judge our bad works (whether motives or actions) through fire, and these works will determine whether we are saved or condemned.

Blessed Assurance — or Blessed Hope?

The Church and the Scriptures repeatedly teach that we hope for salvation, but are not absolutely guaranteed salvation. Our hope in salvation is guaranteed if we are faithful to Christ to the end of our lives. If we persevere to the end, we have a moral certitude that we will be saved. However, if we reject God's grace by failing to persevere in faith and works, we can forfeit the salvation that God died to give us. Thus, by our own choosing (not God's doing), salvation is not a certainty.

The Scriptures are full of examples where the sacred writers call Jesus and the salvation He gives us our "hope":

- In his letter to the Romans, Paul says, "We rejoice in our hope of sharing the glory of God" (5:2).
- "Rejoice in your hope, be patient in tribulation, be constant in prayer" (Rom 12:12).
- To the Corinthians, Paul says, "Since we have such a hope, we are very bold" (2 Cor 3:12).
- To the Ephesians, Paul says, "...that you may know what is the hope to which he has called you" (1:18) and "...you were called to the one hope that belongs to your call" (4:4).
- To the Colossians, Paul refers to "the hope laid up for you in heaven" (1:5) and calls Jesus Christ "the hope of glory" (1:27).
- Paul asks the Thessalonians, "For what is our hope or joy or crown of boasting before our Lord Jesus at his coming?"* He tells them to "helmet the hope of salvation."* Paul also tells them that God has given us "eternal comfort and good hope through grace."*[467]
- In his first letter to Timothy, Paul calls Jesus "our hope" (1:1), and says, "We toil and strive, because we have our hope set on the living God" (4:10).
- Paul tells Titus that he is "in hope of eternal life" and that we are "awaiting our blessed hope, the appearance of the glory of our great God and Savior, Jesus Christ" (2:13). Paul also says we have become "heirs in hope of eternal life" (3:7).
- In the book of Hebrews, Jesus is called "a better hope" (Heb 7:19). "We are his house if we hold fast our confidence and pride in our hope" (Heb 3:6). He desires that we "show the same earnestness in realizing the full assurance of hope until the end" (Heb 6:11), and "seize the hope set before us" (Heb 6:18). We are instructed to "hold fast the confession of our hope without wavering, for he who promised is faithful" (Heb 10:23).
- According to the Apostle John, "...every one who thus hopes in him purifies himself as he is pure" (1 Jn 3:3).

Faith by its very nature is based in hope, according to the author of Hebrews, who explains that "faith is the assurance of things hoped for, the conviction of things not seen" (Heb 11:1). We have assurance in salvation if we hold fast without wavering, but salvation still remains a hope until it is realized. Thus, "Let us run with perseverance the race that is set before us,"* and "...see to it that no one fails to obtain the grace of God."*[468]

In his first epistle, Peter declares, "We have been born anew to a living hope through the resurrection of Jesus Christ from the dead" (1 Pet 1:3), and that we are to "set... hope fully upon the grace that is coming to you at the revelation of Jesus Christ" (1 Pet 1:13). Peter also refers to our hope as he gives us the mandate for apologetics: "Always be prepared to make a defense to any one who calls you to account for the hope that is in you" (1 Pet 3:15).

One has to ask, *"Why all this talk about "hope," if salvation were absolutely assured?"* The sacred writers clearly teach us that salvation is an uncertainty because we could choose to reject it. Paul says: "... that I may know him and the power of his resurrection, and may share his sufferings, becoming like him in his death, that if possible I may attain the resurrection from the dead. *Not that I have already obtained this or am already perfect;* but I press on to make it my own" (Phil 3:11-12).

Paul himself did not view his resurrection with Christ as a certainty. Paul also says, "I am not aware of anything against myself, but I am not thereby acquitted" (1 Cor 4:4). Paul is not presumptuous about his salvation. Paul tells the Romans, "For salvation is nearer to us now than when we first believed" (Rom 13:11). If we already have salvation, how can we only be nearer to it? Peter says, "Like newborn babes, long for the pure spiritual milk, that by it you may grow up to salvation" (1 Pet 2:2). How can we grow up to something we already possess?

Can We Lose Our Salvation?

The Scriptures teach that salvation is not a certainty. This means we can lose our salvation. We can be in God's grace and on our way to heaven, and then, by our free choice, turn away from God and lose heaven. The possibility of losing our salvation is one of the most prominent and pervasive teachings of Jesus and the apostles in Scripture.

- Jesus predicted that some people will receive His Word with joy and believe in Him for a period of time. But when temptation comes, these people who believe in Jesus can also choose to fall away from Him (see Lk 8:13).
- Jesus taught that we can start out as faithful and wise stewards, then fall away and be assigned to a place with the unfaithful (see Lk 12:42-46).
- Jesus also said that those who hear His words, but don't keep them, He will condemn on the last day (see Jn 12:47-48).
- As we have seen in the book of Revelation (see Rev 2:2-5), Jesus tells the Ephesians that they abandoned the love they had at first and have fallen away (v.2-4). Jesus then tells them to repent or they will lose their salvation (v.5).
- Jesus says, "He who conquers, shall be clad thus in white garments, and I will not blot his name out of the book of life" (Rev 3:5). This means that Jesus *can* blot our names out of the book of life.
- Jesus says that some people in Sardis "received the white garment" (a reference to salvation, as demonstrated in Revelation 3:5) but soiled it with sin (see Rev 3:4). These people were "saved," until they sinned.
- Jesus also warns us to "hold fast what you have, so that no one may seize your crown" (Rev 3:11). Jesus is telling us we already have the crown of salvation, but can lose it. If we do not persevere, God will take away our share in the tree of life and the holy city (see Rev 22:19).

As we have already said, the Scriptures never teach that those who believed in Christ had a false faith or were false Christians. Those who believed (faith) and did good (works) were saved, but did not persevere in their faith and works to the end.

"Abide in me..."

Many Protestants contend that those who are in Christ bear good fruit because, as Jesus says, "A sound tree cannot bear evil fruit" (Mt 7:18). In other words, those in Christ cannot fall away. However, in this passage Jesus is not referring to Himself as the good tree (He is talking about both good and bad trees in the context of imperfect human beings). This means there is no guarantee that a sound tree will stay sound. It might rot.

When Jesus refers to Himself as the vine and us as the branches, Jesus says we must *abide* in Him, which means persevere: "Abide in me, and I in you. As the branch cannot bear fruit by itself, unless it abides in the vine, neither can you, unless you abide in me" (Jn 15:4). If we do not abide in Him, Jesus says, we wither, are gathered, thrown into the fire and burned (v.6).

Paul teaches that we can forfeit our salvation

Paul also teaches very clearly that those who are genuinely saved during their lives can lose their salvation if they fail to persevere. In his letter to the Romans, Paul says:

> They were broken off because of their unbelief, but you stand fast only through faith. So do not become proud, but stand in awe. For if God did not spare the natural branches, neither will he spare you. Note then the kindness and the severity of God: severity toward those who have fallen, but God's kindness to you, provided you continue in his kindness; otherwise you too will be cut off. And even the others, if they do not persist in their unbelief, will be grafted in, for God has the power to graft them in again (Rom 11:20-23).

In expounding on Jesus' teaching in John 15, Paul says that the Jews (the natural branches) were broken off by lack of faith,* but says that the Romans stand fast through faith.*[469] So the Romans are saved. However, Paul then says that the Romans can also be cut off if they don't persevere in faith and kindness (Rom 11:22-23). Hence, those saved in faith can lose their salvation by being "cut off." Paul further says that those who are cut off can be grafted back in if they do not persist in their unbelief, because God has the power to graft them in again (v.23).

In his first letter to the Corinthians, Paul teaches quite explicitly that even he could forfeit his salvation:

> Do you not know that in a race all the runners compete, but only one receives the prize? So run that you may obtain it.

Every athlete exercises self-control in all things. They do it to receive a perishable wreath, but we an imperishable. Well, I do not run aimlessly, I do not box as one beating the air; but I pommel my body and subdue it, lest after preaching to others I myself should be disqualified (1 Cor 9:24-27).

The word "disqualified" (in Greek, *adokimos*) means a reprobate. When *adokimos* is used elsewhere in the Scriptures, it always refers to those who are to be condemned by God.[470] It has nothing to do with going to heaven with fewer rewards. No one would reasonably argue that Paul, the divinely inspired apostle, wasn't saved when he wrote this letter. *So if Paul thought that he could lose his salvation, why do many Protestants think that they cannot lose theirs?*

Because 1 Corinthians 9:24-27 is so problematic for the "once saved, always saved" position, some argue that Paul wasn't writing about salvation in these verses. However, this claim is entirely at odds with the Scriptures. When Paul talks about receiving the "prize" (in Greek, *brabeion*), this word has a soteriological implication (meaning it always deals with matters of salvation). For example, in his letter to the Philippians, Paul says, "I press on toward the goal for the prize of the upward call of God in Christ Jesus" (Phil 3:14). The prize of the upward call of God in Christ Jesus is heaven.

When Paul talks about achieving the "imperishable" (in Greek, *aphthartos*) wreath, this word also refers to the eternal. In fact, *aphthartos* only appears one other time in the New Testament in connection with human beings, in Paul's letter to the Corinthians, where Paul says the dead will be raised "imperishable" (1 Cor 15:51). This refers to the resurrection of our salvation. Paul also describes God, the King of ages, as "immortal" (imperishable).[471]

There are many other places in Scripture where Paul teaches about the possibility of losing salvation for those who choose sin. For example, Paul warns the Corinthians that if they do wrong and defraud, they will not inherit the kingdom of God (1 Cor 6:8-9). Paul also writes, "I betrothed you to Christ to present you as a pure bride to her one husband. But I am afraid that as the serpent deceived Eve by his cunning, your thoughts will be led astray from a sincere and pure devotion to Christ" (2 Cor 11:2-3).

The Corinthians already had a sincere devotion to Christ, and earlier in the letter Paul commends them: "You stand firm in your faith" (2 Cor 1:24). Even so, Paul fears that they will fall away from God, just as Eve fell away (and, remember, Eve was created without sin!). And yet, Paul assures the Church in Corinth, God will always provide enough grace for us to overcome whatever temptation assails us (1 Cor 10:13).

Paul also reminds the Corinthians how the Israelites, once saved by God, fell away from God by turning to immorality (1 Cor 10:6-11). Then Paul tells the Corinthians, "Therefore let anyone who thinks that he stands take heed, lest he fall" (1 Cor 10:12). Paul also warns them not to receive the gospel and the grace of God in vain.[472] Paul similarly tells the Colossians that they are in the faith, but exhorts them to "continue in the faith, stable and steadfast, not shifting from the hope of the gospel which you heard" (1:23). Thus, the Colossians have the faith, but can shift away from it.

In his letter to the Galatians, Paul says, "But even if we, or an angel from heaven, should preach to you a gospel contrary to that which we preached to you, let him be accursed" (1:8). By saying "if we . . . should preach a gospel contrary," Paul is telling us he believed *even the sacred writers*, who were currently saved, could fall away from the true faith and teach a heretical gospel. Paul also tells the Galatians that they were formerly in the bondage of idolatry but have now come to know the true God (4:8-9). Paul, acknowledging the possibility of falling away, then says "how can you turn back again to the weak and beggarly elemental spirits, whose slaves you want to be once more?" (4:9). Paul further tells them that they are free in Christ, but warns them to "stand fast therefore, and do not submit again to a yoke of slavery" (5:1). Paul is telling us that we can be slaves, then free, and then slaves again. Paul states plainly that those who choose sin will lose their inheritance[473] because a man reaps what he sows (Gal 6:7-9).

Paul tells Timothy that some people have wandered away from a sincere faith, a pure heart, and a good conscience (1 Tim 1:5-6). They had a sincere (not a phony) faith, and lost it. Paul also tells Timothy to hold fast to the faith and not shipwreck it like Hymenaeus and Alexander shipwrecked their faith (1 Tim 1:19-20).

Paul writes, "Now the Spirit expressly says that in later times some will depart from the faith by giving heed to deceitful spirits and doctrines of demons" (1 Tim 4:1). In fact, Paul says, "For some have already strayed after Satan (1 Tim 5:15). These people strayed away from a true faith. Paul also says if we don't provide for our relatives, we have disowned the faith (1 Tim 5:8). We cannot disown something we do not have. Paul further says the love of money can also lead us away from the faith (1 Tim 6:10). There is never any distinction between true faith and false faith. We can have a true and genuine faith Christ and forfeit it by our own choosing. This is because, even if we know God, our actions can deny Him (Titus 1:16).

It is only at the end of Paul's life that Paul expresses a moral certitude of salvation. In his last letter to Timothy, he writes, "Hence there is laid up for me the crown of righteousness, which the Lord, the righteous judge, will award to me on that Day, and not only to me but also to all who have loved his appearing" (2 Tim 4:8). Paul makes this statement at the end of his life, after a lifetime of teaching that we can lose our salvation. We, like Paul, do have a moral certitude of salvation if we, like Paul, persevere in faith and works to the end of our lives. This is much different than saying that our salvation is guaranteed.

Other apostolic teaching on losing salvation

The author of Hebrews repeatedly warns the faithful about falling from the faith. In fact, these warnings comprise half of his letter:

- "Therefore we must pay the closer attention to what we have heard, lest we drift away from it" (2:1).
- "Take care, brethren, lest there be in any of you an evil, unbelieving heart, leading you to fall away from the living God" (3:12).
- "For we share in Christ, if only we hold our first confidence firm to the end" (3:14).

- "Therefore, while the promise of entering his rest remains, let us fear lest any of you be judged to have failed to reach it" (4:1).
- "Let us therefore strive to enter that rest, that no one fall by the same sort of disobedience" (4:11).
- "Therefore, do not throw away your confidence, which has a great reward" (10:35).
- John gives us a similar teaching: "Look to yourselves, that you may not lose what you have worked for, but may win a full reward"(2 Jn 8).

That we can have a true faith and fall away from it due to our disobedience is clear, when the writer of Hebrews says, "Those who formerly received the good news failed to enter because of disobedience" (Heb 4:6). He also says that those "who have once been enlightened, who have tasted the heavenly gift, and have become partakers of the Holy Spirit, and have tasted the goodness of the word of God and the powers of the age to come" can commit apostasy (Heb 6:4-6). He further says:

> For if we sin deliberately after receiving the knowledge of the truth, there no longer remains a sacrifice for sins, but a fearful prospect of judgment and a fury of fire, which will consume the adversaries (Heb 10:26-27).

Thus, we can know the truth, be enlightened by it, and partake of the Holy Spirit, and still disobey God by rejecting Him and falling away. We need to persevere in our obedience to the truth to attain our reward (see Heb 10:35-38). Quoting from Habakkuk 2:4, the author of Hebrews writes, "'My righteous one shall live by faith, and if he shrinks back, my soul has no pleasure in him.' But we are not of those who shrink back and are destroyed, but of those who have faith and keep their souls."[474] We can be righteous, and still shrink back from the faith. Regarding this possibility of shrinking back from the true faith, James says "if any one among you wanders from the truth and some one brings him back, let him know that whoever brings back a sinner from the error of his way will save his soul from death and will cover a multitude of sins" (James 5:19-20).

As we have seen, James also warns that evil desires can tempt the faithful and, when the desire has conceived, it gives birth to sin, which leads to death (see James 1:14-16). Peter warns that the devil prowls around like a roaring lion seeking someone to devour, and exhorts the faithful to resist him (see 1 Pet 5:8-9). Peter even says that it is difficult for the righteous man to be saved (see 1 Pet 4:18). Peter also says "Therefore, brethren, be the more zealous to confirm your call and election, for if you do this you will never fall" (2 Pet 1:10). In the beginning of the letter we learn that Peter is telling this "to those who have obtained a faith of equal standing with ours in the righteousness of our God and Savior Jesus Christ" (2 Pet 1:1). Peter is teaching that even those with the fervent faith of the apostles can fall away from the faith.

Peter also warns us, "As obedient children, do not be conformed to the passions of your former ignorance" (1 Pet 1:14). Thus, we can be ignorant, receive the truth in obedience, and then reject the truth in disobedience by reverting to our former passions. To those who have obtained a true faith in Christ (2 Pet 1:1), Peter warns that many of them will follow false teachers who teach destructive heresies and even deny the Christ who bought them (2 Pet 2:1-2). Peter says some have already forsaken the right way and have gone astray (2 Pet 2:15). Peter also says:

> "For if, after they have escaped the defilements of the world through the knowledge of our Lord and Savior Jesus Christ, they are again entangled in them and overpowered, the last state has become worse for them than the first" (2 Pet 2:20).

While we can escape the defilements of the world through salvation in Christ, Peter makes it clear that we can again become entangled in them. Thus, Peter warns the faithful not to be carried away with the error of lawless men who may deceive them (2 Pet 3:17). John gives his faithful the same warning (1 Jn 2:24-26). Jude also tells us that even some of the angels, who beheld the face of God, fell away from Him (Jude 6). How much more possible is it for us to fall away? Those who are righteous before God can fall away from Him and commit iniquity, as God tells Ezekiel:

But when a righteous man turns away from his righteousness and commits iniquity and does the same abominable things that the wicked man does, shall he live? None of the righteous deeds which he has done shall be remembered; for the treachery of which he is guilty and the sin he has committed, he shall die.[475]

Some Protestants argue that Christians who fall away from salvation were never saved in the first place. They refer to John's first letter: "They went out from us, but they were not of us; for if they had been of us, they would have continued with us" (1 Jn 2:19). Thus, the Protestant takes the truth about *some* who fall away and applies it to *everyone* who falls away. This type of hermeneutic only leads to exegetical problems. Just because some people who fall away were never true Christians does not mean that everyone who falls away was never a true Christian.

In the preceding verse, John says, "Children, it is the last hour; and as you have heard that antichrist is coming, so now many antichrists have come; therefore we know that it is the last hour" (1 Jn 2:18). Therefore, the people to whom John is referring as falling away in verse 19 are the antichrists of verse 18. These are not ordinary, everyday Christians, but anti-Christians who seek to upset the faith of true believers and destroy Christianity in the process. Paul refers to these people as those who disguise themselves as servants of righteousness and apostles of Christ.[476] Therefore, 1 John 2:19 does not apply to true believers in Christ.

Finally, John is writing about those who fall away to warn his listeners not to fall away themselves! Why is this important? Because John is writing to true believers. John repeatedly calls his audience "children."[477] In fact, some are even priests (see 1 Jn 2:14). John says that his hearers "know the truth" (1 Jn 2:21). Yet John tells them, "Let what you heard from the beginning abide in you. If what you heard from the beginning abides in you, then you will abide in the Son and in the Father" (1 Jn 2:24). Thus, John is actually warning true believers to *abide* in the teachings of Christ, or they will fall away like false believers.

Predestination, the Elect, and Eternal Security

If the doctrine "once saved, always saved" were true, it would be one of the most comforting thoughts a person could have. But if it is false, it represents one of Satan's most harmful deceptions. It gives Christians a false sense of eternal security, and a license to engage in any kind of sin without having to worry about the eternal consequences. Like many teachings that are contrary to Catholic faith, this erroneous belief originated in the Protestant Reformation, and primarily with John Calvin. Much of the error can be attributed to misunderstandings in the theological concepts of "predestination" and "the elect."

There are various Scripture passages that introduce the concept of predestination. For example, in connection with Jesus, Peter says that He was "delivered up according to the definite plan and foreknowledge of God" (Acts 2:23). Peter and John also exclaim that God anointed Jesus "to do whatever thy hand and thy plan had predestined to take place" (Acts 4:28). Jesus similarly says, "For the Son of man goes as it has been determined" (Lk 22:22).

In connection with the baptized, Peter tells the church in Asia Minor that they are "chosen and destined by God the Father and sanctified by the Spirit for obedience to Jesus Christ for sprinkling with his blood" (1 Pet 1:1-2). Paul tells the Ephesians, "He destined us in love to be his sons through Jesus Christ" (Eph 1:5). In his letter to the Romans, Paul also says:

> For those whom he foreknew he also predestined to be conformed to the image of his Son, in order that he might be the first born among many brethren. And those whom he predestined he also called; and those whom he called, he also justified; and those whom he justified he also glorified (Rom 8:29-30).

What does "predestined" mean, in the context of these verses? Predestination (in Greek, *proorizo*) means to know in advance by God's foreknowledge. In other words, God knows what will happen in the future because He is outside of time. This means that God knows who will go to heaven and who will go to hell. The "elect" refer to those people who will go to heaven. Those who are "once saved, always saved" say that they are part of the elect who are predestined to heaven.

However, "predestination" and "elect" always refer to God's knowledge, and never human knowledge. Therefore, no one can ever know if he is part of God's elect, for only God knows the future. Further, though the elect are predestined to heaven, Jesus says that the devil will still try to make them fall. "False Christs and false prophets will arise and show signs and wonders, to lead astray, if possible, the elect" (Mk 13:22).

Predestination is also not the same thing as predetermination, which is another erroneous doctrine introduced by some Protestant Reformers such as Calvin. Predetermination means that God determines in advance who will go to heaven and who will go to hell. Such a theory of fatalism is certainly inconsistent with a God who loves all of us and died on a cross to save us. The theory is also refuted by the Scriptures:

- Paul teaches that God "desires all men to be saved and to come to the knowledge of the truth" (1 Tim 2:4).
- Peter says that the Lord "is forbearing toward you, not wishing that any should perish, but that all should reach repentance" (2 Pet 3:9).
- Jesus also says, "So it is not the will of my Father who is in heaven that one of these little ones should perish" (Mt 18:14).
- God tells Ezekiel, "Have I any pleasure in the death of the wicked, says the Lord God, and not rather that he should turn from his way and live?... For I have no pleasure in the death of anyone, says the Lord God; so turn, and live" (Ez 18:23,32).
- God also says in Sirach (15:11-12), "Do not say, 'Because of the Lord I left the right way'; for he will not do what he hates. Do not say, 'It was he who led me astray'; for he has no need of a sinful man."

God desires every person to be saved; He does not predetermine their eternal fate, for His sovereignty includes, not excludes, our free will. Jesus Christ is the Savior of the world, not just the Savior of the elect.[478] Thus, Christ died for all people, not just the elect, so that all may have eternal life.[479] Because God wants salvation for all people, Scripture teaches that He does not even tempt us (see James 1:13-14). Instead, we are tempted when we are lured and enticed by our own desires. God permits temptation to strengthen our will and desire for holiness, and always provides a way of escape (see 1 Cor 10:13).

Verses that prove "once saved always saved"?

With this as a background, we can greater understand some additional verses Protestants use to try to prove "once saved, always saved":

In *John 10:28-29,* Jesus says, "I give them eternal life, and they shall never perish, and no one shall snatch them out of my hand. My Father, who has given them to me, is greater than all, and no one is able to snatch them out of the Father's hand." This is another passage that deals with God's faithfulness to us. While no external force will snatch us from our Father's hand, this does not mean that we cannot leave the Father's hand by our own choosing. Thus, there is a distinction between God's gift of eternal life (assured) and our possession of it (not necessarily assured). The gift is eternal, and God's promise is guaranteed, if we persevere to the end. We can choose to reject Christ because God gave us free will, creating us in His own image and likeness (see Gen 1:26).

Romans 8:38-39: "For I am sure that neither death, nor life, nor angels, nor principalities, nor things present, nor things to come, nor powers, nor height, nor depth, nor anything else in all creation, will be able to separate us from the love of God in Christ Jesus our Lord." Paul is simply teaching that God will not allow external forces to thwart Christ's love for us. Paul does not even mention salvation in the passage, and even if he did, this would not prove eternal security. It would prove only that God will preserve His elect. Further, all the things Paul mentions are forces beyond an individual's control. God will not allow these external forces to disrupt His plan of salvation. This does not preclude us from succumbing to *internal forces* within us to sever us from Christ.[480]

Romans 11:29. "For the gifts and the call of our God are irrevocable" (Rom 11:29). While often quoted to prove "once saved, always saved," this verse has nothing to do with salvation. It simply addresses God's unmerited gifts and call to us. Moreover, if a person is in the elect, his salvation is irrevocable. But we can never know who is in the elect.

Romans 14:4. Paul writes, "Who are you to pass judgment on the servant of another? It is before his own master that he stands or falls. And he will be upheld, for the Master is able to make him stand" (Rom 14:4). This verse only speaks about what God is able to do for us. It does not speak about what the person is free to do, which is either to accept or reject what God is able to do. The verse also says nothing about salvation.

In *Colossians (3:23-24),* Paul says, "work heartily, as serving the Lord and not men, knowing that from the Lord you will receive the inheritance as your reward." But note that our inheritance depends on us working heartily, and not just accepting Jesus as Lord and Savior. If we persevere in our works, we will indeed receive the inheritance as our reward.

2 Timothy 1:12. In his letter to Timothy, Paul says, "But I am not ashamed, for I know whom I have believed, and I am sure that he is able to guard until that Day what has been entrusted to me." Once again, Paul is not writing about salvation and eternal security. Paul is writing about the revelation of faith with which God has entrusted him, and specifically that God will preserve his ability to teach the faith (through primarily oral Tradition) until the end of his life. This is demonstrated in the next two verses when Paul says, "Follow the pattern of the sound words which you have heard from me, in the faith and love which are in Christ Jesus; guard the truth that has been entrusted to you by the Holy Spirit who dwells within us" (2 Tim 1:13-14).

Psalm 37:28. "For the Lord loves justice; he will not forsake his saints. The righteous shall be preserved for ever, but the children of the wicked shall be cut off." Again, this verse demonstrates the faithfulness of God. He will give the graces necessary for His elect to persevere. But the verse says nothing about our cooperation with His grace, and whether we can ever know who are His elect.

Jeremiah 32:40. God tells Jeremiah, "I will make with them an everlasting covenant, that I will not turn away from doing good to them; and I will put the fear of me in their hearts, that they may not turn from me." This verse describes the faithfulness of God and how He, through His grace, causes the elect to persevere to the end. But there are no teachings in Scripture that reveal who will persevere, and how any human being could know if they are part of God's elect.

1 John 5:18. "We know that any one born of God does not sin" (5:18). Verses like this one fall into a literary genre called "proverbial literature." Proverbial literature tries to make a point by stating an absolute, even though the absolute is necessarily qualified. Notice what the apostle says earlier in the same letter, "If we say we have no sin, we deceive ourselves and the truth is not in us" (Jn 1:8). This verse does not contradict 1 John 5:18 because both verses are divinely inspired. John is making a point about the holiness that is required of a faithful follower of God. He is stating it in absolute terms, even though the absolute is necessarily qualified.

Philippians 1:6. In his letter to the Philippians, Paul says, "And I am sure that he who began a good work in you will bring it to completion at the day of Jesus Christ" (1:6). This verse also falls into the proverbial literature genre; presumably, no one would argue that the whole church at Philippi was saved. Therefore, Paul's statement must be qualified. In fact, Paul does qualify it when he tells the Philippians to work out their salvation in fear and trembling (2:13). He also qualifies it when he says that, if possible, he may obtain the resurrection (3:11), and says that he has not yet received the prize of salvation (3:12-14). Notice also that the verse once again tells us what God will do (He will give all the graces necessary to bring us to completion), but says nothing about our cooperation with God's grace.[481]

2 Timothy 4:18. In this verse, Paul tells Timothy, "The Lord will rescue me from every evil and save me for his heavenly kingdom." Again, this is proverbial literature that demonstrates God's faithfulness to us, but God's ability to save us also depends on our cooperation with His grace. God preserves His elect who are the people who persevere to the end, and only God knows who are in His elect.

1 Peter 1:5. At the beginning of his first letter, Peter says that we "by God's power are guarded through faith for a salvation ready to be revealed in the last time." This is also an example of proverbial literature; no one would likely argue that all of Asia Minor, to whom Peter addresses his letter, was saved. The verse once again simply demonstrates that God's elect are saved (by God's grace and the elect's perseverance), but only God knows who are His elect.

Psalm 121:3,7-8. "He will not let your foot be moved, he who keeps you will not slumber. The Lord will keep you from all evil; he will keep your life.... The Lord will keep your going out and your coming in from this time forth and for evermore." This is another example of proverbial literature about how God will preserve His elect. Again, this depends upon human cooperation, which the verse does not address. Thus, the verse is about how faithful God will be, not how faithful we will be.

With all this talk about the uncertainty of salvation, one might ask, why would anyone want to be Catholic? The obvious answer is because the Catholic faith is the true faith that Jesus Christ revealed to His apostles. Jesus never said our spiritual journey to heaven would be easy. He told us that we must "enter by the narrow gate" (Mt 7:13). By being fully incorporated into Christ's true Church and faithfully receiving the sacraments, Catholics have confidence in God's promise of salvation, even amidst the evil that threatens us. In fact, Catholics have *more* assurance of their salvation than those who believe in "once saved, always saved." Why?

According to the Scriptures, the only distinction between a saved Christian and an unsaved Christian is that *the unsaved Christian will not persevere in faith and works to the end of his life.* But this is something that a Christian can never know during his life; he cannot predict the future. Even though he intends to live in God's grace for the rest of his life, he cannot declare before God that he will never commit an un-confessed, mortal sin in the future. He just doesn't know. This necessarily imposes upon him uncertainty about his salvation until the end of his life. While Catholics know that salvation is ours to lose, Protestants who believe "once saved, always saved" don't know whether salvation is theirs to begin with.

Knowing that salvation is our rightful inheritance, we can have confidence in God as we anticipate the final judgment. John says, "So we know and believe the love God has for us. God is love, and he who abides in love abides in God, and God abides in him. In this is love perfected with us, that we may have *confidence for the day of judgment*, because as he is so are we in this world. There is no fear in love, but perfect love casts out fear" (1 Jn 4:16-18). John tells us that, if we *abide* in God, He will abide in us, and we can face our judgment with confidence. As we have learned, abiding in God means persevering in faith, hope and love. It also means confessing our sins to God, who will be faithful to us and forgive them (see 1 Jn 1:9). Thus, we need not be ashamed, but can have confidence on the last day. "And now, little children, abide in him, so that when he appears we may have *confidence* and not shrink from him in shame at his coming" (1 Jn 2:28).

No salvation outside the Catholic Church

In closing this chapter on salvation, we should briefly explain the Church's infallible decree: "*Extra Ecclesiam Nulla Salus*" ("Outside the Church there is no salvation."). Reformulated positively, this decree simply means that all salvation comes from Jesus Christ through the Catholic Church, which is His body. The Church teaches that no one will be saved who, knowing the Church to have been divinely established by Jesus Christ, refuses to enter it or remain in it, or withholds obedience from the Roman Pontiff, the Vicar of Christ on earth. This affirmation, however, is not aimed at those who, through no fault of their own, do not know Christ and His Church. Those people who are invincibly ignorant of the truths of Christ and the Catholic Church, but seek God with a sincere heart and try to do His will, may also achieve eternal salvation.[482] But this means that Catholics in full communion with the Church are, objectively speaking, in the best position to receive salvation. This is always due to the grace of God and no merit on their part. This also means Catholics have the severe duty to evangelize those outside of the Church to help lead them to the fullness of the means of salvation, so "that they all may be one" in Christ (see Jn 17:11).

CHAPTER EIGHT

Purgatory

Scripture tells us that, without holiness, we cannot see the Lord (see Heb 12:14). Nor can we enter the joys of heaven, where "nothing unclean shall enter it" (Rev 21:27). The word "unclean" (in Greek, *koinon*) refers to a spiritual corruption that must be cleansed before we can enter into God's presence. The Church has always taught that those who die in God's grace and friendship, but who are imperfectly purified, undergo a final purification after death. The Church calls this final purification of God's elect "purgatory."

This purification is entirely different from the punishment of the damned. Those in purgatory are guaranteed to be in heaven with Christ for all eternity. Those in hell have lost heaven for all eternity, and receive their punishments forever. Purgatory is that "interim" state between heaven and hell. When Paul tells us "at the name of Jesus every knee should bow, in heaven and on earth and under the earth," those "under the earth" are in the realm of the righteous dead, which is purgatory (Phil 2:10). These people, who are destined to be with Christ forever, are part of His body in the communion of saints.

The purification we undergo in purgatory includes not only the forgiveness of our venial sins, but also the remission of temporal punishments due to sin. The sins we commit during our lives leave imperfections on the soul. It is like pounding a nail into a piece of wood: When the nail is removed (the sin is forgiven), the nail mark (the consequence of sin) remains. Purgatory smoothes over and refines the marks on our souls so that we become perfected in the image of our heavenly Father (see Mt 5:48). This is why the author of Hebrews says that the spirits of just men are *made* perfect (12:23). These are the souls on their way to heaven, but they are "made perfect" after their death in the refining fires of purgatory.

Those who believe in salvation by faith alone deny the doctrine of purgatory, for once a person accepts Jesus Christ as personal Lord and Savior and His finished work on the cross, Christ's righteousness is imputed to him and all his sins — past, present, and future — are washed away. Therefore, there is no need for God to forgive sins after death. Further, because Christ has paid the penalty for our sins, *sola fide* adherents reject the idea that God could punish the sins of the "saved" after death. However, in the following sections, we see that purgatory is firmly rooted in Scripture, and is a logical extension of God's mercy through the ongoing sacrifice of His Son Jesus.

Suffering and Forgiveness After Death

The Scriptures teach that there is a state of suffering and forgiveness after we die. Jesus says, "And whoever says a word against the Son of man will be forgiven; but whoever speaks against the Holy Spirit will not be *forgiven*, either in this age *or in the age to come*" (Mt 12:32). Here, Jesus teaches that there is forgiveness both during life *and after death*. The phrase "in the age" (in Greek, *en to mellonti*) often refers to the afterlife.[483] While there is forgiveness after death, such forgiveness is not necessary in heaven — and is no longer possible in hell. This means that there is another state after death where forgiveness occurs, and this is the state of purgatory.

Jesus also teaches us, "Make friends quickly with your accuser, while you are going with him to court, lest your accuser hand you over to the judge, and the judge to the guard, and you be put in prison; truly, I say to you, you will never get out till you have paid the last penny."[484] The word "accuser" (in Greek, *antidiko*) is the same word Peter uses to describe the devil in 1 Peter 5:8. The devil is the accuser against man,[485] and God is the judge. If we do not adequately deal with the devil and sin in this life, we will be spiritually "imprisoned" until our entire debt to God is satisfied.[486] This prison is purgatory, where we will not get out until we have paid the last penny. After His death, Jesus preached the good news to these "spirits in prison," declaring that they would be free.[487]

Jesus also says, "And that servant who knew his master's will, but did not make ready or act according to his will, shall receive a severe beating. But he who did not know, and did what deserved a beating, shall receive a light beating" (Lk 12:47-48). Jesus is teaching about the master's will in the context of His second coming and the marriage feast of heaven. This is shown in the previous verses where Jesus describes the "men who are waiting for their master to come home from the marriage feast, so that they may open to him at once when he comes and knocks" (Lk 12:35-36). When Jesus speaks about the master's coming, he is generally speaking about the end of the world and judgment.[488] At the time of His coming, Jesus says some will receive heavy or light beatings, but will still live. In heaven, there are no beatings, and in hell, we will no longer live with the "master." Jesus is describing the sufferings of purgatory.

In Jesus' story about Lazarus and the rich man, we see that the rich man is suffering and in torment after his death.[489] However, the rich man expresses compassion for his brothers on earth, and asks Abraham to warn his brothers about the place of suffering (see Lk 16:27-28). Many exegetes have said that the rich man is in hell. While this is a reasonable interpretation, it is equally plausible to argue that the rich man is in purgatory. This is because compassion for others is a grace from God and those in hell are deprived of God's grace for all eternity. Since the rich man is suffering but shows compassion for his brothers, one may conclude that he is in purgatory.

In the book of Revelation, God also reveals to those who are dwelling with Him that "he will wipe away every tear from their eyes, and death shall be no more, neither shall there be mourning nor crying nor pain any more, for the former things have passed away" (Rev 21:3-4). But this only happens after the coming of the new heaven and the passing away of the first heaven and earth (Rev 21:1-2). Thus, the total elimination of pain and tears for those who are dwelling with God only occurs at the end of time. But there is no mourning or pain in heaven, and God will not wipe away the tears of those in hell. Those who experience this suffering before the end of time are in purgatory.

Paul mentions that people were being baptized on behalf of the dead so that they could be raised to eternal life. "Otherwise, what do people mean by being baptized on behalf of the dead? If the dead are not raised at all, why are people baptized on their behalf?" (1 Cor

15:29). These baptisms were administered to free the dead from their sins. This would only be possible, however, if there was a transitional state before heaven, since in hell there is no longer forgiveness, and in heaven there is no need of forgiveness. This state is purgatory.

Paul's statement directly corresponds to a passage in the book of Maccabees:

> He also took up a collection, man by man, to the amount of two thousand drachmas of silver, and sent it to Jerusalem to provide for a sin offering. In doing this he acted very well and honorably, taking account of the resurrection. For if he were not expecting that those who had fallen would rise again, it would have been superfluous and foolish to pray for the dead. But if he was looking to the splendid reward that is laid up for those who fall asleep in godliness, it was a holy and pious thought. Therefore he made atonement for the dead, that they might be delivered from their sin (2 Mac 12:43-45).

Just as Paul teaches that people are baptized on behalf of the dead so the dead will be raised, Judas Maccabeas teaches that we pray for the dead so that they will be raised. This passage explicitly teaches that prayers for the dead move God to deliver the dead from their sins. As we have seen, those in heaven have no sin, and those in hell can no longer be forgiven of sin. These dead are in purgatory. It has therefore always been the practice of the Church to pray for the dead, especially at the Holy Mass, when God is moved most profoundly by the sacrifice of His Son.

Even for those Christians who have not yet accepted the inspiration of the Deuterocanonical books, this passage confirms that the Jews also believed the dead could be forgiven of sin after death. Therefore, purgatory is not only a Christian doctrine. In another example, Baruch asks God to hear the prayers of the dead of Israel (Bar3:4). This tells us that, not only can we pray for the souls in purgatory, they can also pray for us (because we are part of the one communion of saints). There are other examples in the Old Testament where ritual prayers and penitential mourning were offered for the dead for specific periods of time.[490]

In his letter to Timothy, Paul asks for mercy on deceased One-siphorus on his day of judgment:

> May the Lord grant mercy to the household of Onesiphorus, for he often refreshed me; he was not ashamed of my chains, but when he arrived in Rome he searched for me eagerly and found me — may the Lord grant him to find mercy from the Lord on that Day (2 Tim 1:16-18).

The Scriptures elsewhere show that Paul's phrase "on that day" has an eschatological meaning (that is, dealing with the "last things).[491] It would be useless for Paul to ask God for mercy if One-siphorus were in heaven or in hell. There is no need for mercy in heaven, and there is no mercy in hell. Paul is praying that God releases Onesiphorus from purgatory.

Many non-Catholic Christians argue that, because Jesus sent the good thief right to heaven, there can be no purgatory (see Lk 23:43). But since there was no punctuation in the original New Testament manuscripts, it is possible that there should be no comma after the first "you" in Jesus' statement: "I say to you, today you will be with me in paradise." Jesus could have been saying, "I say to you today, you will be with me in paradise" (meaning that at some point in the future, the good thief would go to heaven). Moreover, even if the good thief did go directly to heaven, this does not prove that there is no purgatory. Those who are fully sanctified in this life — perhaps by a bloody, painful and repentant death like the good thief suffered — are ready for admission into heaven.

Purification After Death by Fire

In the previous chapter on salvation, we studied Paul's teaching to the Corinthians about how God judges our works by fire after we die. This is also one of the key passages that demonstrate the reality of purgatory. Again, Paul says:

> Now if any one builds on the foundation with gold, silver, precious stones, wood, hay, straw — each man's work will become manifest; for the Day will disclose it, because it will

be revealed with fire, and the fire will test what sort of work each one has done. If the work which any man has built on the foundation survives, he will receive a reward. If any man's work is burned up, he will suffer loss, though he himself will be saved, but only as through fire" (1 Cor 3:12-15).

Because Paul says, "...the Day will disclose it," he is speaking to the Corinthians about God's final judgment. We just saw how Paul uses the phrase "the Day" in an eschatological context.[492] Paul elaborates about God's judgment in the next chapter when he says, "Therefore, do not pronounce judgment before the time, before the Lord comes, who will bring to light the things now hidden in darkness and will disclose the purposes of the heart. Then every man will receive his commendation from God" (1 Cor 4:5). We have also seen how Paul speaks about this same judgment in 2 Corinthians 5:10 and Romans 14:10. Further, when Paul says, "he himself will be saved," the word "saved" (in Greek, *sothesetai*) refers to the salvation that God gives us at the end of our lives.

As we studied in the chapter on salvation, Paul uses metaphors to describe what people have done during their earthly lives. The metaphors he uses are building and temple (for people), gold, silver and precious stones (for good works), and wood, hay and stubble (for bad works). God judges us by revealing with fire what kind of works we performed during our lives. If we have done only good works, we will receive a reward (see 1 Cor 3:14). If we have done both good and bad works, the bad works are burned up, but we are still saved through fire (v.15). If we have done only bad works, we have destroyed the temple, and God will destroy us (v.17). The polarity of Paul's teaching in Romans 2:6-8 is also present in this passage — the opposite of saved (all good works) is destroyed (all bad works). That is, if people are damned for bad works, it follows that people are saved (not just rewarded) for good works.

In regard to the person who did both good and bad works, the Scripture says that he will "suffer loss" (in Greek, *zemiothesetai*). Protestants attribute the phrase "suffer loss" to a loss of rewards. However, whenever this phrase is used throughout Scripture, it always refers to *punishment*. For example, in Exodus 21:22 and

Proverbs 19:19, we see the same word (in Hebrew, *anash*) meaning "punish" or "penalty." The root word (in Greek, *zemioo*) also refers to punishment.[493] Therefore, the person who did bad works during his life was *punished* after his death, *but was still saved*.

A salvation that is preceded by a fiery punishment is foreign to Protestant theology. However, since they have no other explanation for the post-death, punishment/salvation process that Paul describes, they deny that *zemiothesetai* means "punishment" in this context. This rebuttal is incredible, for God is clearly punishing (that is, destroying) those whose bad works destroyed the temple (see 1 Cor 3:17).

Some Protestants argue that Paul is addressing two classes of people — the saved (who did good works in verses 14 and 15) and the unsaved (who did bad works in verse 17). In other words, they argue that God is punishing those who did bad works in verse 17, and rewarding (not punishing) those who did good works in verses 14-15. This argument exposes additional flaws in their exegesis:

First, the text does not support an arbitrary distinction between the saved and the unsaved. In fact, the text does not create any distinctions among the Corinthians at all. To the contrary, Paul is writing "to the whole church of God which is at Corinth" (1 Cor 1:2). These are the same people that Paul tells to "strive to excel in building up the church" (1 Cor 14:12). Paul tells the whole Corinthian church "you are God's building" and "you are God's temple."[494] These statements are bookends to Paul's judgment by fire metaphor.[495] This means that the metaphor applies to all the members of the Corinthian church. Therefore, God is punishing those who did bad works in both verses fifteen and seventeen, but the punishment in verse fifteen is less severe than in verse seventeen because the person is still saved. Paul does change the metaphor from building (verse nine) to temple (verses sixteen to seventeen), but this does not mean that Paul is creating two classes of Christians. Such an exegesis displays the fallacy of "anachronism."[496] Paul calls Jesus Christ the "foundation" of the building (1 Cor 3:11), but this does not mean that Jesus is not the foundation of the temple as well.

We have already addressed the contention that the bad works in verse fifteen are bad motives rather than sins, showing that Scripture *also judges bad motives as sins.* But there is a further problem with arguing that in verse fifteen God is only removing rewards from those who are saved: The person who "suffers loss" *does not lose his reward.* He is still saved, because salvation *is the reward,* as Paul also teaches.[497] While Protestants argue that "suffer loss" refers to the loss of rewards, the phrase actually refers to the *bad works* that are burned up. Paul says, "If any man's work is burned up, he will suffer loss" (1 Cor 3:15). The "man's work being burned up" is how he "suffers loss."

Those who believe in a one-time, actual salvific justification by a "faith alone" acceptance of Christ must argue that the man forever loses his reward but is still immediately saved. Otherwise, they would have to admit that *the man's salvation is delayed on the basis of his works,* for he must first pass through fire to be saved. In other words, they would have to admit that *works* determine the degree to which and whether *salvation is attained,* and not how salvation is enjoyed. Such a concept is inimical to Protestant theology.

This brings us to another scriptural truth that we have just touched upon, and that Protestants cannot adequately explain. After Paul says that a man's work is burned up and he will suffer loss, he says "though he himself will be saved, but only as through fire" (1 Cor 3:15). The phrase "but only" (in Greek, *houtos*) means "in the same manner." This means that the man who did bad works must, *in the same manner,* pass through the fire that burned up those bad works in order to be saved. Protestants have no real explanation for this temporary fire in their theology, without admitting that works serve as a basis to advance or retard salvation. The reason why the man must pass through this same fire is to be purged of the things that led him to produce the bad works in the first place. As we have seen, the phrase "suffer loss" means to punish. Thus, the man who passes through the fire undergoes an expiation of temporal punishment for his bad works before he can behold the face of God. If there is any dross in him, the fire will remove it, just as the fire removed the bad materials from the building it burned. This is God's purpose for purgatory.

Thus, Paul's teaching in 1 Corinthians 3:14-17 reveals the three possible conditions of a person's soul at death:

- the state of righteousness (v.14 — a man receives a reward);

- the state of venial sin (v.15 — a man "suffers loss" but is still saved); and,
- the state of mortal sin (v.17 — a man is destroyed).

This passage also proves that "works" (in Greek, *ergon*) are tested by God with fire after death. If works are sufficiently good, they lead to salvation; if works are sufficiently bad, they lead to damnation.

Sacred Scripture often refers to this purgatorial fire which tests and refines us like gold:

- The Lord Jesus tells us from heaven, "Therefore I counsel you to buy from me gold refined by fire, that you may be rich, and white garments to clothe you and to keep the shame of your nakedness from being seen, and salve to anoint your eyes, that you may see. Those whom I love, I reprove and chasten; so be zealous and repent" (Rev 3:18-19).
- Peter also says, "In this you rejoice, though now for a little while you may have to suffer various trials, so that the genuineness of your faith, more precious than gold which though perishable is tested by fire, may redound to praise and glory and honor at the revelation of Jesus Christ" (1 Pet 1:6-7).
- Jude instructs us to "save some, by snatching them out of the fire; on some have mercy with fear, hating even the garment spotted by the flesh" (Jude 23).

We see similar references to fire, testing, refining, purifying, gold and salvation in the Old Testament:

- "Having been disciplined a little, they will receive great good, because God tested them and found them worthy of himself; like gold in the furnace he tried them, and like a sacrificial burnt offering he accepted them" (Wis 3:5-6).
- "For gold is tested in the fire, and acceptable men in the furnace of humiliation" (Sirach 2:5).
- "The crucible is for silver, and the furnace is for gold, and the LORD tries hearts" (Prov 17:3).
- In connection with the last things, Daniel says, "Many shall purify themselves, and make themselves white, and be refined" (Dan 12:9-10).

Regarding the second coming and final judgment, Malachi prophesies: "But who can endure the day of his coming, and who can stand when he appears? For he is like a refiner's fire and like fullers' soap; he will sit as a refiner and purifier of silver, and he will purify the sons of Levi and refine them like gold and silver, till they present right offerings to the LORD" (3:2-3).

In reference to the saving fires of purgatory, God also tells Zechariah: "In the whole land, says the LORD, two thirds shall be cut off and perish, and one third shall be left alive. And I will put this third into the fire, and refine them as one refines silver, and test them as gold is tested. They will call on my name, and I will answer them. I will say, 'They are my people'; and they will say, 'The LORD is my God'" (13:8-9).

This analysis demonstrates the explicit, biblical basis for the Church's doctrine of purgatory. As members of the one body of Christ through baptism, we need to pray for the holy souls in purgatory, that God may release them from their trial by fire.

We also need to thank God for purgatory. If God didn't give us this final state of purification, most of us would not be pure enough to enter into the heavenly kingdom. God is indeed a consuming fire — a fire of love in heaven, a fire of suffering and damnation in hell, and a fire of purgation in purgatory.[498]

Appendix A

Deuterocanonical References in the New Testament

Matthew 2:16. Herod's decree of slaying innocent children was prophesied in Wisdom 11:7 — slaying the holy innocents.

Matthew 6:19-20. Jesus' statement about laying up treasure in heaven follows Sirach 29:11 — lay up your treasure.

Matthew 7:12. Jesus' Golden Rule: "Do unto others..." is the converse of Tobit 4:15 — what you hate, do not do to others.

Matthew 7:16,20. Jesus' statement, "You will know them by their fruits" follows Sirach 27:6 — the fruit discloses the cultivation.

Matthew 9:36. The people were "like sheep without a shepherd" is same as Judith 11:19 — sheep without a shepherd.

Matthew 11:25. Jesus' description, "Lord of heaven and earth" is the same as Tobit 7:18 — Lord of heaven and earth.

Matthew 12:42. Jesus refers to the wisdom of Solomon, which was recorded and made part of the Deuterocanonical books.

Matthew 16:18. Jesus' reference to the "power of death" and "gates of Hades" references Wisdom 16:13.

Matthew 22:25; Mark 12:20; Luke 20:29. The gospel writers refer to the canonicity of Tobit 3:8 and 7:11, regarding the seven brothers.

Matthew 24:15. The "desolating sacrilege" Jesus refers to is taken from 1 Maccabees 1:54 and 2 Maccabees 8:17.

Matthew 24:16. Let those "flee to the mountains" is taken from 1 Maccabees 2:28.

Matthew 27:43. If He is God's Son, let God deliver him from His adversaries follows Wisdom 2:18.

Mark 4:5,16-17. Jesus' description of seeds falling on rocky ground and having no root follows Sirach 40:15.

Mark 9:48. Jesus' description of hell, where "worm does not die and the fire is not quenched," references Judith 16:17.

Luke 1:42. Elizabeth's declaration of Mary's blessedness follows Uzziah's declaration in Judith 13:18.

Luke 1:52. Mary's Magnificat addressing "the mighty falling from their thrones" and replaced by "the lowly" follows Sirach 10:14.

Luke 2:29. Simeon's declaration that he is ready to die after seeing the Child Jesus follows Tobit 11:9.

Luke 13:29. The Lord's description of men coming from the east and west to rejoice in God follows Baruch 4:37.

Luke 21:24. Jesus' words "fall by the edge of the sword" follows Sirach 28:18.

Luke 24:4 and Acts 1:10. Luke's description of the two men in dazzling apparel reminds us of 2 Maccabees 3:26.

John 1:3. All things were made through Him, the Word, follows Wisdom 9:1.

John 3:13. Jesus' explanation that "who has ascended into heaven but He who descended from heaven" references Baruch 3:29.

John 4:48; Acts 5:12; 15:12; 2 Corinthians 12:12. Jesus, Luke and Paul refer to "signs and wonders," following Wisdom 8:8.

John 5:18. Jesus claiming that God is His Father follows Wisdom 2:16.

John 6:35-59. Jesus' Eucharistic discourse is foreshadowed in Sirach 24:21.

John 10:22. The identification of the feast of the dedication is taken from 1 Maccabees 4:59.

John 10:36. Jesus accepts the inspiration of Maccabees as He analogizes the Hanukkah consecration to His own consecration to the Father in 1 Maccabees 4:36.

John 15:6. Jesus' explanation of fruitless branches that are cut down follows Wisdom 4:5, where branches are broken off.

Acts 1:15. Luke's reference to the 120 may be a reference to 1 Maccabees 3:55 — leaders of tens / restoration of the twelve.

Acts 10:34; Romans 2:11; Galatians 2:6. Peter and Paul's statements that God shows no partiality are taken from Sirach 35:12.

Acts 17:29. Paul's description of false gods as like gold and silver made by men follows Wisdom 13:10.

Romans 1:18-25. Paul's teaching on the knowledge of the Creator and the ignorance and sin of idolatry follows Wisdom 13:1-10.

Romans 1:20. Specifically, Paul's description of God's existence being evident in nature follows Wisdom 13:1.

Romans 1:23. Paul's condemnation of the sin of worshiping mortal man, birds, animals and reptiles follows Wisdom 11:15; 12:24-27; 13:10; 14:8.

Romans 1:24-27. This idolatry results in all kinds of sexual perversion, which follows Wisdom 14:12,24-27.

Romans 4:17. Paul's quote that Abraham is a "father of many nations" is taken from Sirach 44:19.

Romans 5:12. Paul's description of death and sin entering into the world is similar to Wisdom 2:24.

Romans 9:21. Paul's reference to the potter and the clay making two kinds of vessels follows Wisdom 15:7.

1 Corinthians 2:16. Paul's question, "Who has known the mind of the Lord?" references Wisdom 9:13.

1 Corinthians 6:12-13; 10:23-26. Paul's warning that, while all things are good, beware of gluttony, follows Sirach 36:18 and Sirach 37:28-30.

1 Corinthians 8:5-6. Paul acknowledges many "gods" but one Lord follows Wisdom 13:3.

1 Corinthians 10:1. Paul's description of our fathers being under the cloud passing through the sea refers to Wisdom 19:7.

1 Corinthians 10:20. Paul's statement that "what pagans sacrifice they offer to demons and not to God" is taken from Baruch 4:7.

1 Corinthians 15:29. Paul's teaching that if there was no expectation of the resurrection, it would be foolish to be baptized behalf of the dead follows 2 Maccabees 12:43-45.

Ephesians 1:17. Paul's prayer for a "spirit of wisdom" follows the prayer for the spirit of wisdom in Wisdom 7:7.

Ephesians 6:14. Paul's description of the breastplate of righteousness is the same as that in Wisdom 5:18. See also Isaiah 59:17 and 1 Thessalonians 5:8.

Ephesians 6:13-17. The whole discussion of armor, helmet, breastplate, sword, and shield follows Wisdom 5:17-20.

1 Timothy 6:15. Paul's description of God as "Sovereign" and "King of kings" is from 2 Maccabees 12:15; 13:4.

2 Timothy 4:8. Paul's description of a crown of righteousness is similar to Wisdom 5:16.

Hebrews 4:12. Paul's description of God's Word as a sword is similar to Wisdom 18:15.

Hebrews 11:5. Paul's teaching that Enoch was taken up into heaven is also referenced in Wisdom 4:10 and Sirach 44:16. See also 2 Kings 2:1-13 and Sirach 48:9 regarding Elijah.

Hebrews 11:35. Paul teaches about the martyrdom of the mother and her sons described in 2 Maccabees 7:1-42.

Hebrews 12:12. Paul's "drooping hands" and "weak knees" is taken from Sirach 25:23.

James 1:19. James' instruction that every man should be "quick to hear and slow to respond" follows Sirach 5:11.

James 2:23. James' quote that it was reckoned to him as righteousness follows 1 Maccabees 2:52 — it was reckoned to him as righteousness.

James 3:13. James' instruction to perform works in meekness follows Sirach 3:17.

James 5:3. James' teaching about silver that rusts and laying up one's true treasure follows Sirach 29:10-11.

James 5:6. James' condemning and killing the "righteous man" follows Wisdom 2:10-20.

1 Peter 1:6-7. Peter teaches about testing faith by purgatorial fire as described in Wisdom 3:5-6 and Sirach 2:5.

1 Peter 1:17. Peter's teaching that God judges each one according to his deeds refers to Sirach 16:12 — God judges man according to his deeds.

2 Peter 2:7. Peter's reference to God's rescue of a righteous man (Lot) is also described in Wisdom 10:6.

Revelation 1:4. The seven spirits who are before God's throne is taken from Tobit 12:15 — Raphael is one of the seven holy angels who present the prayers of the saints before the Holy One.

Revelation 1:18; Matthew 16:18. Jesus' power of life over death and gates of Hades follows Wisdom 16:13.

Revelation 2:12. The reference to the two-edged sword is similar to the description of God's Word in Wisdom 18:16.

Revelation 5:7. God is described as "seated on His throne," as He is in Sirach 1:8.

Revelation 8:3-4. The prayers of the saints presented to God by the hand of an angel follows Tobit 12:12,15.

Revelation 8:7. The raining of hail and fire to the earth follows Wisdom 16:22 and Sirach 39:29.

Revelation 9:3. The raining of locusts on the earth follows Wisdom 16:9.

Revelation 11:19. The vision of the Ark of the Covenant (Mary) in a cloud of glory was prophesied in 2 Maccabees 2:7.

Revelation 17:14; 19:16. The description of God as King of kings follows 2 Maccabees 13:4.

Revelation 19:1. The cry "Hallelujah" at the coming of the New Jerusalem follows Tobit 13:18.

Revelation 19:11. The description of the Lord on a white horse in the heavens follows 2 Maccabees 3:25; 11:8.

Revelation 21:19. The description of the New Jerusalem with precious stones is prophesied in Tobit 13:17.

Exodus 23:7. Do not slay the innocent and righteous follows Daniel 13:53 — do not put to death an innocent and righteous person.

1 Samuel 28:7-20. The intercessory mediation of deceased Samuel for Saul follows Sirach 46:20.

2 Kings 2:1-13. Elijah being taken up into heaven follows Sirach 48:9.

APPENDIX B

What Is the History of Your Church?

Church	Year Established	Founder	Where
Catholic	33	Jesus Christ	Jerusalem
Orthodox	1054	certain Catholic bishops	Constantinople
Lutheran	1517	Martin Luther	Germany
Anabaptist	1521	Nicholas Storch and Thomas Munzer	Germany
Anglican	1534	Henry VIII	England
Mennonites	1536	Menno Simons	Switzerland
Calvinist	1555	John Calvin	Switzerland
Presbyterian	1560	John Knox	Scotland
Congregational	1582	Robert Brown	Holland
Baptist	1609	John Smyth	Amsterdam
Dutch Reformed	1628	Michaelis Jones	New York
Congregationalist	1648	Pilgrims and Puritans	Massachusetts
Quakers	1649	George Fox	England
Amish	1693	Jacob Amman	France
Freemasons	1717	Masons from four lodges	London
Methodist	1739	John and Charles Wesley	England
Unitarian	1774	Theophilus Lindley	London
Methodist Episcopal	1784	sixty preachers	Baltimore, MD
Episcopalian	1789	Samuel Seabury	American Colonies
United Brethren	1800	Philip Otterbein and Martin Boehn	Maryland
Disciples of Christ	1827	Thomas and Alexander Campbell	Kentucky
Mormon	1830	Joseph Smith	New York
Methodist Protestant	1830	Methodists	United States

Churches of Christ	1836	Warren Stone and Alexander Campbell	Kentucky
Seventh Day Adventist	1844	Ellen White	Washington, NH
Christadelphian (Brethren of Christ)	1844	John Thomas	Richmond, VA
Salvation Army	1865	William Booth	London
Holiness	1867	Methodists	United States
Jehovah's Witnesses	1874	Charles Taze Russell	Pennsylvania
Christian Science	1879	Mary Baker Eddy	Boston
Church of God in Christ	1895	various Churches of God	Arkansas
Church of Nazarene	c. 1850 -1900	various religious bodies	Pilot Point, TX
Pentecostal	1901	Charles F. Parkham	Topeka, KS
Aglipayan	1902	Gregorio Aglipay	Philippines
Assemblies of God	1914	Pentecostals	Hot Springs, AZ
Iglesia ni Christo	1914	Felix Manalo	Philippines
Four-square Gospel	1917	Aimee Semple McPherson	Los Angeles, CA
United Church of Christ	1961	Reformed and Congregationalist	Philadelphia, PA
Calvary Chapel	1965	Chuck Smith	Costa Mesa, CA
United Methodist	1968	Methodist and Evangelical United Brethren Churches	Dallas, TX
Born-again	c. 1970s	various religious bodies	United States
Harvest Christian	1972	Greg Laurie	Riverside, CA
Saddleback	1982	Rick Warren	California
Non-denominational	c. 1990s	various	United States

Notes

[1] Early Christian writers say that Ignatius was ordained by the Apostle Peter, the chief shepherd of the infant Church. Many also believe that Ignatius was an auditor of the Apostle John, during whose lifetime Ignatius may have written his letter to the Smyrnaeans.

[2] Scripture passages quoted here are from the *Revised Standard Version — Catholic Edition* translation of the Bible, unless otherwise noted. This translation closely follows, and is based on, the King James Version commonly used by Protestant Christians.

[3] Because *sola Scriptura* is not taught in the Bible, Protestants have developed many different definitions of the doctrine. This makes the doctrine all the more difficult to understand.

[4] The canon of Scripture refers to the list of books in the Bible. For example, the New Testament canon includes the twenty-seven books of the New Testament that all Christians agree are divinely inspired.

[5] Sometimes this book is called "the Apocalypse."

[6] The Council of Trent (1545-1563) dogmatically affirmed the canon of Scripture in response to the Protestant Reformation. The Council of Trent also declared the Latin Vulgate Edition of the Scriptures, translated by Jerome in the fourth century, to be the authentic translation of God's Word. The Latin Vulgate is the source from which the Douay-Rheims was translated, and is viewed as the official translation of the Catholic Church.

[7] The Deuterocanonical books are Tobit, Judith, Baruch, Sirach (Ecclesiasticus), Wisdom of Solomon, 1 and 2 Maccabees and parts of Daniel and Esther.

[8] See Mk 12:20; Lk 20:29.

[9] Eph 6:13-17; 1 Cor 10:20; 1 Tim 6:15.

[10] The Catholic Church has traditionally held that Paul is the author of the letter to the Hebrews. The Catholic Councils of Florence (1438 – 1445) and Trent (1545 – 1563) refer to "fourteen Epistles of Paul the Apostle." The Church's Pontifical Biblical Commission also affirmed Paul's authorship of Hebrews (1914). Nevertheless, to accommodate the viewpoints of other Christian traditions, we will not expressly refer to Paul when quoting from Hebrews.

[11] Whenever a word from Scripture is italicized for emphasis, please assume it is my emphasis unless otherwise noted.

[12] Mk 16:15; see also Lk 24:47; Mt 28:20.

[13] The only place where Jesus commands anyone to write is in the book of Revelation (see Rev 1:11,19). But John, the author of Revelation, was in exile in Patmos and could not preach the word, which was the normative way in which the gospel was spread. Further, Jesus' command to write is limited to the book that John wrote, the book of Revelation, and has nothing to do with the other Scriptures.

[14] 1 Cor 11:34; see also 1 Cor 11:23-34.

[15] See Mt 15:3-6; Mk 7:8-9.

[16] See Deut 4:2; 12:32.

[17] See Jn 14:26; 16:12-13.

[18] See 1 Thess 2:13; Mt 10:20; 22:43; Acts 4:8.

[19] See 1 Cor 15:11. See 1 Cor 15:1-2

[20] See 2 Tim 1:13-14.

[21] See 2 Tim 4:2,6-7.

[22] In fact, knowing who wrote the Gospel of Matthew is also a Tradition of the Church. (The Gospel of Matthew, as well as the other Gospels, do not identify the authors.

[23] See Ex 17:1-17 and Num 20:2-13.

[24] See Jude 9. See Jude 14-15.

[25] See Col 4:16.

[26] See 2 Pet 3:15-16.

[27] See 2 Pet 3:16.

[28] See Acts 17:4. See Acts 17:12.

[29] Paul was warning the Corinthians that they were imbibing the same mentality as the Jews by boasting about their works, as if God now owed them what they were receiving. Just as the Jews were boasting about having the law of Moses, the Gentiles were boasting about having the Christian religion, and were falling into the sin of pride. Paul also accuses the Gentiles of boasting (see Rom 2:17, 23; 3:27; 4:2; and Eph 2:8-9). By accusing the Corinthians of being "puffed up," Paul introduces the faith versus works, or grace versus law paradigm, which is at the heart of his teaching in justification (which we study in the chapter on justification).

[30] See 1 Sam 3:1-9.

[31] See Titus 1:2.

[32] See 1 Cor 14:33.

[33] See Mt 16:18. See Mt 16:19. See Jn 21:15-17.

[34] See Eph 2:20; Mt 18:18.

[35] Caesarea Philippi, which was a district built by Herod's son Philip as a dedication to Caesar, had a massive rock formation at the base of Mount

Hermon. It was against this metaphorical backdrop that Jesus chose to rename Simon the "rock."

[36] Mt 16:17-19; see also Mt 16:13-16.

[37] See Gen 17:5,15. See Gen 32:28. See 2 Kings 23:24.

[38] See 2 Sam 22:2-3,32,47; 23:3; Ps 18:2,31,46; 19:4; 28:1; 42:9; 62:2, 6-7; 89:26; 94:22; 144:1-2.

[39] The word *Cephas* is a transliteration of the Aramaic word *Kepha*, which means rock.

[40] This is why the Scriptures generally refer to Peter as Simon during Christ's ministry, and Peter after Christ's Ascension into heaven.

[41] Notice that non-Catholics first try to prove that Peter is not the rock on which Christ builds the Church. But if Peter really is the rock (as the Scriptures demonstrate), then non-Catholics argue that he is just a small one, and thus cannot be the foundation of the Church.

[42] Jesus' use of *Bar-Jona* in Matthew 16:17 proves that He was speaking Aramaic (in Aramaic, *Bar* means son and *Jona* means John; Simon was the son of John). See also Mark 15:34, where Jesus speaks Aramaic as He utters from the cross the first verse of Psalm 22, declaring that He is the Christ.

[43] See Rev 21:1-2.

[44] See 2 Sam 7:12,14,16; see also Ps 89:3-4; 1 Chron 17:12,14.

[45] See Jer 23:5; 33:17; Dan 2:44.

[46] See Mt 1:1; Lk 3:31.

[47] See Mt 9:27; 15:22; 20:30-31; 22:40; Mk 10:47-48; Lk 18:38-39.

[48] Is 22:15,19-22.

[49] See Mt 18:18.

[50] See Rev 1:18; 3:7; 9:1; 20:1.

[51] The Douay-Rheims translates Matthew 16:18's phrase "powers of death" as "gates of hell" (see Rev 1:18). This further demonstrates that Peter's keys represent power over the supernatural.

[52] See Mt 16:18-19, Lk 22:31-32 and Jn 21:15-17.

[53] The Latin word for chair is *cathedra*, and is used to describe the chair of Peter and his successors as the legitimate seat of authority in the Church. When the pope formally teaches a matter of faith and morals, it may rise to the level of an *ex-cathedra* (from the chair) teaching.

[54] See Lk 12:41-42.

[55] Lk 22:31-32 — brackets with "plural" and "singular" added.

[56] Rev 12:5; 2:27; see Mt 2:6; Ps 2:9.

[57] See Mt 13:24-30.

[58] See Mt 13:31-32; Mk 4:26-32; Lk 13:19-20.

[59] See Mt 13:33.

[60] See Mt 13:47-48.

[61] See Mt 25:1-2.

[62] See Mt 12:18; Lk 17:21. Mk 1:15; Lk 11:20.

[63] See Is 22:19-22.

[64] See Mt 10:2; Mk 1:36; 3:16; Lk 6:14-16; Acts 1:3; 2:37; 5:29. The only two exceptions are in 1 Cor 3:22 and Gal 2:9.

[65] Lk 8:51; 9:28; 22:8; Acts 1:13; 3:1,3-4,11; 4:13,19; 8:14.

[66] See Mt 16:16; Mk 8:29; Jn 6:69.

[67] See Mt 18:21. See Mk 11:21.

[68] See Mt 19:21; Mk 10:28.

[69] See Lk 7:40-50.

[70] See Lk 8:45.

[71] See Lk 9:33.

[72] See Lk 12:41.

[73] See Jn 13:6-9.

[74] See Mt 17:24-27.

[75] See Acts 1:15ff.

[76] See Acts 2:14ff.

[77] See Acts 2:38.

[78] Acts 3:12-26; 4:8-12.

[79] Acts 10:34-38; 11:1-18.

[80] See Acts 5:3.

[81] See Acts 8:14. We will examine this more closely in the chapter on the sacraments.

[82] See Acts 8:20-23.

[83] It is a common practice of bishops gathered in a regional or ecumenical council to speak and render judgments in support of a papal teaching. James' affirmation of Peter's teaching in Acts 15:13-19 is an example of this. (James was the bishop of Jerusalem, where this first council of the Church was held.)

[84] See 1 Pet 5:1. See 2 Pet 3:16.

[85] See Lk 24:12; Jn 20:4-6.

[86] Gal 1:18; see also Acts 9:3-5; 22:6-8; 26:12-15.

[87] See Mt 14:28-29.

[88] See Acts 3:6-7. See Acts 5:15.

[89] See Acts 9:32-34; Acts 9:38-40.

[90] See Acts 10:5. See Acts 12:6-11.

[91] See Rev 14:8; 16:19; 17:5; 18:2,10,21.

[92] See Jn 13:36; 21:18. See 2 Pet 1:14.

[93] See Mt 23:11; Mk 9:35; 10:44.

[94] See Acts 20:17,28; Phil 1:1; 1 Tim 3:1; Titus 1:7. See Acts 20:17,28; 1 Tim 5:17; Titus 1:5; James 5:14. See Phil 1:1; 1 Tim 3:8.

[95] See 1 Cor 12:28; Eph 4:11.

[96] See Mt 16:18; 18:18.

[97] Paul also calls his position a divine "office" (Col 1:25). Of course, an office has successors and therefore does not terminate at death. Otherwise, it's not an office.

[98] 1 Tim 4:14. 2 Tim 1:6.

[99] See Ex 18:25-26.

[100] See Num 27:18-20.

[101] See Ex 28:1. See Ex 19:6; 28:1. See Ex 19:6.

[102] See Heb 3:1. See Rom 15:16; 1 Tim 3:1,8; 5:17; Titus 1:7. See 1 Pet 2:5, 9; Rev 1:6.

[103] See 2 Cor 1:21-22; 2:17.

[104] See 2 Cor 5:20; 10:8; Titus 1:5; Lk 10:1.

[105] See 1 Thess 5:12-13; 1 Tim. 5:17; Heb. 13:7, 17.

[106] See 1 Pet 5:5; Jude 8; 1 Pet 2:18. See 2 Pet 2:10.

[107] See 1 Pet 2:25.See Acts 20:28.

[108] See Deut 17:10-13.

[109] See Jn 5:30; 14:10; see also Num 16:28. See Jn 7:16-17; 8:28; 12:49.

[110] Jn 17:18. Mt 28:20.

[111] See Is 35:8; 54:13-17.

[112] See Acts 9:2; 22:4; 24:24,22.

[113] Mt 10:20; Lk 12:12.

[114] See Jn 14:16, 26.

[115] See Jn 16:13.

[116] Mt 12:25; Mk 3:25; Lk 11:17.

[117] See Jn 17:11,21,23.

[118] See Mt 13:24-30.

[119] See Mt 13:47-50.

[120] See 2 Tim 2:20.

[121] See Jer 24:1-10.

[122] See Rom 3:3-4.

[123] See 2 Tim 2:13.

[124] See Mt 16:18.

[125] In the Eastern rite, infants generally receive confirmation right after baptism.

[126] In addition, the sacraments of penance, holy orders and anointing of the sick can be celebrated only by ministerial priests (in the case of holy orders, bishops ordain new priests, and the pope ordains new bishops).

[127] The Protestant doctrine of "believer's baptism" and the Catholic requirement of professing faith in Christ before baptism are addressed later in the chapter. For now, we are simply demonstrating that John 3:3-5 is about baptism and its salvific power.

[128] Many scholars believe that the phrase "not as a removal of dirt from the body" is a reference to circumcision, especially because baptism is the "new circumcision" of the New Covenant (Colossians 2:11-12).

[129] Similar to the "water and the Spirit" in John 3:5 and Titus 3:5.

[130] Acts 22:16; see Acts 9:18.

[131] See Acts 8:12-13; 36; 10:47; 16:15, 31-33; 18:8; 19:2,5.

[132] Ez 36:25-27.

[133] The Church calls adults who are candidates for baptism "catechumens."

[134] See Mt 9:2; Mk 2:3-5.

[135] See Mt 8:5-13.

[136] See Mk 9:22-25.

[137] See Ex 12:24-28. Those who are tempted to delay their children's baptism should also note that, in the book of Joshua, God punished Israel because they had not circumcised their children, based on the parents' faith (Josh 5:2-7). They should further remember that, while Christendom has a two-thousand-year history of baptizing babies, there is nothing at all in the Scriptures about a "believer's baptism."

[138] See Mt 18:4; Mk 10:14.

[139] See Lk 18:15; Mt 18:2-5.

[140] See Eph 1:1; Col 1:2.

[141] In verse 39 when Peter says, "to all that are far off," he was referring to those who were at their homes (primarily infants and children).

[142] See also Lk 19:9; Jn 4:53; Acts 11:14; 1 Tim 3:12; Gen 31:41; 36:6; 41:51; Josh 24:15; 2 Sam 7:11; and 1 Chron 10:6.

[143] See Acts 16:33. See Acts 10:47-48.

[144] See Gen 17:12; Lev 12:3.

[145] See 1 Cor 7:14.

[146] See Mt 20:22-23; Mk 10:38-39; Lk 12:50.

[147] See Mt 3:11; Mk 1:8; Lk 3:16.

[148] See Acts 2:17-18,33.

[149] See Heb 10:22; see Heb 6:2.

[150] See Mt 20:22-23; Mk 10:38-39; Lk 12:50.

[151] See Acts 9:18; 22:16.

[152] See Acts 10:47-48. See Acts 16:33.

[153] See Mt 3:16; Mk 1:9; Lk 3:21; Jn 1:31-32.

[154] See Mt 3:6; Mk 1:5.

[155] See Mk 2:7; Lk 5:21; Mt 9:3.

[156] See Mt 9:6; Mk 2:10; Lk 5:24. When the sacred writers use the title "Son of man," they are emphasizing Jesus' humanity. When they use "Son of God," they are emphasizing His divinity.

[157] Anyone who has experienced God's mercy and forgiveness in the sacrament of reconciliation understands the significance of this verse.

[158] See Mt 26:26-28; Mk 14:22-24; Lk 22:19-20; 1 Cor 11:23-25.

[159] The Church has traditionally explained transubstantiation using the philosophical concepts of "accidents" and "substance." Accidents describe what we perceive in the matter by our senses (color, texture, taste, size, smell). Substance describes what the matter truly is (the essence or substance). Changes that can take place with water are commonly used analogies to explain transubstantiation, but in the opposite way. For example, when the temperature of water reaches 32° F, the accidents of the water change (from liquid to solid), but the substance stays the same (it's still H_2O). When the temperature of water reaches 212° F, the accidents of the water change (from liquid to gas), but the substance stays the same (it's still H_2O). In a similar but opposite way, the substance of the bread and wine change (into Christ's body and blood), but the accidents stay the same (they still appear to be bread and wine).

[160] From the Greek word *eucharistein*, which means "thanksgiving."

[161] Lk 22:19; in Greek, *touto esti to soma mou to uper hymon didomenon*.

[162] 1 Cor 11:24; see also 1 Cor 10:16.

[163] Mt 26:27-28; in Greek, *touto gar estin to haima mou to tes kaines diathekes to peri pollon ekchynnomenon eis aphesin hamartion*; cf. Mk 14:24; Lk 22:20; 1 Cor 9:25.

[164] Lk 22:20; in Greek, *touto to poterion he kaine diatheke en to haimati mou, to yper hymon ekchynnomenon*.

[165] Mt 26:28; Mk 14:24; similar words are used in Lk 22:20; 1 Cor 11:25.

[166] Exodus 24:8; in Greek, *idou to haima tes diathekes*.

[167] Lk 22:19; 1 Cor 11:24-25.

[168] See also Lev 2:2,9,16; 5:12; 6:15; 24:7 and Num 5:26, where the same word for "memorial" (in Hebrew, *azkarah*) is used in connection with a sacrifice currently offered and made present in time.

[169] See Ex 13:9; see Ex 12:1-27.

[170] See Lev 2:2,9,16; 5:12; 6:5. See Acts 10:4.

[171] See also Mt 26:13; Mk 14:9.

[172] Jn 15:13; 10:17-18.

[173] 1 Jn 2:1-2 (NIV); see Rom 3:25. In connection with explaining the efficacy of Christ's sacrifice, we should briefly address the erroneous Protestant doctrine of penal substitution. This doctrine says that Jesus paid the full legal and eternal penalty for our sins. If this were true, however, God would legally owe us salvation and no one would go to hell. That is because God would not require two payments for the same sin. But we know that this cannot be true because Jesus said people would go to hell. In fact, if Christ paid the eternal penalty for our sins, He would still be suffering in hell. Therefore, the atonement of Christ is about propitiation, not legal payment.

[174] See Heb 10:29. See Heb 10:35.

[175] When God created the world, He employed the inviolable principle of *representation*. This principle required one person to represent the whole, and be held responsible for the good or bad that would come to the whole (see Rom 5:18-19). Thus, just as Adam's sin condemned the whole world, by God's principle of *representation*, Jesus Christ's sacrifice can save the whole world.

[176] For example, in the book of Exodus, God decides to destroy the Israelites for worshiping the golden calf (Ex 32:10); Moses pleads with God to relent of His wrath (Ex 32:11-13); and, God decides not to destroy them as a result of Moses' intercession (Ex 32:14). God deals with His people on a moment-by-moment basis, and is moved by sacrifice.

[177] See Heb 9:14; 1 Pet 1:19.

[178] One of the main differences between the Old and New Covenant is that, in the Old Covenant, the sacrifices based their power on the *anticipated* work of Christ, whereas, in the New Covenant, the "sacrifices" base their power in the *accomplished* work of Christ.

[179] See Heb 5:6,10; 6:20; 7:15,17.

[180] See Gen 14:18; Ps 76:2.

[181] See Jer 33:18. See Zech 9:15-16.

[182] See, for example, Lev 7:12-15; 22:29-30; cf. Ps 20:2-4; 50:14, 23; 116:13, 17 which also refer to these "thanksgiving offerings" or "sacrifices of praise."

[183] Mal 1:11; Heb 9:23.

[184] See 1 Pet 2:9; Rev 20:6.

[185] See, for example, Lev 24:6; Ez 41:22; 44:16; and Mal 1:7,12 where the phrase "table of the Lord" refers to an altar of sacrifice.

[186] See Num 8:11,13,15,21.

[187] Rev 19:13. Rev 7:14.

[188] See Mt 6:11; Lk 11:3.

[189] See Heb 2:17; 3:1; 4:14; 8:1; 9:11,25; 10:19,22.

[190] See 2 Chron 7:1; cf. Mk 16:19; Lk 24:51; Acts 1:10.

[191] See Heb 2:18; 5:7-8.

[192] See Heb 9:6-7. See Heb 9:12,26; 10:10.

[193] See Heb 8:2; 9:24.

[194] See 1 Jn 2:2. See Heb 7:25; Rom 8:34.

[195] Heb 13:8. Heb 4:3.

[196] See Ps 2:6; 132:13.

[197] See especially vv. 17-18, 20, 33-34; 14:23, 26. Christians met on Sunday to celebrate the Eucharist because Christ rose from the dead on Sunday. This was a departure from the Jewish tradition of meeting in the synagogue on Saturday. See, for example, Acts 20:7; 1 Cor 16:2; Col 2:16-17; Heb 4:8-9; Rev 1:10; see also Heb 7:12.

[198] See Rev 1:10.

[199] See Rev 1:12; 2:5.

[200] See Rev 4:4; 5:14; 11:16; 14:3; 19:4. See Rev 14:4. See Rev 1:13; 4:4; 6:11; 7:9; 15:6; 19:13-14.

[201] See Rev 7:3; 14:1; 22:4.

[202] See Rev 2:5,16,21; 3:3; 16:11.

[203] See Rev 15:3-4. See Rev 19:1,3,4,6.

[204] See Rev 5:1. See Rev 5:8; 8:3-4.

[205] See Rev 4:8. See Rev 4:8-11; 5:9-14; 7:10-12; 18:1-8. See Rev 5:14; 7:12; 19:4.

[206] See Rev 15:5. See Rev 15:7; 16:1-4,8,10,12,17; 21:9. See Rev 2:17.

[207] See Rev 8:3; 11:1; 14:18; 16:7. See Rev 6:9.

[208] Rev 11:12.

[209] Rev 8:1.

[210] See Rev 12:1-6,13-17. See Rev 5:8; 6:9-11; 8:3-4; 12:7.

[211] See Rev 7:9; 14:6.

[212] Rev 5:6ff.

[213] Rev 19:9.

[214] See Lev 7:15; 19:22.

[215] See Ex 12:5. See Ex 12:47; Num 9:12. See Ex 12:7,22-23.

[216] See Ex 12:8,11.

[217] See 2 Chron 30:15-17; 35:1,6,11,13; Ezra 6:20-21; Ez 6:20-21.

[218] See Ex 12:12.

[219] See Ex 12:43-45; Ez 44:9. Ex 12:49. See Ex 12:14,17,24; Ex 24:8.

[220] See Ex 16:4-36; Neh 9:15.

[221] See Ps 78:24-25; 105:40; see 2 Kings 4:43.

[222] See Jn 1:29,36; Acts 8:32; 1 Pet 1:19.

[223] See Jn 6:4,11-14.

[224] *Trogo* is never used metaphorically in the Scriptures. In fact, *trogo* is only used two other times in the New Testament (Mt 24:38; Jn 13:18). Both times, it means "to chew food."

[225] See Jn 1:13,14; 3:6; 8:15; 17:2; Mt 16:17; 19:5; 24:22; 26:41; Mk 10:8; 13:20; 14:38; Lk 3:6; 24:39.

[226] See Ps 27:2; Is 9:20; 49:26; Mic 3:3; 2 Sam 23:17; Num 23:24; Ez 39:17-20; Rev 16:6; 17:6,16.

[227] See Jn 3:6; Mk 14:38.

[228] See 1 Cor 2:14; 3:3; Rom 8:5; Gal 5:17.

[229] Jn 6:63. Anyone making this argument must also explain why there is not a single place in Scripture where "spirit" means "symbolic."

[230] See Jn 6:53-54,57-58.

[231] See Mk 4:34. See Jn 3:5,11; Mt 16:11-12.

[232] Mt 26:26-28; Mk 14:22-24; Lk 22:19-20; 1 Cor 10:16-21; 11:23-30.

[233] Gen 9:4-5; Lev 17:11,14; Deut 12:16,23-24.

[234] Rom 14:14-18; 1 Cor 8:1-13; 1 Tim 4:3.

[235] See Mt 26:29; Mk 14:25; Lk 22:18.

[236] See Mt 3:7; 12:34; 23:33.

[237] See 1 Cor 11:26-27.

[238] See Mt 26:2; Mk 14:12; Lk 22:7.

[239] The hymn was usually based on Ps 115-118. See Mt 26:30; Mk 14:26.

[240] See Mt 26:39; Mk 14:36; Lk 22:42; Jn 18:11.

[241] See Lk 23:4,14; Jn 18:39; 19:4,6; Heb 9:14; see Ex 12:5.

[242] See Jn 1:29,36; Acts 8:32; 1 Pet 1:19.

[243] See Mt 27:34; Mk 15:23.

[244] See Ex 28:4; Lev 16:4.

[245] Jn 19:28-29. See Jn 19:30; Mt 27:48; Mk 15:36.

[246] See Jn 19:29. See Ex 12:7,22-23.

[247] See Jn 19:30 (DR).

[248] See Ex 12:47; Num 9:12.

[249] See Mt 26:26; see Mk 14:22; Lk 22:19; 1 Cor 11:24.

[250] See Mt 26:26-28; Mk 14:22-24; Lk 22:19-20.

[251] See Lk 24:30-31; cf. Lk 24:35.

[252] See Mt 19:6; Mk 10:8.

[253] See Eph 1:22-23; 5:23,30-31; Col 1:18,24.

[254] People who are prepared to receive the sacrament are called "confirmands."

[255] The Church's use of oil is rich in meaning. Oil is a sign of abundance and joy (see Deut 11:14; Ps 23:5; 104:15) that heals bruises and wounds (see

Is 1:6; Lk 10:34). Oil is thus used not only in confirmation, but also in the sacraments of baptism, holy orders and anointing of the sick.

[256] This "seal" is a mark or sign of their total belonging to Christ (see Gen 38:18; 41:42; Deut 32:24).

[257] See Heb 6:2 (DR).

[258] Jn 6:27. See Rev 9:4; Rev 14:1; 22:4; Ez 9:4-6.

[259] A priest or deacon of the Church, preferably in the context of the Eucharistic liturgy, must witness this consent.

[260] See Mt 19:6; Mk 10:8.

[261] See 1 Cor 6:16; Eph 5:31.

[262] See Eph 5:22-32.

[263] See Mal 2:14.

[264] See Mk 10:11-12; Lk 16:18; Mt 19:9.

[265] Mt 19:9; Mt 5:32.

[266] See 1 Cor 7:12-15.

[267] See Ezra 10:1-14. This provision is rarely used by the Church.

[268] See Rev 19:9; Jn 2:1-11.

[269] This is why the Church also prohibits in-vitro fertilization, surrogate motherhood, and any other procedure where life is created outside the marital act. The unitive (love) and procreative (life) components of the conjugal union between a husband and wife are inseparable.

[270] See Gen 1:28; 9:1,7; 35:11.

[271] See Ex 23:25-26; Deut 7:13-14; 1 Chron 25:5

[272] Tobit 6:16-17 (DR).

[273] Tobit 6:22 (DR).

[274] Lev 18:22-23; 20:13; see also Gen 19:24-28.

[275] See Rom 1:26-27; 1 Cor 6:9; 1 Tim 1:10.

[276] See Lev 21:20. See Deut 23:1.

[277] See Hos 9:11; Jer 18:21.

[278] See Rev 9:21; 21:8; 22:15; Gal 5:20. Chemical contraception (e.g., "the Pill," the patch, injections, etc.) can cause spontaneous abortions by preventing an embryo from attaching to the uterine wall. That women often do not realize that they may be killing their unborn children with these forms of contraception is one of Satan's greatest deceptions.

[279] See also Eph 5:33; 1 Pet 3:5-7; 1 Cor 14:34-35; 1 Tim 2:10-15; and Is 3:12. Paul's requirement that wives be subject to their husbands is based not on sexism or cultural conditions, but divine command "as even the law says" (see 1 Cor 14:34,37). Further, Paul says that a wife symbolizes that she is under authority by covering her head when she prays or prophesies "because of the angels" (1 Cor 11:10).

[280] Eph 5:24 (DR).

[281] See Judg 17:10; 18:19.

[282] See Gen 2:21-22.

[283] See Gen 2:18; 1 Cor 11:9; 1 Tim 2:12-13.

[284] See Acts 1:20; 6:6; 13:3; 8:18; 9:17; 1 Tim 4:14; 5:22; 2 Tim 1:6.

[285] See Judg 17:10; 18:19.

[286] See Acts 7:2; 22:1.

[287] See 1 Jn 2:1,13,14.

[288] See 1 Cor 4:17; 1 Tim 1:2,18; 2 Tim 1:2-3.

[289] See 2 Cor 12:14.

[290] See 1 Jn 2:1,18,28; 3:18; 5:21; 3 Jn 4.

[291] Mt 3:9; Lk 3:8; 16:24,30; Jn 8:56

[292] See Jn 7:22.

[293] Mt 15:4-5; 19:19. See Eph 6:2.

[294] Acts 7:11-12,15,19,38,44-45,51,52.

[295] See Is 56:3-7. See Jer 16:1-4.

[296] In heaven, those consecrated to virginity are honored (Rev 14:4).

[297] See 1 Cor 7:1,7.

[298] In fact, while marriage is a sacrament, consecrated virginity is not.

[299] See Mk 14:17,20; Lk 22:14.

[300] See Gen 14:10; Heb 5:6,10; 6:20; 7:15,17.

[301] See Lk 7:37-50. See Jn 8:3-11. See Mk 16:9.

[302] Judg 17:10; see also Judg 18:19.

[303] Because women were usually naked when they were baptized by immersion, women helpers were needed to prepare the candidates in order to prevent scandal.

[304] See Lk 2:36-37.

[305] See 1 Cor 14:34-35; 1 Tim 2:12.

[306] See Num 16:1-50.

[307] See Num 16:31-34,49.

[308] See Gen 3:1-6; Rev 12:1-6,13-17.

[309] Catholics place a tremendous significance on Mary's choice to accept the motherhood of Jesus Christ. She was neither required nor coerced to accept the role, and probably could not comprehend the suffering that would attend it. But, like Christ, her sacrificial love for God and humanity moved her to offer her fiat to God. This voluntary dimension of Mary's fiat corresponds to the voluntary dimension of Christ's sacrifice before the Father, which moves God to have mercy on us and forgive our sins.

[310] In other words, Mary was created and redeemed *at the same time*. Interestingly, even Martin Luther agreed with this.

³¹¹ In this passage, Luke uses a linguistic construction called a "circumlocution" to describe Mary's blessedness.

³¹² Lk 1:43. In Hebrew, the translation of Lord is *Adonai*.

³¹³ The Church gave Mary the title *Theotokos* at the Council of Ephesus in 431.

³¹⁴ The tabernacle contains the Eucharist — the consecrated hosts of bread which have become the body and blood, soul and divinity of Jesus Christ through the offering of His memorial sacrifice. The tabernacle is generally located in the center of Catholic churches behind the altar, or some other prominent place in the church.

³¹⁵ See 2 Sam 6:7; 1 Chron 13:9-10.

³¹⁶ See Ex 24:15-16; 40:34-38; 1 Kings 8:10-11; Job 14:4; and 2 Mac 2:4-8.

³¹⁷ See 2 Sam 6:11 and 1 Chron 13:14.

³¹⁸ Remember that Rev 11:19 and Rev 12:1 are directly connected; there were no chapter and verse divisions at the time these texts were written.

³¹⁹ See Rev 12:2. God increased the pain of childbirth due to the original sin (Gen 3:16).

³²⁰ Jer 13:21; see also 4:31.

³²¹ Is 7:14 (DR).

³²² See Gen 5:24; Heb 11:5; 2 Kings 2:11-12; 1 Mac 2:58.

³²³ See Zeph 3:14; Zech 2:10; 9:9.

³²⁴ See 1 Kings 2:19; Neh 2:6; Ps 45:9.

³²⁵ 2 Chron 22:10; see also 1 Kings 15:13.

³²⁶ See Rev 12:1. See 2 Tim 4:8. See James 1:12; Rev 2:10. See 1 Pet 5:4; Wis 5:16.

³²⁷ In addition, when Jesus uses the title "woman," He is also using it as a title of dignity and respect (in Greek, *gnyai*). It is the equivalent of Lady or Madam, and was a title commonly used to address women during the time of Jesus.

³²⁸ That Satan perceived her as a danger is clear from the fact that he sought to destroy her even after the Savior was born (see Rev 12:13-16).

³²⁹ Rev 12:17.

³³⁰ Jn 2:4 (DR).

³³¹ Those who think Jesus rebuked Mary at the wedding feast of Cana, or anywhere else, are implying that Jesus violated the Torah — here, the Fourth Commandment. This argument is blasphemous because it essentially says that God committed sin by dishonoring His mother.

³³² Mt 12:46-48; see Mk 3:33-35; Lk 8:21.

³³³ See Mt 12:46; Mk 3:31-32; Lk 8:19-20; Jn 7:3,5,10.

[334] In Hebrew and Aramaic, the word "sister" can also mean "cousin." Whatever their exact relationship, it is clear that the Virgin Mary and Mary of Clopas were immediate family members. This explains why Mary of Clopas was with the Virgin Mary at the crucifixion.

[335] Mt 27:61; 28:1. While many translations call this Mary the "wife of Clopas," the Greek grammar says Mary was "of Clopas." This means Mary could have either been the wife or daughter of Clopas.

[336] See Mt 27:56; Mk 15:40,47. Note also that Alphaeus is the father of James (Mt 10:3; Mk 3:18; Lk 6:15; Acts 1:13). This makes Alphaeus and Mary of Clopas the parents of the James of Matthew 13:55 and Mk 6:3. As a result, "of Clopas" can have three possible meanings: (1) Mary is the daughter of Clopas and the wife of Alphaeus; (2) Mary was married to Alphaeus when she had James, and then remarried Clopas; or, (3) Alphaeus and Clopas (also translated "Cleophas") refer to the same man. In any case, the Scriptures prove that James and Joseph are the children of Mary of Clopas, not Jesus' biological brothers.

[337] Gen 11:26-27.

[338] Gen 13:8; 14:14,16.

[339] See 2 Sam 1:26; 1 Kings 9:13; 20:32.

[340] See Deut 23:7; 2 Kings 10:13-14; 1 Chron 15:5-18; 23:21-22; Jer 34:9; Neh 4:14; 5:1,5,7-8,10,14; Tobit 5:11.

[341] See, for example, Acts 7:26; 11:1; 13:15,58; 15:3,23,32; 28:17,21.

[342] Lk 1:34 (DR).

[343] See Jn 7:3-4 and Mk 3:21.

[344] See Gen 3:19; Ps 16:10.

[345] See Rev 12:1-2,17.

[346] See Rev 6:9. See Rev 12:1.

[347] Gen 5:24; Heb 11:5.

[348] 2 Kings 2:11-12; 1 Mac 2:58.

[349] See Rom 12:5; Eph 3:15; 1 Cor 12:12,27.

[350] See Rom 8:35-39.

[351] See Eph 1:22-23.

[352] For verses that describe those on earth as saints, see Acts 9:13,32,41; 26:10; 1 Cor 6:1-2; 14:33; 2 Cor 1:1; 8:4; 9:1-2; 13:13; Rom 8:27; 12:23; 15:25,26, 31; 16:2,15; Eph 1:1,15,18; 3:8; 5:3; 6:18; Phil 1:1; 4:22; Col 1:2,4,26; 1 Tim 5:10; Philem 1:5,7; Heb 6:10; 13:24; Jude 1:3; Rev 11:18; 13:7; 14:12; 16:6; 17:6;18:20,24; Rev 19:8; 20:9. For verses that describe those in heaven as saints, see Mt 27:52; Eph 2:19; 3:18; Col 1:12; 2 Thess 1:10; Rev 5:8; 8:3-4; 11:18; 13:10.

[353] See Dan 4:13,23; 8:23.

[354] See 1 Cor 12:14-25; Rom 12:4-5.

[355] See Mt 22:32; Mk 12:27; Lk 20:38.

[356] See James 5:16; Ps 15:8,29.

[357] 1 Sam 28:7; 1 Chron 10:13-14.

[358] See Mt 4:11; Mk 1:13.

[359] See Mt 17:1-3; Mk 9:4; Lk 9:30-31.

[360] See 1 Sam 28:7-20; Sir 46:13,20.

[361] This was one reason why Luther removed Maccabees from the Old Testament canon.

[362] See Mt 27:47,49; Mk 15:35-36.

[363] See similar prayers in Ps 35:1; 59:1-17; 139:19; Jer 11:20; 15:15; 18:19; Zech 1:12-13.

[364] See Rev 5:8; 8:3-4.

[365] See Mt 5:44-45. See Mk 11:24.

[366] See 2 Cor 9:14. See 2 Cor 13:7,9.

[367] Col 1:9; see also Col 1:3; 4:12.

[368] See Rom 15:30. See Eph 6:19. See 2 Thess 3:1.

[369] See Heb 13:18-19. See Col 4:4; 1 Thess 5:25.

[370] Gal 6:2,10; 1 Thess 5:11.

[371] Rom 1:9. See 2 Tim 1:3. 1 Thess 5:17. See Col 4:2.

[372] See, for example, Exodus 32:11-14, 30-34; 34:9; Num 14:17-20; 21:7-9.

[373] See Jer 37:3. See Jer 42:1-6.

[374] See Tobit 12:12,15. See Is 6:6-7. See Zech 1:12-13.

[375] This is an ancient (more than 800-year-old) devotional prayer to God through the Blessed Mother, in which one "Our Father" and ten "Hail Mary" prayers are offered in succession as one reflects on a particular mystery in the life of Jesus and Mary. Traditionally this sequence is repeated five times, once for each of five mysteries in that day's Rosary.

[376] The prayer responses in each litany, such as "have mercy on us" (if prayed to God) or "pray for us" (if prayed to God through a saint), are repeated many times in succession.

[377] See Dan 3:52-66.

[378] See Phil 3:17; 1 Thess 1:6; 2 Thess 3:7.

[379] See Heb 6:12; 13:7.

[380] Sacramentals are sacred signs that call to mind the grace of the sacraments (but do not confer grace in the same way the sacraments do). They also signify the spiritual effects that are obtained through the intercession of the Church.

[381] See Ex 25:18-22; 26:1,31.

[382] See 1 Kings 6:23-36; 7:27-39; 8:6-67.

[383] See 1 Chron 28:18-19.

[384] See 2 Chron 3:7-14.

[385] See 2 Kings 13:21.

[386] See Acts 19:11-12.

[387] See Acts 5:15.

[388] See Mt 9:21; Mk 5:28.

[389] See Mk 16:1; Lk 24:1.

[390] Holy water is water that has been specially blessed by a priest.

[391] See Ex 29:4; Lev 8:6.

[392] See Ex 30:18-19.

[393] Jn 19:34; see Zech 13:1.

[394] See 1 Pet 3:21; Heb 10:22. See Titus 3:6.

[395] See 1 Cor 6:11. See Jn 3:3,5.

[396] See 1 Thess 1:3; 2 Thess 1:11; Rev 3:10. See Rom 1:5; 6:17; 15:18; 16:26; 2 Cor 9:13; Heb 5:9.

[397] See Eph 6:23; Col 1:4; 1 Thess 1:3; 3:6; 5:8; 1 Tim 1:14; 2 Tim 1:13; 3:10; Titus 2:2; Philem 5; Gal 5:6.

[398] See Lk 24:47; Acts 2:38; 3:19; 17:30.

[399] See Rom 3:28 and Gal 2:16.

[400] See Gen 4:4-5 (NIV).

[401] See Gen 6:8 (NIV).

[402] See 4:9-17; Gal 5:2-4.

[403] In the eighth century, B.C. (see Rom 11:2-4).

[404] See Gal 3:10,13; James 2:10.

[405] See Gal 5:14; Rom 13:9.

[406] Rom 7:12. See Rom 2:13.

[407] James 2:17; see also James 2:26.

[408] See Eph 3:17; 1 Thess 3:6,12-13; 2 Thess 1:3; 1 Jn 3:23; and Rev 2:4-5,19.

[409] The theological virtues are faith, hope, and love.

[410] See James 1:19. See James 1:26; 3:6-12; 4:11. See also James 5:12. See James 4:4.

[411] See James 5:7-8. See James 4:6; 5:1. See James 1:12.

[412] See Num 25:10-13; Ps 106:31.

[413] See Mt 5:2-11; Lk 6:20-38.

[414] See Mt 5:44-47; 22:39; Mk 12:31.

[415] See Mt 7:19-23.

[416] See Jn 5:36; 10:37-38.

[417] See Jn 8:31-32.

[418] See Jn 5:39-42.

[419] Jn 13:34; see also Jn 15:12; Jn 14:15; see also Jn 14:21; 15:10; 1 Jn 1:3-4; 5:2-3.

[420] 1 Jn 2:3-5; 3:23; 4:7-21; 5:2-3; 2 Jn 6.

[421] See Deut 1:31; Ps 89:26; Is 63:16; 64:8; Wis 2:16; 14:3; Sir 23:4; 51:10; Jer 3:4,19; 2 Cor 6:18; Gal 4:1-7.

[422] Rom 8:16-17; see also Heb 12:5-11.

[423] When Paul says God made Christ "to be sin," this does not mean Christ literally became sin. Such a view would be heretical, because Christ is the sinless Son of God. Paul uses this phrase to underscore that Christ became a sin offering, but not sin itself.

[424] Mt 23:25-28.

[425] Lk 11:39-40.

[426] Eph 4:22-24; see also Col 3:10.

[427] Rom 5:1-2,5.

[428] Ps 51:2,6-7,9-10.

[429] Ez 36:26-27; see also Ez 37:23.

[430] Acts 22:16; see also 1 Cor 6:11.

[431] 1 Jn 1:7,9.

[432] Mt 5:3,5,8.

[433] Mt 5:6; Lk 6:21.

[434] Mt 15:18; Mk 7:15.

[435] See Mt 9:2-8.

[436] See Mt 3:8,10; 7:16-20; 12:33; 13:23; 21:41,43; Mk 4:20; Lk 3:8-9; 6:43-44; 8:14-15; 13:6-7,9; Jn 4:36; 12:24; 15:2,4-5,8,16.

[437] See Heb 7:25.

[438] Since God fulfilled His promise, the word "justify" in verse 8 means the same thing as "blessed" in verse 9. Because Paul is actually quoting from Gen 12 in these verses, this is further proof that Abraham was justified in Gen 12.

[439] Gen 14:19,22-23.

[440] As we have addressed, most Protestants say that Abraham was first justified in Gen 15:6 because the Scripture says God "credited Abraham with righteousness." They use Romans 4:2-3 to prove Abraham was justified in Gen 15:6.

[441] 2 Sam 12:7-15.

[442] See Rom 4:7-8.

[443] Ps 32:1.

[444] Mt 26:75; Mk 14:72; Jn 18:17, 25-27.

[445] Jn 21:15-17.

[446] See Lk 15:18-19,21.

[447] Acts 9:3-5; 22:6-8; 26:12-15.

[448] See Acts 9:6-9; 22:10-11; 26:16-18.

[449] See Acts 9:18; 22:16.

[450] See Jn 12:48; James 4:12; 5:9; 1 Pet 1:17; Acts 10:42; 1 Cor 4:4-5; 2 Thess 1:5-10; Heb 12:23; Rev 20:11-15.

[451] Mt 10:22; 24:13; Mk 13:13.

[452] John 3:16 is a favorite verse among Protestants, but its sacrificial import can only be fully appreciated from a Catholic theological perspective. First, when Jesus decided to become human, He knew that His current state of being (pure Spirit) and relationship with the Father would be forever altered. Jesus would now relate to the Father in human form for all eternity. Second, Jesus knew that His new form (divine being with a human nature) would be required to propitiate the Father in sacrifice for the sins of the world. Thus, John 3:16 is about sacrifice — the Father sacrificed to clothe His Son with humanity, and the Son offers the sacrifice of His humanity back to the Father forever. This is what John means when he says "God *gave* us His only begotten Son."

[453] Jer 25:14; see Jer 50:29-30.

[454] Ez 9:10; see Ez 11:21; 36:19.

[455] Hos 4:9; see Hos 9:15; 12:2.

[456] Sir 16:12,14; see Sir 28:1; 35:19.

[457] Mt 25:14-30. See also Mt 13:41-42.

[458] Mt 25:40; see also Mt 25:45.

[459] Mt 25:46; see also Mt 16:27; Lk 14:14.

[460] Rev 2:23; see also Rev 3:2-5,8,15,16.

[461] Mt 10:22; 24:13; Mk 13:13.

[462] 2 Cor 11:15. See Rom 2:6-10,13; 2 Tim 4:14.

[463] We will also examine this passage in the chapter on purgatory.

[464] 1 Cor 3:9; 1 Cor 3:16-17; 1 Cor 3:11-12.

[465] In the chapter on purgatory, we explain that the person must pass through this same fire to expiate himself of the things that led to his production of the bad works before entering heaven.

[466] See Rom 14:10,12. Rom 14:4,10,13.

[467] 1 Thess 2:19. 1 Thess 5:8. 2 Thess 2:16.

[468] Heb 12:1. Heb 12:15.

[469] See Rom 11:20. See Rom 11:21.

[470] See Rom 1:28; Titus 1:16; 2 Tim 3:8; Heb 6:8; 2 Cor 13:5-7.

[471] 1 Tim 1:17.

[472] 1 Cor 15:1-2; 2 Cor 6:1.

[473] Gal 5:19-21; Eph 5:5-6.

[474] Heb 10:38-39; see 1 Jn 2:28.

[475] Ez 18:24; see Ez 3:20; 33:12-13,18.

[476] 2 Cor 11:13,15.

[477] 1 Jn 2:1,12,18,28; 3:1,2,7,18; 4:4; 5:21.

[478] See Jn 4:42; 1 Tim 4:10; Titus 2:11; 1 Jn 2:2; 4:14.

[479] See Rom 5:6,18; 2 Cor 5:14-15; 1 Tim 2:6.

[480] This is a constant theme in the verses used to "prove" eternal security — the assurance of God's love and faithfulness to us (versus the possible *lack of assurance* of our love and faithfulness to Him).

[481] Some Protestants point out that Paul also mentions his fellow workers are in the book of life (Phil 4:3). But we have already seen that Jesus warns us He will blot our names out of the book of life if we fail to persevere (Rev 3:5).

[482] In today's world of electronic, satellite and other forms of global communication, the gospel is able to reach more people than ever before. This means that "invincible ignorance" of Christ and His Church is an exception (not the rule) to the teaching *Extra Ecclesiam Nulla Salus.*

[483] See, for example, Mk 10:30; Lk 18:30; 20:34-35; and Eph 2:1 for similar language.

[484] Mt 5:25-26; 18:34; Lk 12:58-59.

[485] See Rev 12:10; Zech 3:1; Job 1:6-12.

[486] Luke's version of the Lord's Prayer equates "debt" (in Greek, *opheilonti*) with "sin" (in Greek, *hamartias*): "forgive us our sins as we forgive our debtors" (Lk 11:4). This further demonstrates that Luke (and Matthew) is referring to paying the penalty for "sins" when he teaches that the imprisoned will not go free until they have satisfied their entire "debt" to God.

[487] See 1 Pet 3:19; 4:6

[488] See Mt 24:45-50; 25:18-26; Mk 13:35.

[489] Lk 16:23-24,28.

[490] See Gen 50:10; Num 20:29; Deut 34:8; Zech 9:11.

[491] See, for example, Rom 2:5,16; 1 Cor 1:8; 3:13; 5:5; 2 Cor 1:14; Phil 1:6,10; 2:16; 1 Thess 5:2,4,5,8; 2 Thess 2:2-3; and, 2 Tim 4:8.

[492] See, for example, 2 Tim 1:16-18.

[493] See, for example, Deut 22:19; Prov 17:26; 19:19; 21:11; 22:3.

[494] 1 Cor 3:9; 1 Cor 3:16-17.

[495] See 1 Cor 3:12-15.

[496] An "anachronism," in this context, is an artificial division within a group of people. Protestant apologists often advance anachronistic argu-

mentation in an effort to refute Catholic teachings that have strong scriptural support.

[497] See Rom 2:6-7; 2 Cor 5:10.

[498] See Heb 12:29.

Our Sunday Visitor ...
Your Source for Discovering the Riches of the Catholic Faith

Our Sunday Visitor has an extensive line of materials for young children, teens, and adults. Our books, Bibles, pamphlets, CD-ROMs, audios, and videos are available in bookstores worldwide.

To receive a FREE full-line catalog or for more information, call **Our Sunday Visitor** at **1-800-348-2440, ext. 3**. Or write **Our Sunday Visitor** / 200 Noll Plaza / Huntington, IN 46750.

Please send me ___ A catalog
Please send me materials on:
___ Apologetics and catechetics
___ Prayer books
___ The family
___ Reference works
___ Heritage and the saints
___ The parish

Name _____
Address _____ Apt._____
City _____ State _____ Zip_____
Telephone (   ) _____
                                                      A53BBBBP

Please send a friend ___ A catalog
Please send a friend materials on:
___ Apologetics and catechetics
___ Prayer books
___ The family
___ Reference works
___ Heritage and the saints
___ The parish

Name _____
Address _____ Apt._____
City _____ State _____ Zip_____
Telephone (   ) _____
                                                      A53BBBBP

OurSundayVisitor

200 Noll Plaza, Huntington, IN 46750
Toll free: **1-800-348-2440**
Website: www.osv.com